Beautiful Terrible Ruins

Detroit and the Anxiety of Decline

DORA APEL

Rutgers University Press
New Brunswick, New Jersey, and London

Library of Congress Cataloging-in-Publication Data
Apel, Dora, 1952– author.
Beautiful terrible ruins : Detroit and the anxiety of decline / Dora Apel.
pages cm
Includes bibliographical references and index.
ISBN 978–0–8135–7407–3 (hardcover : alk. paper) — ISBN 978–0–8135–7406–6 (pbk. : alk. paper) — ISBN 978–0–8135–7409–7 (e-book (web pdf)) — ISBN 978–0–8135–7408–0 (e-book (epub))
1. Detroit (Mich.)—In art. 2. Ruins in art. 3. Regression (Civilization) in art. 4. Arts and society—United States—History—20th century. 5. Arts and society—United States—History—21st century. I. Title.
NX653.D48A64 2015
704.9'49977434—dc23
2014040073

A British Cataloging-in-Publication record for this book is available from the British Library.

Visit our website: http://rutgerspress.rutgers.edu

Manufactured in the United States of America

Beautiful Terrible Ruins

For Joan Weinstein

Contents

Illustrations

Acknowledgments

I am grateful to everyone who has supported this project, beginning with the students in my seminar on ruin imagery, who explored the subject of city ruination with great emotional and intellectual investment. Special thanks go to Katherine Toole for her work as my research assistant on this project.

At Rutgers University Press, I owe a great debt of gratitude to my editor, Leslie Mitchner, whose invaluable insights and guidance have greatly improved this book. This is our fourth book together, and I deeply appreciate her support of my work. Lisa Boyajian, Marilyn Campbell, and everyone else at the press was meticulous and helpful, as always; Patti Bower was a diligent copy editor.

At Wayne State University, I thank the indefatigable Walter Edwards and the Advisory Board of the Humanities Center for the Marilyn Williamson Distinguished Faculty Fellowship in support of this project; Matthew Seeger, dean of the College of Fine, Performing and Communication Arts; and John Richardson, chair of the James Pearson Duffy Department of Art and Art History, for their support of a sabbatical leave and a further course release in conjunction with the Marilyn Williamson Fellowship, which provided time and resources for research and writing.

Shane McGowan offered an inspiring exchange on the topic of ruins and romantic apocalyptic imagery at the Apocalyptic Imagination conference sponsored by the Humanities Center at Wayne State University. I thank him for sending me his stimulating work and for pointing me toward other useful sources. For inviting me to present my research at the Harvard Graduate School of Design, I thank Ewa Harabasz as well as the audience for that lecture, and the audiences at the Marilyn Williamson Distinguished Faculty Fellowship Lecture and the James Pearson Duffy Department of Art and Art History Colloquium at WSU.

I am grateful to the artists who graciously supplied images of their work. For their support in collegial and other invaluable ways, I thank Susan Aaron-Taylor and Harry Taylor, Jeffrey Apt, Matthew Biro, John Ganis, Lisa Homann, Kay Perreault, Sandra Schemske, Buzz Spector, and Millee Tibbs. For sending articles my way, I thank the clippings maestro, Dennis Nawrocki, as well as Mariam Noland and my Facebook friends and colleagues who have posted dozens of articles on Detroit or related subjects, including Danielle Aubert, Hartmut Austen, Vince Carducci, Darlene Carroll, Laura Crary, Maureen Devine, Jonathan Flatley, Richard Grusin, Rebecca Hart, renée hoogland, Lisa Langlois, Diana Linden, Ruth Lopez, and Martha Rosler. I appreciate the work on aspects of this inquiry produced by my Wayne State colleagues Jerry Herron, Chera Kee, John Patrick Leary, and Steven Shaviro. I also thank Michael Ashmore and my friends at the MTCI for helping to sustain me, especially after the death of Stephen Britt, a remarkable teacher and tai chi chuan master extraordinaire.

I am particularly grateful to Joan Weinstein, a groundbreaking scholar and visionary leader, for her remarkable acuity, sense of humor, and generosity of spirit. For her longtime support and friendship, and our treasured moments together in Detroit, this book is dedicated to her.

I could not have written this book, however, without the tireless support of my husband, Gregory Wittkopp, whose acute observations often led me to new insights and down new paths of inquiry and whose critique of the manuscript in its early stages was invaluable. More than anyone, he has encouraged me to write this book. I also thank our daughter, Rachel, for sending me articles and also proving to be a thoughtful reader for parts of the manuscript in its early stages. Finally I thank the artists and creative enthusiasts who have helped make Detroit such an interesting place to be, despite all its troubles.

Beautiful Terrible Ruins

Introduction

Modernity in Ruins

The disaster unfolds before our eyes: dense fiery clouds mushroom outward; the shocking downward crash; the skewed fragments standing in an otherworldly landscape like a modern-day Dante's Inferno. When the World Trade Center was attacked in 2001, the nation was inundated with images of fire and smoke, ashes and rubble. The country as a whole felt violated and vulnerable, a feeling that only deepened in the following weeks and months as the planes repeatedly flew into the towers that fell again and again. The visual trauma of bodies falling from the towers was largely suppressed in favor of focusing on the architectural collapse, which was traumatic enough. The smoldering remains and terrifying steel lattice ruins that stood in place of the towers signaled a metaphorical blow to American imperialist pretensions. This humbling of imperial power surely drove the rush to rebuild, to fill the void of loss in the Manhattan skyline. It also drove the launching of two grueling, costly, and destructive wars, the limitless War on Terror and the vastly expanded security state by President George W. Bush and his administration. They were eager to replace those videos and photographs of catastrophe and defeat with images of triumph and the victory of "freedom." But the "shock and awe" campaign failed, and the recently opened National September 11 Memorial & Museum instantiates the experience of highly intensified security and surveillance, producing what one critic calls "a celebration of liberty tightly policed."[1] The memorialized footprints of the towers, however, have become a kind of ur-ruin that casts its shadow forward over the new millennium. In the current era, ruins and scenes of ruination rank among its most iconic images.

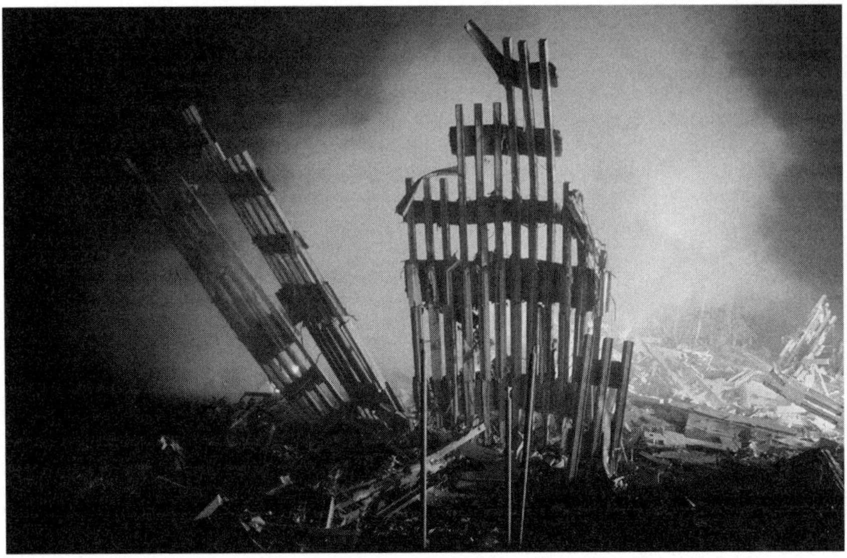

FIG. 1 Steve McCurry, *New York City, 2001. Wrecked Remains of the World Trade Center's Twin Towers.* © Steve McCurry/Magnum Photos.

The aesthetic appeal of the postapocalyptic ruins in the aftermath of the 9/11 attacks is unmistakable, prompting another observer to ask, "Is it unseemly now or ever to talk about the beauty of the World Trade Center's ruins?"[2] The pictured ruins, such as those taken by Steve McCurry on the day of the attack, or those of the clean-up by Joel Meyerowitz have an eerie splendor even as they convey a sense of ghostliness and suspended time (figure 1). Still haunted by the loss of almost three thousand lives, the pictures make it possible to "empathize and even identify with the ruins."[3] We must recognize that the implicit warning against imperial hubris and the burden of grief imparted by the images are in conflict with the impulse to find beauty in the ruins. Yet these contradictory narratives coexist—the beautiful and the terrible—indeed, one mediates the other, beauty making the terrible bearable. The looming trauma of the ruins may be mastered through the safe remove of representation. This is the ameliorating function and inherent contradiction of ruin imagery.

Natural disasters wreak another kind of ruinous havoc. When Katrina hit New Orleans in 2005, thousands of poor and black people were trapped for days before any action was even taken to try to rescue them. The nation looked on in horror while the Federal Emergency Management Agency (FEMA) claimed ignorance about conditions in the Louisiana Superdome that everyone else in the country was watching on television. Here the power of imagery was evident in a whole new way, exposing FEMA's shocking mismanagement and lack of preparation for the disaster in which more than eighteen hundred people died. All too aware of the effects of images, FEMA urged that no reporters accompany rescue boats and that no photographs of the dead be published.[4] Media controversy flared nonetheless when a photo of a young black man wading chest deep through floodwater while carrying a case of soda and pulling a floating plastic bag was described as "looting," while in a similar photo, a white couple holding bags of food were described as "finding bread and soda from a local grocery store."[5] Along with the exaggerated and false media reports of black violence and criminal activity in the storm's aftermath, these captioned images expressed the racist attitudes that demonized blacks as looters and rapists, justifying the callous and discriminatory treatment of displaced black citizens in the majority black city.[6] Such images—the displacement of eight hundred thousand people in New Orleans and the catastrophic strike at the center of global capital in New York—reverberate with a challenge to the ability of the state to protect its citizens and to the idea of progress and rationality in the capitalist order.

The imagery of abandonment and decay produced by deindustrialization and urban decline also resounds with such challenges, and no city is more repeatedly pictured in the national media for its stark deterioration than Detroit. The travails of the city are featured in dozens of stories in the *New York Times*, for example, including many with front page headlines and two-page inside spreads with enormous photographs. The *New York Times* even initiated a "Ruin and Renewal" series that specifically tracks efforts to revive an area defined as Detroit's North End, and produced a magazine cover story profiling Detroit-based entrepreneurs considering investment in the city, "Detroit, Through Rose-Colored Glasses."[7] Although deindustrial decline is widespread across the country and abroad, most notably in the former leading manufacturing centers, Detroit has become the preeminent example of urban decay, the global metaphor for the current state of neoliberal capitalist culture and the epicenter of the photographic genre of deindustrial ruin imagery.

What the city has become best known for, through the pervasive reproduction and circulation of ruin imagery, are the abandoned factories and skyscrapers; derelict hotels, libraries, schools, churches, and businesses; the acres of vacant residential lots dotted here and there with lone houses; and the derelict homes that run into the tens of thousands. After the attacks of 9/11, hurricanes intensified by global warming such as Katrina and Sandy, the global economic crisis of 2008 that caused millions of people to lose their jobs and their homes, and the nuclear meltdown in Japan in 2011, the imagery of ruination has only grown and speaks to the overarching fears and anxieties of our era: increasing poverty, declining wages and social services, inadequate health care, unemployment, homelessness, ecological disaster and degradation, and fear of the other. These issues play an important role in positioning the ruins of Detroit at the center of a vast network of ruin images, making the former Motor City the poster child of ruination in the advanced capitalist countries today. Although images are never the same as the real, the global network of ruin imagery visually constructs the nature of modern decline and shapes collective ways of seeing.

Repeatedly construed in the national media as a postapocalyptic landscape, Detroit is often compared to war zones, hurricane wreckage, conditions of the poorest developing nations, the aftermath of nuclear explosion or destruction by alien invaders. To the annoyance of Detroit's residents, the city's deterioration tends to overwhelm any sense of its vitality, or, more acutely, its living population of nearly seven hundred thousand people. But the effects of ruination are stark: 40 percent of the streetlights do not work, the school system is abysmal, and the fire department functions without adequate equipment. The unemployment rate, at 23 percent in the 2010 census, is the highest among the nation's fifty largest cities and well above the national average, while the higher education rate is well below it. Though city services are slow and inadequate, property taxes are high, continually threatening poor residents with home foreclosures and threatening the city with yet more blighted, abandoned houses. Nearly 40 percent of the city's population lives below the poverty line. About a fifth of the city's residents cannot afford a car, and Detroit has one of the worst public transit systems of any major city in the nation, which, moreover, is not integrated with a regional public transit system so that people can get to work in the suburbs. Indeed, there is no regional integration of most resources, so that what is now the poorest city in the nation, which is overwhelmingly black, is also bordered on the north by some of the wealthiest suburbs in the nation, which are overwhelmingly white.

Is the nation's former leading manufacturing center a metonym for global urban decline or a racially unique city? Does it matter what happens to Detroit, or is it obsolete and expendable? What are the cultural and political implications of Detroit's ruin imagery? The ruination of cities is always more complicated than it may seem at first, and their representation is significant for the ways in which images reveal or conceal relations of power.

We might think of Detroit as embodying two cities—the real one with all its complexities and histories, and the one fashioned through ruin images. In his 1993 study of Detroit, Jerry Herron observed, "Detroit is the most representative city in America. Detroit used to stand for success, and now it stands for failure. In that sense, the city is not just a physical location; it is also a project, a projection of imaginary fears and desires. This is the place where bad times get sent to make them belong to somebody else."[8] As a repository for the cultural fears and anxieties of the nation, Detroit as constructed through images may be appalling or amazing, but photographs, by their nature, tend to explain very little about the complex causes of decline or the ramifications of ruination for the city's future, or the nation's. Instead the city produced through images takes on different meanings in different contexts; even the same images may be used to serve different political agendas. Detroit is seen as both representative of urban decline *and* as a uniquely mismanaged city. As the former leading manufacturing center in the world and now a failing black city, Detroit is construed as both exemplifying inevitable economic trends for which no one is to blame and as a highly racialized city that has caused its own decline through incompetent or corrupt leadership. Detroit is thus regarded as "demonstrating" either the historical inescapability of decline or its own history of "irresponsibility."

In this way, the rest of the country may be lulled into believing that Detroit's downward spiral is either deserved or unavoidable, or a combination of the two. These constructions of the city allow the real agents of decline—the corporations and the state—to evade responsibility and justify the state takeover of Detroit, its forced bankruptcy, the attack on workers' pensions, privatization of city services, and other threatened austerities, which ultimately serve as disciplinary warnings to declining cities and towns from Maine to California. By establishing crucial precedents that place the burden of debt on poor, black, and working people in the face of a shrinking economy, and under cover of blaming no one or blaming the city itself, Detroit and its representations assume a pivotal role in helping to shape the future of city life in America. As the central locus for the anxiety of decline, Detroit's ruins loom over the nation and beyond.

The anxiety of decline may be understood as the dark side of modernity, which is founded on a set of universalist values stemming from the Enlightenment that supported ideals of progress and rationality through science and technology. Yet modernity has also fostered the growth of disaster capitalism—the unparalleled power of the security and surveillance state, the stateless subject, the capacity for mass death on an enormous scale, the ability to destroy the earth's ecology, and new ways of immiserating masses of people, all in the service of producing extraordinary wealth and power for a tiny privileged elite.[9] Faith in progress and rationality erodes as economic and ecological crises, poverty and urban deterioration grow. As national economic imperatives clash with the demands of globalized capital, the continuing decline and ruination of cities feeds a pervasive cultural pessimism that foresees violent disintegration and collapse—whether through viral pandemics, global warming, ecological destruction, warfare, or deindustrialization and the explosive growth of social inequality and discriminatory practices. Thus we have the paradoxical appeal of ruin imagery: the beauty of ruins helps us to cope with the terror of apocalyptic decline. Put another way, the hold of apocalyptic fear on the cultural imagination is produced by the widespread anxiety of decline and the search for ways to mitigate its effects.

As faith erodes in a future that promises to exclude the many and privilege the few, the global network of ruin imagery expands and grows denser with a variety of contact or nodal points that connect to social issues. I want to suggest that the crucial nodal point of this network is the imagery of the postapocalyptic deindustrialized city for which Detroit serves, in the cultural imagination, as the paradigmatic example. The abandoned factories and blighted schools, churches, shops, and homes of the modern ruined city constitute the iconic ruin forms in the era of industrial disinvestment and globalization. When German news media crowned the debt-ridden city of Oberhausen "Germany's Detroit," it clearly invoked the universal signifier of urban decline. In the cultural imagination, the *idea* of Detroit as the repository of widespread industrial decay, shorn of its actual complexities, histories, and contradictions, serves as the quintessential urban nightmare in a world where the majority of people live in cities.

The reasons for Detroit's pivotal position are rooted in the relationship of modernity to Detroit's own history. The period from 1870 to 1914 has been called the "first globalization" of finance and trade, which saw the invention of the electric light, film, radio, and the ocean liner as well as international investment and the automobile.[10] As the birthplace of the automobile and Fordism—the industrialized and standardized form of mass production that became the basis of modern industry—Detroit was seen as the industrial powerhouse of the nation and the motor force of modernity in the twentieth century (figure 2). The city greatly expanded in the 1920s when the downtown skyscrapers were built. But manufacturing disinvestment began in the immediate post–World War II period and developed into a cascade of closing auto factories in the latter half of the twentieth century up to the present. The resulting deindustrialization and continuing ruination of the city have come to signify modernity itself in ruins. In Detroit and hundreds of other cities, the hopes and dreams for continuous prosperity and progress in a meritocratic democracy have been steadily undermined as the unemployed and underemployed come to feel increasingly marginalized.

The effects of industrial disinvestment last for decades, especially in those cities where one industry has dominated, destabilizing communities through the loss of jobs, homes, health care; reductions in the tax base in turn lead to cuts in public services; crime increases, as does suicide, drug and alcohol abuse, family violence, and depression; landscapes decay and cultural resources decline, as does faith in government. Deunionized workers who find new jobs often do so at far lower wage rates, contributing to an almost inescapable cycle of continuing decline. John Russo and Sherry Lee Linkon, authors of a study on deindustrialization, explain this downward spiral in deunionized wages:

> The pay and benefits negotiated by unions rippled through the national economy, raising the standard of living for all workers in what economists call wage pull. But deindustrialization and associated deunionization have had the reverse effect. As unionized industries close, wages and benefits have fallen across the board, for all workers. At the same time, benefits are declining as workers are being asked to pay for all or part of their health insurance. To put this differently, one of the social costs of deindustrialization is the declining economic security of the entire American middle and working class. Even workers who were never displaced by plant closings or industry decline have been affected.[11]

Thus deindustrialization not only harms the communities and the workers whose jobs have been eliminated but also undermines the quality of the jobs that remain. Conservative observers and economists often argue that these are "natural" economic trends, and claim that the manufacturing economy has given way to a service economy. But this shift has contributed to the nation's growing inequality because manufacturing jobs have been replaced by low-wage jobs. Even when displaced workers find new jobs, they tend to earn only about 40 percent of their previous income.[12] This is true not just in America but is reflected in the global economy. Even in China, seen as the

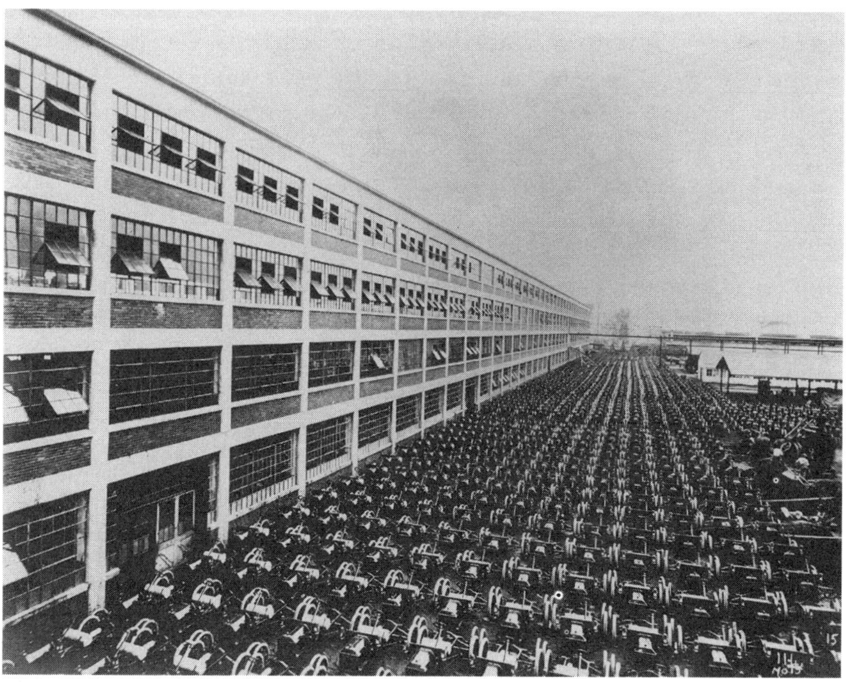

FIG. 2 One thousand Ford Model T chassis, one shift's output, outside the Highland Park Plant, 1913. The collections of The Henry Ford (P.O. 716/ THF109225).

leader in industrial jobs, workers have been displaced, first by privatization and more recently by companies moving factories to Indonesia and other countries where labor is even cheaper and environmental regulations fewer.[13]

Sometimes former manufacturing centers with new office buildings, riverfront parks, and gentrified neighborhoods appear to have made recoveries, often depending on tourism or entertainment. Despite such new development, poverty rates remain high because the jobs associated with these industries represent a dramatic decline in job quality. In 2014 Buffalo, for example, was named one of New York's "10 most exciting places" while other press headlines announced a "feeling of resurgence" in Cleveland, which has revitalized its lakefront area with new museums and gentrified old working-class neighborhoods with ethnic restaurants and loft housing. Yet Cleveland today has the highest poverty rate in the nation after Detroit; its joking mantra is, "At least we're not Detroit." Buffalo has the fourth-highest poverty rate in the country, after Rochester, New York. As a mill and steel town on the southern shores of Lake Erie, with the added advantage of Niagara Falls as a source of energy, Buffalo was once known as the City of Light. But like every city on the Great Lakes and the Mississippi River that depended on water for shipping, Buffalo declined when rail became more efficient and industries left for areas with cheaper labor costs. The city has yet to recover. Pittsburgh has shown the most economic growth since the collapse of the steel industry in the 1970s and 1980s and ranks as one of the country's "most livable cities" with its diversified economy, low cost of living, and concentration of cultural and educational institutions. Yet many people struggle in low-wage jobs. A two-year conflict between low-wage workers at the University of Pittsburgh Medical Center, the city's largest employer, erupted in downtown protests by hundreds of demonstrators against the UPMC in 2014. Like Detroit, all three cities have lost more than half their populations since midcentury.[14]

Across the country, inequality grows as the gap between the wealthy elite and the poor has widened exponentially and continues to widen. For the first time in decades, the current generation has a lower standard of living than that of its parents.[15] Although corporate profits have soared, incomes have declined, with one-third of all working families making below the poverty threshold.[16] While nonwhites have an astounding 90 percent risk of economic insecurity, more than 76 percent of whites today are also subject to periods of joblessness and the need for welfare.[17] They too are at risk of becoming marginalized. The American dream—the idea of individual upward mobility based on merit instead of class, available to all if only they work hard enough—has become an empty phrase that ignores the downward pressure on the middle and working classes. It ignores the need for adequate food, housing, education, and health care, not to mention social institutions, social services, and functioning communities that support the efforts and provide the opportunities that make the success of individuals possible. For most people who work very hard all their life, upward mobility will never arrive. One of the effects of capitalism is this ideological privileging of the individual at the expense of the collective, despite the realities.

Ruination, then, as Ann Laura Stoler suggests, must be understood as both a noun and a verb—"an *act* perpetrated, a *condition* to which one is subject, and a *cause* of loss."[18] Ruins are not just objects to be historicized but "unfinished histories" with different possible futures; how we understand the causes of ruination affects ongoing urban policy. But ruins also convey a sense of downward progress for a majority of Americans, which has an impact on every aspect of life. Even safely historicized ruins meant to celebrate significant American landmarks often lead to thoughts of inevitable collapse. In *American Ruins*, for example, a coffee-table photography book by Arthur Drooker that focuses on preserved and protected picturesque sites—Chaco Canyon in New Mexico or Harper's Ferry in West Virginia—historian Douglas Brinkley muses aloud in the foreword, "Given global warming and chemical weapons and nuclear reactors, you wonder whether everyplace might someday become a candidate for Drooker's ruins portfolio."[19]

In addition to picture books and websites, the explosion of ruin imagery in the last fifteen or twenty years has been gathered in exhibitions such as *Irresistible Decay: Ruins Reclaimed* at the Research Library of the Getty Research Institute (1997); *Visions of Ruin* at the Sir John Soane's Museum (1999), which looked at the "cult of ruins" in the eighteenth and nineteenth centuries; *The Ruins of Detroit* at the Wilmotte Gallery at Lichfield Studios in London (2012); *American Ruins: Challenging Ideas of Progress*, produced online by the Snite Museum of Art at the University of Notre Dame (2013); *Living in the Ruins of the Twentieth Century* at the UTS Museum in Sydney (2013); and *The Evolution of Neglect: Scenes of Ruin and Ruins from the Menil Collection* in Houston (2014). The Tate Britain mounted the exhibition *Ruin Lust*, curated by Brian Dillon and focused on the work of British artists, which included ruins in art from the seventeenth century to the present day (2014). Detroit ruin images in particular have proliferated at dizzying speed, including in the news media, reiterating and reinforcing the city's pivotal position in the network of ruin images. From the Broadway play *Detroit* to Chrysler's "Imported from Detroit" advertising campaign to proposals for colonizing hundreds of acres in the city for a zombie theme park, the borders between art, media, advertising, and popular culture have become increasingly permeable as visual imagery easily ranges across these formats and as people produce their own imagery on websites and social media.

My premise is a simple one: the anxiety of decline feeds an enormous appetite for ruin imagery. But it matters whether we understand ruination as historically inevitable, the fault of its own victims, or as the result of industrial disinvestment and capitalist globalization. In this book, I want to explore the politics of ruination in order to better understand the pleasure, horror, and continuing fascination that ruin imagery exerts across cultural spheres and visual formats. As fears of decline grow, the threshold for compensatory aesthetic pleasure also grows higher, requiring more expressions of ruin and disaster to be mentally mastered in order to achieve a sense of safety. The appetite for ruin imagery grows larger, in other words, as the fears of ruination, which drive the need to contain and control those fears, grow more intense, imbuing ruin imagery with ever greater cultural power. Thus the fascination with Detroit's abandoned downtown skyscrapers, empty urban spaces, decaying factories, and derelict neighborhoods intensifies as the city negotiates the crisis of bankruptcy. Despite the narrative that seeks to marginalize and isolate the city as responsible for its own decline, Detroit has become emblematic of failing cities everywhere as the paradigmatic city of ruins.

Yet Detroit is also the mecca of urban explorers, architects, urban planners, and geographers as well as photographers, artists, musicians, writers, and the curious who are drawn to a city that seems to embody not only disaster but also open-ended possibility. As a result, some loyalists insist on hopeful or upbeat images of the city. But it is not my aim to prescribe the kinds of images photographers "should" or "shouldn't" produce in order to serve particular social or political agendas. Instead, my approach is to understand how we see Detroit through the imagery that already exists and continues to be produced, to understand how this imagery engages the anxiety of decline and to consider what cultural and political work it does.

Images work affectively, as sensory-emotional experiences, and ideologically, in ways that are quite separate from overt or "activist" intention by their makers. Aesthetic perception is conditioned by and works within a social field; it is subject to its pressures and anxieties. In other words, how we make images and how we interpret them is always transformed by our engagement with everyday life. This approach to imagery is what Jill Bennett calls "practical aesthetics," which links visual perception to actual events or problems and the social effects of images.[20] As Bennett notes, the connection of visual imagery to the practices of everyday life "occurs on an aesthetic continuum (rather than in a rarified realm)" and this understanding therefore "resists the idea that useful art must conform to a single ideal of 'activist' art measured in inaesthetic terms" and instead asks "what art and imagery *does*—what it *becomes*—in its very particular relationship to events."[21] Similarly, I examine the politics of ruin imagery to understand the symbolic work that it does.

Different trends within ruin imagery emerge, offering a variety of perspectives on ruination. Images may lament the decline of the city as a deindustrialized wasteland or, conversely, engage in romanticized reveries on the struggle between nature and culture; they may represent ruins as sites of exotic discovery and transgressive pleasure or, conversely, as places of danger and threat; they may construct ruins as a backdrop to a resilient and determined city heading toward a brilliant comeback or, conversely, envision a future that regresses to an idealized preindustrial past; or they may visualize postapocalyptic landscapes that implicitly critique the status quo and offer grounds for a new beginning. These approaches imply different political perspectives, but all of them grapple with a pervasive and growing cultural pessimism, loss of faith in progress, and deepening fear that we are living in the end times. Yet just as ruin imagery challenges the idea of the capitalist state as effective protector of its citizens and source of progress and rationality, it also challenges us to consider how our declining cities may be reclaimed and reimagined as part of an egalitarian society where cities meet the needs of their collective populations, provide the basis for individual fulfillment, and help sustain the earth's environment.

1

Ruin Terrors and Pleasures

Many writers since the nineteenth century have tended to see ruins in quasi-sacred metaphysical terms, that is, as aestheticized and dehistoricized landscapes that find their locus of fascination in the beautiful and melancholic struggle between nature and culture. This fascination produced what became known as *ruin lust.* German theorist and cultural critic Georg Simmel, at the beginning of the twentieth century, perhaps best articulated this view: "The aesthetic value of the ruin combines the disharmony, the eternal becoming of the soul struggling against itself, with the satisfaction of form, the firm limitedness, of the work of art." This equation requires equilibrium between matter and nature, "a pillar crumbled—say, halfway down," for "a maximum of charm" and a sense of unity in which "purpose and accident, nature and spirit, past and present" create a balance of tensions, although the higher pull of spirit is ultimately privileged over the lower pull of nature in a vertical hierarchy of balance.[1] The dehistoricized classical ruins that are the subjects of Simmel's contemplation, however, constitute a different category of ruination and more easily lend themselves to this sort of subjective ennobling and romanticizing as compared to contemporary deindustrial ruins. On a formal level alone, modernist architecture refuses the return of culture to nature in the manner of ancient ruins in large part because the building materials of concrete, steel, and glass do not delicately crumble in the picturesque way that stone does.

Moreover, the classical ruin has already reached its absolute form as an aesthetic artifact, defining its status as a ruin, and its preservation in this state is enforced and maintained by the guardians of the ruins; the remaining pillars and arches are regarded as eternal. The contemporary ruin, however, is in a continuous state of flux, of "becoming and unbecoming," as the British philosopher Dylan Trigg observes. The glass continues to break, the paint peels away, the floor and the roof are transformed through stages of collapse, all of which constantly redefine the form and therefore our relationship to the form. The sense of the eternal is replaced by a sense of impermanence, the sense of certainty by uncertainty, "by an unfolding of content in which the phenomenology of detail takes precedence."[2] Far more recent in their abandonment and decay, industrial ruins are more likely to be structurally dangerous architectural hulks subject to the depredations of strippers, urban explorers, animals, weather, and other forces. In a continual state of transformation as they decay, industrial ruins largely embody formless decline and disordered space, mirroring the irrationality of the system that has produced them. Contemporary ruins are thus nothing like the Roman, Grecian, and other ancient objects of traditional romantic ruin gazing, which offered modernity a way of conceiving itself in relation to the remains of the ancient past.

Ruin Lust

Ruin gazing engendered ruin lust by the late eighteenth century, when the wealthy went so far as to build fake ruins both for aesthetic and political reasons. Fragments of monasteries and medieval castles, known as follies, were commissioned for English pleasure gardens both for their beauty and for the pleasure their patrons took in seeing the institutions these artificial ruins represented—the papacy and feudal aristocracy—in visible collapse.[3] English and French garden follies also took the form of fake Roman temples, to symbolize classical virtues or ideals, as well as Chinese temples, Egyptian pyramids, or Tatar tents, in orientalizing gestures, or they took the form of rustic villages, mills, and cottages, to symbolize rural virtues. One of the most famous examples of such a rustic folly was built at Versailles, allowing Marie Antoinette to play at being a shepherdess.

Ruins of the classical world, consumed through the travel gaze of Europeans, tended to confirm for these viewers the status of European countries as the historical apex of civilization. The British in the eighteenth century, through the Grand Tour of the continent that included the Roman Empire, Greece, and the Middle East, confirmed their own sense of superiority by gazing on the ruins of other civilizations, evoking the terror and delight of the Burkean sublime. The most important aspect of this experience was that the civilizations the ruins represented were always *other*. The Grand Tour became a kind of ideological exercise intended to cultivate historical consciousness and prepare the upper class for their future position of leadership in the flourishing empire.[4] Such scenes prompted travelers to make comparisons between past and present civilizations, and these comparisons inevitably privileged contemporaneous conditions over those in the past. Thus, as literary scholar Shane McGowan notes, "The act of ruin gazing reaffirmed the Enlightenment's teleological narrative of progress, which depicted history as humanity's inevitable journey from Oriental despotism to Occidental rationality."[5] This view necessarily regarded the ruins of antiquity, despite their grandeur, as vestiges of a more barbaric age, making ruin gazing a "ready tool of nationalism" as well as "an even more valuable tool of imperialism and colonialism."[6]

By the nineteenth century, however, critique of empire entered the romantic lexicon in literature and art. Edward Gibbon's multivolume history, *The Decline and Fall of the Roman Empire* (1776), firmly established the idea of the unstable and transitory nature of all power, and after the 1793 Reign of Terror, romantics became increasingly skeptical of enduring faith in reason and progress. J. M. W. Turner's painting *The Decline of the Carthaginian Empire*, produced at the height of Great Britain's wealth and power following the collapse of Napoleon's empire in 1815, offered another warning of imperial decline, while Joseph Gandy's painting *An Imagined View of the Bank of England in Ruins* (1830) pictured the collapse of the major financial underwriter of the Napoleonic Wars (figure 3). Gandy's aerial perspective of the interlocking maze of offices became reality almost a century later when the bank's interiors were demolished in the 1920s. Thomas Cole's series *The Course of Empire*, depicting the rise and fall of an imaginary city that refers to Carthage, was influenced by Turner and carried the warning of imperial decline into 1830s America. Ed Ruscha then reimagined the fall of American empire in the post-9/11 era, producing a series of works representing industrialized modernity in decay as part of the exhibition *The Course of Empire* shown at the Whitney Museum of American Art in conjunction with Cole's series in 2006, transforming spectators into ruin gazers and witnesses to the decline of empire once more.[7] Hovering over the Whitney exhibition were the spectral images of the Twin Towers as the most chilling warning of contemporary imperial decline.

The Third Reich provides an example of ruin lust in the form of planned future ruins. Albert Speer's conception of "ruin value" in Nazi monumental architecture was designed with an eye toward its future picturesque decay through the use of stone rather than concrete and steel. The concept of ruin value was meant to assert both German imperial power far into the future and German mastery over its own ruination. While Speer asserted that his theory of ruin value arose in response to Hitler's definition of architecture as a "bridge" across time, German studies scholar Julia Hell suggests that Speer reinvented the ruin gazer in the Third Reich because the Nazis were preoccupied with countering the specter of imperial decline, especially after publication of Oswald Spengler's highly influential *The Decline of the West*

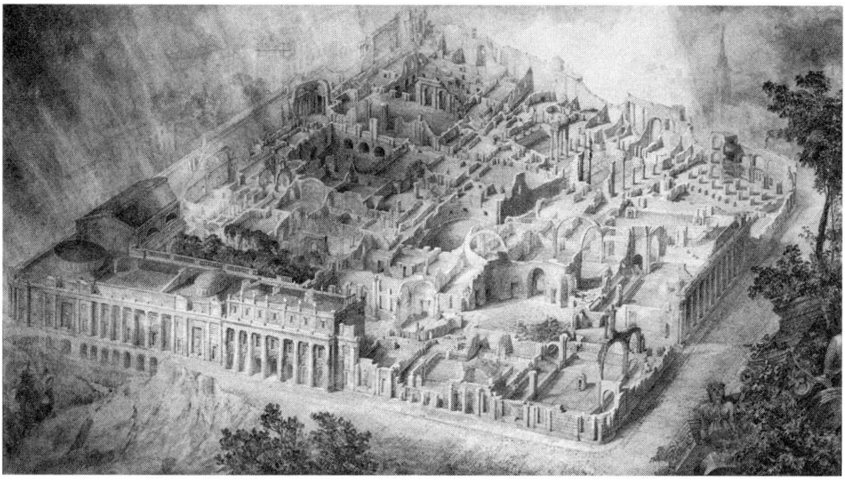

FIG. 3 Joseph Gandy, *An Imagined View of the Bank of England in Ruins*, 1830. Courtesy of the Trustees of Sir John Soane's Museum.

(the first volume was published in 1918 and revised in 1922; the second volume was published in 1923), which embraced modernity's ruination.[8] While Spengler allows for the possibility of a future barbarian ruin gazer from a foreign culture, Hell argues that Hitler and Speer were at pains to construct a future Aryan ruin gazer who would marvel at the spectacle of Nazi imperial power while keeping the future "barbarian" ruin gazer out of sight through their program of slavery and genocide.[9] Hell also suggests that the unique Nazi articulation of imperial creation and destruction represents an anxious awareness and fear of the retaliation that awaited them for the crimes of monstrous proportions they knew they were committing. It was this awareness that ultimately drove the Nazi mania for ruins, a plan that was nevertheless foiled.[10] Although Hitler insisted that his architects build for "eternity," Speer's Reich's Chancellery, his most famous building, completed in 1939, did not crumble picturesquely like the Roman ruins shown to Hitler by Mussolini on his visit to Rome. Instead, the Chancellery was bombed by Allied air raids four years later and then razed by the Soviets, defeating the future realization of Aryan ruin gazing.

What distinguishes the experience of contemporary ruin gazing from that of viewing ancient ruins is not only the difference in the physical nature and materials of the ruin but also the greater mental effort required to distance oneself. This distancing is what facilitates a sense of political and cultural superiority over the disaster of ruination. But what happens when those ruins are in one's own homeland? Modern ruins cannot be safely ensconced in obsolete civilizations that only demonstrate the superiority of our own. Unlike eighteenth-century follies and Grand Tours that reinforced notions of cultural and political superiority in relation to the failed empires of past foreign cultures, contemporary ruins function as a critique of our own social conditions and thus are more closely aligned with the critical perspective of late romantic art and literature. The warnings of imperial decline through a postapocalyptic aesthetic, which began to picture ruins within the West itself in the late romantic period, suggest a critique of empire that begins at home.[11]

The phrase "ruin lust" was coined by English novelist and essayist Rose Macaulay. When Macaulay returned to her flat in London following the death of her sister in 1941, she discovered that her home and all her possessions, including her beloved library, had been destroyed in a bombing a few nights before. Macaulay was haunted by the loss. Yet in 1953 she published *Pleasure of Ruins*, in which she discussed the history of ruin lust and meditated on the nature of "new ruins" and the pleasure they inspired:

> New ruins have not yet acquired the weathered patina of age, the true rust of the barons' wars, not yet put on their ivy, nor equipped themselves with the appropriate bestiary of lizards, bats, screech-owls, serpents, speckled toads and little foxes which, as has been so frequently observed by ruin-explorers, hold high revel in the precincts of old ruins. . . . But new ruins are for a time stark and bare, vegetationless and creatureless; blackened and torn, they smell of fire and mortality. . . . What was last week a drab little house has become a steep flight of stairs winding up in the open between gaily-coloured walls, tiled lavatories, interiors bright and intimate like a Dutch picture or a state set; the stairway climbs up and up, undaunted, to the roofless summit where it meets the sky.[12]

In her phrases describing the "smell of fire and mortality" and the "roofless summit" of a staircase meeting the sky, Macaulay captures the rawness of new ruins while asserting that "ruin pleasure must be at one remove, softened by art," as well as poetry and fantasy. For ruin pleasure, she asserts, is "merely a phase of our fearful and fragmented age."[13] Macaulay's acute insight into the need for a "remove" in order for ruin pleasure to occur merits further exploration through the concept of the sublime.

The Deindustrial Sublime

The strategies of contemporary ruin imagery are necessarily in dialogue with romanticism and the aesthetic of the sublime. The romantic sublime came to apply to catastrophic events and to the act of ruin gazing in the eighteenth century; scenes of ruin became both spectacles of eerie beauty and testaments to the humbling power of nature in which the spectator could delight in experiencing its visual effects while escaping its ravages. For both Edmund Burke and Immanuel Kant, the two most important theorists of the sublime in the latter half of the eighteenth century, the experience of the sublime depended upon distance and safety as conditions that were crucial for the enjoyment of a scene that would otherwise be too terrifying to endure. This distance could be spatial or temporal, but it was always mental.

Mental, temporal, and spatial distance thus allows for the conceptual grasp and rationalization, or the domestication and taming of the terror before us, permitting its aestheticization and enjoyment. As Kant explained in his *Critique of Judgment*, sublimity is, in fact, never found in nature but only in the mind: "Hence sublimity is contained not in any thing of nature, but only our mind, insofar as we can become conscious of our superiority to nature within us, and thereby also to nature outside us (as far as it influences us). Whatever arouses this feeling in us, and this includes the *might* of nature that challenges our forces, is then (although improperly) called sublime."[14] Kant asserts that the forces in nature that arouse sublime experience are improperly called sublime because it is the internal mental act of mastery that transforms the terrifying into a thrilling sense of superiority.

This understanding of the sublime as aesthetic experience arrived at through contemplation made possible by safety and distance—the sublime as a "taming category" by which the terrifying is made enjoyable—helps to explain the compelling power and pleasure of contemporary ruin gazing and ruin imagery. Since the taming of terror is a crucial component of the sublime, it follows that catastrophe, destruction, and ruination can produce subjectively sublime experience. In addition to events such as fires, droughts, floods, tsunamis, tornados, hurricanes, meteor crashes, and viral pandemics, in modern times, catastrophe and the ruined landscape also can proceed through the quicker or slower events of nuclear power plant meltdowns, explosions and warfare, climate change, deindustrialization, and economic collapse. The terror these events produce are aestheticized not only by picturing the beauty of actual decay but also through fantasy disasters, from the Cold War era sci-fi thrillers of killer monsters, mutants, robots, and aliens to contemporary zombie invasions and other apocalyptic catastrophes.

It is telling that the romantic sublime was conceptualized following one of the most catastrophic events in Europe: the Lisbon earthquake of 1755. Combined with subsequent fires and a tsunami, the earthquake almost totally destroyed the city of Lisbon, killing over sixty thousand people and causing much suffering. The destruction of the earthquake sent shock waves throughout Europe, with many written eyewitness accounts.[15] The association of ruination with the Lisbon earthquake may have been further underscored by the fact that the Portuguese empire was already in decline.[16] Still one of the deadliest earthquakes in recorded history, it was a calamity of such epic and terrifying proportions that it was unequaled by any then-known natural disaster. It was widely discussed by European Enlightenment philosophers and proved to be a shattering force that was foundational to theorizing the sublime in Burke's *A Philosophical Enquiry into the Origin of Our Ideas of the Sublime and Beautiful*, published only two years later in 1757, and Kant's *Critique of Judgment* first published in 1790.

Kant also published three separate texts on the Lisbon earthquake, and his attempts to explain its geological causes may have represented, as Walter Benjamin suggests, the beginning of modern geology and seismology.[17] English scholar Alexander Regier argues that the secular and scientific "disciplining" of the catastrophe by Kant has a parallel in the realm of the aesthetic. However, since the aesthetic experience depends on the initial fragmenting or shattering effect of the event, the taming or domesticating tendency of the sublime is, paradoxically, predicated on a radically destabilizing premise. Kant implies this as a distinction between the sublime and the beautiful when he writes: "In presenting the sublime in nature the mind feels *agitated*, while in an aesthetic judgment about the beautiful in nature it is in *restful* contemplation."[18] The sublime thus relies on inherent anxiety about the violence of disaster and its fragmenting effects. In Regier's words, "The secular sublime, together with its ruins, discloses a disruptive and breaking quality at its core."[19]

The Lisbon earthquake serves as a prototype for the modern postapocalyptic ruin imaginary and the aesthetic of the sublime. It may be argued that contemporary ruin imagery constitutes a new deindustrial sublime, which also has a disruptive quality at its core and fragmenting effects. At the same time, the deindustrial sublime serves to domesticate the terrifying forces of capitalist disinvestment, privatization, and wealth inequality, the shattering effects of which are well represented in Detroit ruin imagery. The contemporary experience of the deindustrial sublime, which occurs when contemplating ruins and ruin imagery, becomes a way of containing and controlling the anxiety produced by the economic and social breakdown that has resulted from capitalist globalization, especially since the 1970s.

This domesticating of the terrible also occurs in many other works of modern and contemporary art and visual culture. To take just one example, the experience of observing, up close and personal, Damien Hirst's preserved shark in his work *The Physical Impossibility of Death in the Mind of Someone Living* is quite capable of producing a frisson of pleasurably controlled terror (figure 4). Critic Luke White argues that Hirst took Burke's work on the sublime as a "handbook for cultural production," which Burke apparently intended it to be, and echoes Burke's fascination with the body, mortality, violence, and pain. Burke writes, "Whatever is fitted in any sort to excite the ideas of pain, and danger, that is to say, whatever is in any sort terrible, or is conversant about terrible objects, or operates in a manner analogous to terror, is a source of the sublime."[20] Although White regards Hirst's shark as more Hollywood than high art ("more Steven Spielberg than it is Barnett Newman,"

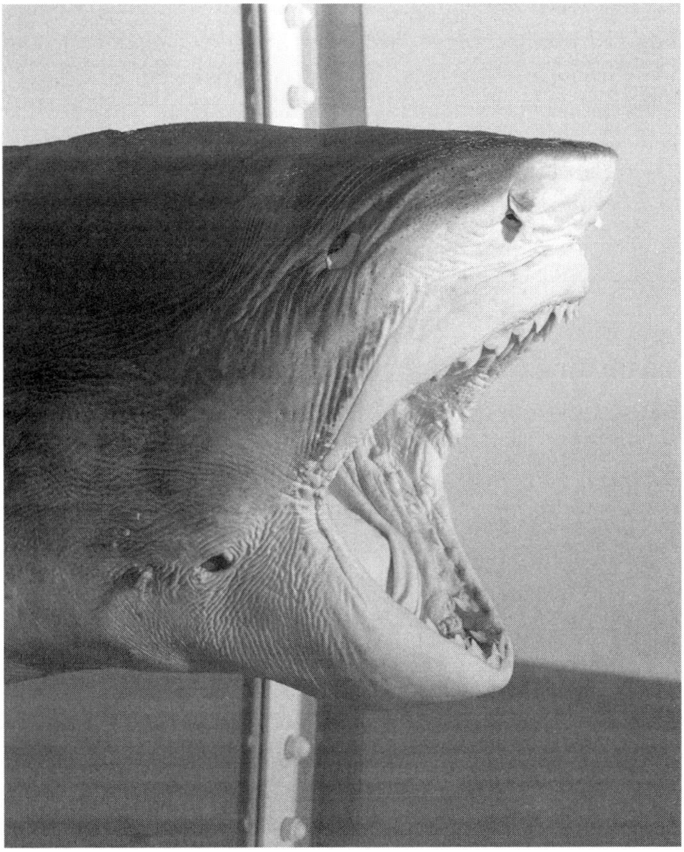

FIG. 4 Damien Hirst, *The Physical Impossibility of Death in the Mind of Someone Living*, 1991 (detail). © Damien Hirst and Science Ltd. All rights reserved / DACS, London/ARS, NY 2014. Photo: Prudence Cuming Associates Ltd.

in a reference to Newman's 1948 article "The Sublime Is Now"), he argues that the continual appearance of the sublime in contemporary art is a kind of haunting that speaks to an overarching modernist trauma defined by imperial instability and precariousness—captured in Marx's phrase "all that is solid melts into air"—as well as the limits to human power and progress imposed by environmental catastrophe. "The shark provides," writes White, "throughout its modern history, an image not only of nature as hostile but furthermore, and more precisely, of nature being as rapacious, insatiable, and unfeeling as capital accumulation itself."[21]

Shark horror has been a constant theme in contemporary culture, figuring in the flow of colonialist slave-trading capital in works such as John Singleton Copley's *Watson and the Shark* and stories such as Hergé's *Tintin and the*

Red Sea Sharks about smuggling enslaved Africans while on the pilgrimage to Mecca. Films such as Spielberg's *Jaws*, Renny Harlin's *Deep Blue Sea*, and James Contner's *Shark Swarm* of course depend on shark horror. The latest incarnation is *Sharknado*, a Syfy channel B movie about a freak hurricane that causes shark-filled water spouts or "sharknados" to flood Los Angeles. *Sharknado* aired several times in the summer of 2013 and was included in Syfy's week-long "Sharkathon." Like the shark figurations that invoke the sublime through the terrifying in nature, ruin imagery pictures abandonment and decay as a way of mastering and making pleasurable the fears they provoke and embody.

The Problematic Concept of "Ruin Porn"

The proliferation of ruin imagery has activated a debate that has been raised in the past over photographs of starvation in Africa, poverty in Depression-era America, Holocaust atrocities, or victims of lynching. On one level the question is whether such photographs are exploitative or whether they make visible what might otherwise remain hidden from history and even denied as factual. While such photos may be instrumentalized for ideological purposes by the state, they also may serve as forms of historical witnessing and potential tools of resistance.

The specific form the debate takes in relation to ruin imagery is whether or not it should be dismissed as "ruin porn," a phrase that has been playfully applied to many subjects (cabin porn, food porn, shoe porn, etc.). Art critic Richard Woodward in *Art News* describes ruin porn as "a phrase so immature and gawky it isn't sure how seriously to take itself" and "a smirking neologism that may or may not aspire to be a social critique."[22] The phrase appears to have been coined by writer and photographer James D. Griffioen, who writes the Detroit-based blog *Sweet Juniper.* Commenting on the constant requests from outside reporters for tours of Detroit, Griffioen told *Vice Magazine*, "At first, you're really flattered by it, like, 'Whoa, these professional guys are interested in what I have to say and show them.' But you get worn down trying to show them all the different sides of the city, then watching them go back and write the same story as everyone else. The photographers are the worst. Basically the only thing they're interested in shooting is ruin porn."[23] The term has found acceptance in various publications and as an academic topic.[24] But as Griffioen tells Woodward, "I take pictures of ruins, too, but I put them in the context of living in the city. These photographers were showing up with $40,000 cameras to take pictures of houses worth less than their hotel bills."[25] After years of shooting the city, it is difficult for local photographers to see others arrive from the outside with better equipment and connections to the art world and walk off with credit for "revealing" the blight of Detroit.

But history is rife with scenes of ruin and decay that photographers are drawn to photograph and people want to see. The problem with ruin porn as a tool of cultural analysis, as Woodward notes, is that it would invalidate a great many "images of blasted lives and places that carry a whiff of 'exploitation or detachment'" and would "do away with a sizable chunk of pictorial and written history."[26] It may be argued that the very act of picturing the abject carries "a whiff of exploitation," yet those pictures act as witnesses to history. Like all witnesses, they are subjective and imperfect but offer perspectives, usually those of the oppressed, that might otherwise be unseen and unheard. The medium of photography itself has limitations; it is able to document specific moments in time but is ill equipped to explain complicated causes and chains of events. This does not mean, however, that photography is not uniquely capable of producing powerful effects. Moreover, these effects may be mobilized to help produce desirable outcomes. One of the first photographic projects in the world was commissioned by the French government in the 1840s, not long after the camera was invented, to catalogue the nation's deteriorating medieval architecture in order to arouse public support for its preservation.[27] Likewise, more recent disasters such as September 11, Katrina, the earthquake and tsunami in Japan, Hurricane Sandy as well as recent wars and conflicts, including the events in Ferguson, Missouri, in response to the police shooting of Michael Brown, and the Israeli war in Gaza, are captured most powerfully in pictures. The influx of photographers may be disturbing at times, and local photographers may have better knowledge of the locale, but the story is always larger than the local. As Woodward observes about such conflicted feelings, "As someone living in Detroit and raising a family there, Griffioen might not appreciate strangers cruising through neighborhood streets and selling prints of local despair for $50,000 each. However, he, like others, doesn't want to censor efforts to record Detroit's struggle. The city's travails began long before the present recession and the problems are those of other once-prosperous northern cities."[28]

Griffioen understands the appeal of ruins and has himself posted many ruin images on his website, including several photographic series on such topics as "feral" houses that are overgrown with vegetation, lost neighborhoods, vacant schools, and the former Detroit Public Schools Book Depository (jamesgriffioen.net). His ruin photographs have been published in such magazines as *Vice, Harper's*, and *O, The Oprah Magazine* and exhibited in such venues as the Cirrus Gallery in Los Angeles, the Kiang Gallery in Atlanta, and the David Weinberg Gallery in Chicago. For Griffioen, his photographs began as a way to illustrate the stories he was writing about Detroit on his blog. The mood of his photograph *The Tree, Detroit Public Schools Book Depository*, for example, hints at the frustration he conveys in a blog post that details the

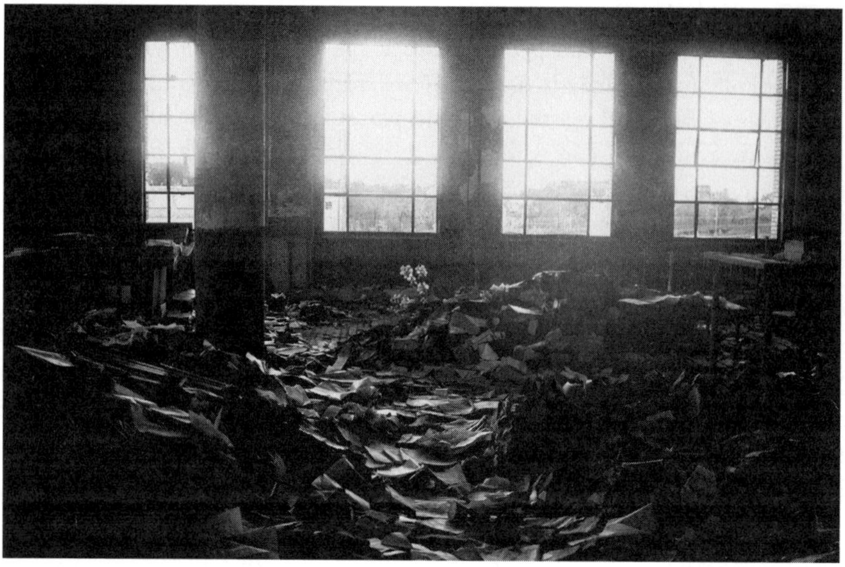

FIG. 5 James D. Griffioen, *The Tree*, from *Detroit Public Schools Books Depository*, 2007–2012. Courtesy of the artist.

inexplicable waste of many pallets of undamaged and still unwrapped textbooks, flash cards, workbooks, art paper, pencils, scissors, maps, and more that were abandoned by Detroit's deeply troubled public school system following a fire in the mid-1980s (figure 5). His photo portrays a stifling and musty darkness set against the bright sunshine beyond the windows, mitigated only by the slender Box Elder sapling that has taken root in a carpet of rotting books.

A comparison of Griffioen's photo with another by New York–based "outsider" Andrew Moore, considered by Griffioen the main exemplar of ruin porn, demonstrates that many photographers, both local and outside the city, are drawn to the same scenes of ruination (and even tapped Griffioen for the sites of some of his photos), although they convey different moods. In Moore's photo, *Birches Growing in Decayed Books, Detroit Public Schools Depository*, the books have turned mostly to mulch while young trees reach through the open roof toward the sky (figure 6). The receding diagonal perspective and warm light create a sense of renewal in adversity, a kind of comforting perspective, while Griffioen's photo generates greater tension between the promise of regeneration and the bleakness of decay. Despite his resentment of well-heeled outsiders with expensive camera equipment, paid assistants, and connections to the art world, Griffioen, whose own work has received wide attention, claims never to have considered himself an artistic photographer.[29] His concern, nonetheless, seems to be an insistence that insiders retain a kind of "ownership" of the ruins.

The ruin porn critique thus depends on a dichotomy between insiders and outsiders, between those who regard themselves as city loyalists whose lives and work are affected by the city and have therefore earned the right to profit from it and those whose photos they regard as voyeuristic and exploitative, feeding off the city's misery while understanding little about its problems, histories, or dreams. But for many poor local residents who have internalized an image of the city as a site of failure, or who suddenly see their city from another perspective, Detroit ruin imagery in the national media becomes a source of demoralization and embarrassment, regardless of who has taken the photos.

Michael Chanan, who made the 2005 film *Detroit: Ruin of a City* with sociologist George Steinmetz, proposes something similar when he notes that the resistant responses to outside filmmakers and photographers may "arise from a fear of representation, of the exposure to ridicule of an object of attachment." Chanan suggests that what the defensive insider "fails to allow is the validity of the stranger's perspective, and the representation of what the other sees. Behind this rejection is the fear that what others say *may turn out to be true.*"[30] This view is echoed by Detroit-based photographer Michelle Andonian, who observes that people in Detroit are angered by ruin imagery because they may suddenly see their own city through a different lens—the eyes of outsiders—compelling them to recognize that they have become so accustomed to ruination that they stopped seeing it long ago.[31] Chanan also reminds us that both insiders and outsiders produce work shaped by subjective perspectives. And it cannot be otherwise. The goal of the self-aware contemporary photographer

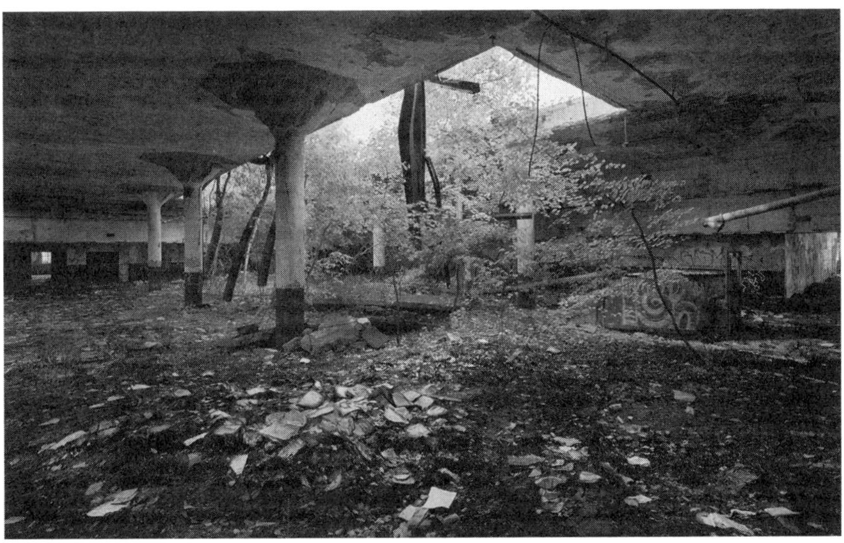

FIG. 6 Andrew Moore, *Birches Growing in Decayed Books, Detroit Public Schools Book Depository*, from *Detroit Disassembled*, 2010. © Andrew Moore.

is no longer a pretense of objectivity but rather an attempt to make his or her subject position and point of view visible, to claim the frame by which the image is constructed and meaning structured.

The larger fear, then, fueled by the proliferation of ruin imagery, is that of irreversible marginalization and alienation of the city from a host nation that views the ruins of Detroit from a position of aestheticized fascination at a comfortable remove. Whether the images have been produced by insiders or outsiders, national viewers make little of the distinction. And there are plenty of local photographers who shoot the ruins, drawn by the aesthetics of decay and the allure of transformation as well as the effects of ruins on the city. In response to the ruin porn critique, Andrew Moore asserted, "I think ruin porn is a mask for bigger issues. People are very anxious about this country, its direction and future. I think Detroit is a metaphor for both the good and the bad in this moment. Detroit is America's city. Detroit is not just about local issues. It's not just about providing good PR for Detroit. It's talking about America as a place, and where we're headed."[32]

It is more useful, then, to focus on *why* we are so drawn to ruins and ruin imagery and to examine the larger social and cultural roles that images play. This is more easily accomplished by distancing ourselves from the condemnatory use of the term "porn" in order to look more broadly and openly at the effects of ruin imagery and its ideological implications. As Linda Williams points out in discussing the early days of academic discourse on sexual pornography, there was often a fight over the very existence of porn, although no one denied its popularity or its power to arouse. Williams's solution in her study of pornography was to "avoid condemnation or defensiveness."[33] Similarly, my goal is to begin with an acknowledgment of the widespread popularity of ruin imagery and to seek a dispassionate perspective that examines the ability of ruin images to move and arouse us (intellectually or emotionally), not to debate the right of photographers to photograph ruins, even though some, inevitably, may care more about how, when, and why such ruination developed than others. Although sexual pornography has been notoriously contentious and difficult to define, most agree, suggests Williams, that the objective of porn is the production of pleasure or arousal, or both. Even if we take the term "ruin porn" at face value and see the objective of ruin imagery as the production of pleasure or arousal, to condemn the massive proliferation of ruin images on this basis leads to no new insight or knowledge. The more productive questions are how ruin images please, move, or arouse and what purposes this serves. Understanding the concept of the deindustrial sublime as a means of tempering the anxiety of decline helps to explain the attraction of photographers to the ruins of Detroit and the global appeal of contemporary ruin imagery.

"Discovering" Detroit's Ruins

George Steinmetz argues that the city's ruins, which are often perceived as "embarrassing and ugly," have long been invisible to society at large because they are not memorialized in any way and because there is no consensus about what caused them. Unlike the cathedral at Coventry bombed by the Luftwaffe in World War II, Ground Zero in Hiroshima, or the World Trade Center in New York, Detroit's ruins were not caused by an act of war or some other spectacular event but are instead the result of "more gradual and hidden processes of disinvestment, emigration, and racialized discrimination."[34] The ruins lack specific signification and are perceived more as rubble, a view that is compounded by the fact that they tend to be located in poor and minority neighborhoods. Detroit's ruins were "discovered" by the national media during the buildup to the 2006 Super Bowl game held in Detroit, when reporters who came to the city to produce pregame stories saw for the first time the acres of abandoned factories, storefronts, office buildings, churches, schools, houses, and vacant lots with which Detroiters have been living, in states of continuous transformation, for decades.

Detroit again made national news in 2009 when a man was found encased in ice at the bottom of an elevator shaft in the Roosevelt Warehouse (formerly known as the Detroit Schools Book Depository, designed by Albert Kahn), an abandoned building owned by billionaire Manuel "Matty" Moroun. The frozen man, with only his legs sticking out, had been submerged in ice for at least a month before authorities were notified and his body was removed. Homeless men who frequented the building and knew the body was there did not tell police for fear they would be routed from the building in the middle of a brutal winter, which is exactly what happened. A medical examiner ruled out death by murder or drowning since there were no wounds on the body or water in the lungs, and ruled it a cocaine overdose. Detroit journalist Charlie LeDuff, who broke the story, speculates that he was "tossed down the elevator shaft by a panicky friend," something that happens "all the time" among drug addicts. One of nineteen thousand homeless people in Michigan, the frozen man was soon identified as Johnnie Lewis Redding, a fifty-six-year-old second cousin to famed American singer-songwriter Otis Redding. Nearly three hundred people attended his funeral.[35]

Steinmetz notes that the insider mentality often lends itself to forms of city boosterism and defensiveness that obscure or ignore the immensity of the city's problems: "Politicians, local developers, city planners, and many community activists are virtually compelled to strike an optimistic, even Pollyannaish pose . . . in the hope of luring residents and investors back to the crumbling city."[36] Artists in particular, who have embraced the city, often feel vulnerable and betrayed by what they perceive as bad press. LeDuff notes that "the small, white 'art community' in Detroit" complained to him that he was too focused on the negative "in a city with so much good." At local forums on urban problems and at showings of city films, a similar complaint is often heard: What about all the good things? There are indeed many good things in the city, including its do-it-yourself spirit; its neighborhood initiatives; its waterfront development, art institutions, colleges, and universities; its galleries, museums, opera, symphony, art, dance, theater, food, music, performance, and literary scenes; and its hardworking, dedicated citizens. In his own account of good people in Detroit, LeDuff refers to "community elders trying to make things better, teachers who spend their own money on the classroom, people who mow lawns out of respect for the dead neighbor, parents who raise their children, ministers who help with funeral expenses. But these things are not supposed to be news. These things are supposed to be normal. And when normal things become the news, the abnormal becomes the norm."[37]

It may be argued nonetheless that Detroit has lost control of its own representation and that a "voyeuristic pathologization" of the city has overtaken it through the proliferating images of decay that have turned the urban dystopia into a city whose "ruination bleeds metonymically into a discourse about 'human ruins' who are blamed for the damaged condition of their environment," as Steinmetz suggests.[38] Many outsiders, in other words, including many whites in Detroit's suburbs, blame the city's own population for its ruination. As an overwhelmingly black city, this racist perspective constructs the city as the nation's "dark other" in both literal and figurative terms, a city to be isolated, feared and cut off from the body of the nation, as if ruins were not to be found in hundreds of other declining cities across America. By examining the effects of ruin images from a position that neither boosts nor criticizes the city, we may consider how ruin imagery obscures or reveals the ongoing relations of capital, power, and the city that structure the processes of ruination and its profound effects on the lives of people.

2

Fear and Longing in Detroit

Contemplating ruins within one's own nation greatly undermines the function of ruin gazing as an exercise in national superiority. The ruins of the homeland, represented in proliferating media, produce a trenchant challenge to assumptions about capitalist justice and democracy, notions of Western superiority and narratives of progress through technology. Yet even as ruin images picture the evidence of decline and collapse, they fail to account for the specific political and historical processes that lead to deindustrialization and city decline. By examining the causes of Detroit's ruination, we may better understand the decline of all cities and the status of this decline as an active and ongoing process. The plight of Detroit throws into sharp relief the effects of deindustrialization and capitalist disinvestment in cities across the nation—from Trenton, Baltimore, and Philadelphia to Oakland, Fresno, and Sacramento—even as the black city of Detroit (and other majority black cities in Michigan) is uniquely targeted for "emergency management" based on the official presumption that its own profligacy and fiscal irresponsibility led to its decline.

Capitalism and City Bankruptcy

In a television appearance on *Sunday Morning with George Stephanopoulos* in July 2013, Republican George Will clearly articulated the conservative view of Detroit's condition during a discussion of possible federal intervention in Detroit's bankruptcy. Will suggested that "cultural problems," including unwed mothers, were to blame for Detroit's financial collapse. In response to Steve Rattner, who argued, "Eighty percent of the pain in this restructuring is being borne by the workers and the retirees if this plan goes through. Detroit needs investment, and that's where the federal government and the state, particularly, can and should help," Will responded, "You can't solve their problems because their problems are cultural. You have a city, 139 square miles, you can graze cattle in vast portions of it. Dangerous herds of feral dogs roam in there. You have 3 percent of fourth graders reading at the national math standards. Forty-seven percent of Detroit residents are functionally illiterate. Seventy-nine percent of Detroit children are born to unmarried mothers. They don't have a fiscal problem, Steve, they have a cultural collapse." Katrina vanden Heuvel said, "I find that really insulting to the people of Detroit. There is a serious discussion about the future of cities in a time of deindustrialization, but in many ways, Detroit has been a victim of market forces. I think that what Steve said is so critical, that retirees and workers should not bear this. This story should not be hijacked as one of about greedy, fiscal public unions." Will replied, "What Steve said in his op-ed was that the people in Detroit are no more to blame than the victims of Hurricane Sandy because apart from voting—well, what did they vote for? For sixty years they voted for incompetents, malcontents, and in some cases criminals."[1] By construing Detroit as a city whose problems can't be solved because they are "cultural"—meaning that the population is poor and black—Will not only absolves the real agents of decline, the corporations and their political spokesmen, but also justifies harsh fiscal austerities imposed on the city and paves the way for such austerities to be imposed on other cities once the precedent has been established in Detroit.

Since the 1970s, following the policies of Chicago School economist Milton Friedman, capitalism has taken a turn toward what has become best known as neoliberalism (but is also known as free trade and globalization). Neoliberal capitalism focuses on advancing corporate goals by seeking to privatize government services, deregulate corporate industries, and deeply cut social services and social spending. These measures, including massive assaults on privacy, democratic rights, and unions and labor rights are not limited to the efforts of Republicans or Tea Partyers. Measures such as the "free trade" NAFTA agreement in 1994, established by the Clinton administration, played an important role in exacerbating the effects of disaster capitalism, impoverishing much of the Mexican population and causing a huge agricultural crisis as the United States exported tons of corn to Mexico. At the same time, it moved manufacturing plants from the United States to Mexico, where resources and labor are cheaper and more easily exploited for higher profits. The AFL-CIO estimates that plant closures in the United States caused the loss of seven hundred thousand American manufacturing jobs.[2] Neoliberal policies also compromise the environment through lack of oversight as exemplified by the faulty safeguards on nuclear power plants that led to the Fukushima Daiichi meltdowns in Japan in 2011 and the ongoing problems with inadequate radiation containment; genetically modified organisms, pesticides, and other agribusiness practices; or the significant soil and water pollution often left behind when companies abandon factories. The ongoing rebellions against entrenched repressive regimes across North Africa and against austerity measures across Europe, the United States, and Brazil are responses to "free market reforms." In reality, these are austerity measures and the results of deregulation and globalization that have led to an onslaught of human, economic, and environmental disasters, including the 2008 global financial collapse, as well as the acceleration of deindustrialization in the traditional manufacturing centers.[3]

Because the vast majority of people derive no benefit from the transfers of wealth from the public coffers of the government to private corporate hands, the spreading discontent, opposition, and protest also have produced an increased need for aggressive domestic surveillance and bottomless spending on security as well as mass incarceration, shrinking civil liberties, and a liberal use of torture, all veiled in secrecy and resistance to accountability. At the same time, the practices of neoliberal capitalism support financial elites on the grounds that banks are "too big to fail" and that the duty of state power is to protect financial institutions at all costs and provide a good business climate. "Only now," writes social theorist David Harvey, "as the state steps in to bail out the financiers, has it become clear to all that the state and capital are more tightly intertwined than ever, both institutionally and personally. The ruling class, rather than the political class that acts as its surrogate, is now actually seen to rule."[4]

The effects of neoliberal practices, especially state support of corporations over the poor and working population, are all too evident in Detroit, now the largest municipality in the country to file for Chapter 9 bankruptcy (on June 18, 2013). Detroit was placed under state control by Michigan Republican governor Rick Snyder in March 2013, when Snyder turned over management of all city resources and finances to an emergency manager (EM), the bankruptcy lawyer Kevyn D. Orr, whose sweeping powers included the ability to privatize city services, sell off municipal assets, and alter collective bargaining agreements with public sector unions. Although Michigan voters repealed the emergency manager law in a ballot referendum in 2012, Snyder forced through a new version in a lame-duck session of the Republican-controlled State Legislature in order to install the EM in the majority black city—effectively a coup against the elected city government. By the very fact of selecting a bankruptcy lawyer as EM, Snyder signaled his agenda of taking the city through bankruptcy.

In one of Orr's first political acts as EM, following a long history of city corruption, he hired his own former law firm, Jones Day, to help restructure

Detroit's long-term debt, despite the fact that Jones Day already represented some of the very banks holding this debt, including JPMorgan Chase and Bank of America.[5] Such an act clearly demonstrates that the banks always come first in the current capitalist order. The banks, however, are not hurting; on the contrary, they continue to show fat profits as the leveraging and speculation in derivatives using taxpayers' money in unregulated markets, which produced the financial crisis of 2008, continues apace as if nothing happened. The banks know they will be protected, encouraging further greed and recklessness.

Although the state blames municipal budget problems primarily on public employees' retirement benefits, the pension fund monies often have been used to enact expensive tax cuts or provide corporate subsidies. Public employees, whose pensions average just $19,200 per year ($1,600 per month), strenuously opposed Orr's demand to further cut their retirement benefits, which are firmly protected in the Michigan state constitution, and filed suit against the city. When state attorneys filed for Detroit bankruptcy, however, they used a deceptive stratagem to outmaneuver the pensioners and derail their lawsuit. As the *Detroit Free Press* reported, "An attorney for the pension funds who was seeking a temporary restraining order in Ingham County to block the historic bankruptcy filing said he felt blindsided because he agreed to delay an emergency hearing by five minutes at the request of attorneys for Snyder. During those five minutes, he said, attorneys filed the bankruptcy petition in Detroit, which generally results in a stay in all other pending lawsuits involving the city."[6] In December 2013 bankruptcy judge Steven W. Rhodes of the United States Bankruptcy Court ruled that the pension checks of retirees could be reduced even though they were protected by the state constitution.

More than thirty-two thousand active and retired Detroit city employees face a pension rip-off, which must be understood as the theft of workers' earnings as well as a harbinger of what lies in store for public workers across the nation. Known as the "grand bargain" and largely crafted by federal mediators, the bargain involves sweetheart deals for the banks and a battering for the workers who could either vote for major give-backs or else be subject to a "cram down" by Judge Rhodes on whatever terms he decided. This was a "lose-lose" situation for city workers. The grand bargain would result in a 4.5 percent cut to most pension checks (exempting police and firefighters) and also calls for a "claw back" of "overly generous" interest earned in pensioners' retirement accounts, in effect doubling or tripling the actual reduction in monthly pension payments. Cost-of-living increases would be reduced and retiree health care coverage *eliminated*. For the seventy-five hundred retirees too young for Medicare, this would be a major blow. The city would jettison a $4.3 billion liability in return for setting up a $450 million health care trust that would offer Detroit retirees a mere $175 per month to help buy insurance under the Affordable Health Care Act (also known as "Obamacare") that can cost around $5,000 per year for mid-range coverage and includes hefty out-of-pocket expenses. The imagery of city ruination thus may be understood as the visual expression of the financial ruination of unionized workers, which leads to the physical ruination of the body, the home, and hopes for a peaceful old age.

To ensure that the devastating effects of the grand bargain are not undone, unelected authorities vested with special powers will oversee the slashing of benefits and wages for at least the next thirteen years. State lawmakers approved a legislative package that subjects the city to an oversight committee, composed mainly of state officials or people appointed by Governor Snyder. Modeled on a board that controlled New York City following a 1975 municipal fiscal crisis, the commission will have control over labor contracts and will exert authority over elected city officials. Meanwhile, the EM and Judge Rhodes made a deal with Bank of America and UBS Investment Bank that granted them $85 million to settle claims stemming from wildly speculative financial "swaps" from which the banks have already profited. Ironically, the city made these transactions in the mid-2000s to shore up the pension plans, which went bust in the 2008 financial crisis.

Also linked to the bankruptcy are plans to privatize the Detroit Water and Sewerage Department (DWSD), another attack on a unionized workforce. In addition, starting in the spring of 2014, the DWSD sent out work crews, under orders from Kevyn Orr, to shut off water in up to three thousand homes *each week* that are behind in their bill payments. Between March and June 2014, service was cut off to more than fifteen thousand households and small businesses. Two-thirds of the water cutoffs involved homes with children, so that in some cases child welfare authorities took action to remove children from their homes since working utilities are legally required in all homes with children. People were given no warning and had no time to fill bathtubs and buckets, leaving everyone, include sick people, without water to drink, without toilets, without the ability to bathe or cook.[7] No such threats to cut off water service were made to the large corporations and institutions, such as the Red Wings' hockey arena or the Ford football stadium, that are also delinquent on their bills, and thousands of vacant and abandoned buildings in Detroit still have running water, often gushing through broken pipes.[8]

How could this happen? As the population has declined, water bills have risen 119 percent in a decade in a city with already high rates of unemployment and poverty. Moreover, as one report notes, "As a cost-cutting measure, the DWSD stopped sending bills, expecting residents to just figure out their own bills. 'Smart meters' were then installed that read backwards and many families were hit with bills in the thousands of dollars. Many of these bills were from former tenants, and many included water bills from nearby abandoned houses. But that didn't matter to the authorities."[9] As more than a thousand demonstrators marched in a downtown protest organized by National Nurses United, the largest labor union of registered nurses in the country, a report from Demos, a public policy organization, characterized the shutoff program as "mass enforcement to discipline the people" and a "misuse of the right to deny service." Amnesty International asserted, "Access to water is a human right for all people without discrimination," and a United Nations team of experts determined that "disconnection of water services because of failure to pay due to lack of means constitutes a violation of the human right to water and other international human rights."[10]

Amid growing anger in the city and international concern, Judge Rhodes admonished Orr to limit the damage to the city's reputation. But the EM asserted that his approach was "necessary" and claimed that of the fifteen thousand suspended accounts, half were made current within twenty-four hours and service was restored. Many of the people who settled up after being cut off, however, were able to do so only after receiving emergency cash from churches, charities, or friends, or by raiding funds set aside for such things as prescriptions for their elderly parents.[11] Yet even as another ninety-two thousand customers remained at risk for service cutoffs, Orr maintained that the city debt of $5.4 billion related to water and sewer bonds would be paid in full to creditors.

Opponents claim that Orr is simply cleaning up the DWSD's account books to prepare for privatization, which could push water rates even higher. Indeed, turning off the water of thousands of Detroit households seems designed to drive out the city's remaining poor residents not only to make the sale of the city's water system to a private company more attractive but also to help facilitate what has been called "hyper-gentrification"—a deliberate and strategic plan to "take back" urban areas.[12] As John Russo and Sherry Lee Linkon, authors of "The Social Costs of Deindustrialization," point out, "Over time, a struggling community may become divided, as those who promote a new vision of the city blame displaced workers for the area's problems" and come to regard them as "useless to the future of the town."[13] In other words, conservatives blame the city's failure on its own struggling residents, denying the effects of plant shutdowns and the resulting dissolution of the city's social fabric. This is true not just for Detroit but all deindustrialized cities.

In June 2014 the Detroit City Council approved yet another 8.7 percent increase on water prices, pushing household bills to almost twice the national average. The abrupt service shutoffs disproportionately affect African Americans in a city with a long history of racial discrimination, and, as activist groups assert, the exorbitant water rates place the burden of the city's fleeing tax base on the shoulders of its poorest citizens. In the rush to enforce austerity, no payment assistance programs were put in place and publicized before the shutoffs began, and a hastily established program set criteria for assistance that is difficult for many poor families to meet. As environmental writer Martin Lukacs observes:

> The official rationale for the water shut-downs—the Detroit Water Department's need to recoup millions—collapses on inspection. Detroit's high-end golf club, the Red Wings' hockey arena, the Ford football stadium, and more than half of the city's commercial and industrial users are also owing—a sum totaling $30 million. But no contractors have showed up on their doorstep. The targeting of Detroit families is about something else. It is a ruthless case of the shock doctrine—the exploitation of natural or unnatural shocks of crisis to push through pro-corporate policies that couldn't happen in any other circumstance.[14]

In response to growing national pressure over the mounting water crisis, full-scale media coverage, and a series of protest actions, Orr finally announced a moratorium on shutoffs and relinquished control over the DWSD to the city's mayor, Mike Duggan.[15] By October, 350 to 400 residents were again losing water service daily under Duggan's watch after Judge Rhodes ruled that there is no "enforceable right" to water, renewing the humanitarian crisis.[16]

But even as the hockey arena and football stadium are in arrears on their water bills, Snyder plans to spend $283 million of taxpayer money to help subsidize a new hockey stadium for the Detroit Red Wings as the centerpiece of a proposed downtown development project. This project is led by Olympia Development, which is owned by the billionaire founder of Little Caesars Pizza, Mike Ilitch, who also owns the Red Wings hockey team and the Tigers baseball team. City taxpayer funds were previously used to support the new baseball and football stadiums of Comerica Park and Ford Field, part of a longstanding pattern of granting corporate subsidies while cutting services and tax credits to low-income families.[17]

Critics noted more than a decade ago that such sports stadiums as well as gambling casinos are primarily meant to serve the suburban population "by recasting the redundant city as an a-historical destination theme park banking on Detroit's historical name brand."[18] As one television commercial for the Motor City Casinos has it, "a million miles away and just down the road." Moreover, tourist attractions such as sports stadiums or convention centers (Youngstown's Chevrolet Center or Detroit's Cobo Center), amusement parks (Flint's Auto World), casinos (Detroit and Gary), golf courses (Anaconda, Montana), shopping malls (Homestead, Pennsylvania), or historic sites built on abandoned industrial sites (Bethlehem, Pennsylvania) rarely bring high quality jobs after the initial construction jobs.[19]

Although about 40 percent of Detroiters live in poverty (more than 2.5 times the national rate), city bankruptcy enriches the bankers while further impoverishing the resident population not only by cutting pensions for city workers but also by privatizing city services. In addition to water, these services include trash pickup, electricity, and bus services, inevitably resulting in decreased quality and higher rates as well as lower wages and benefits for privatized workers. Privatizing bus operations, for example, will raise bus fares for residents who depend on the system as their primary mode of transportation. In his June 14, 2013, restructuring proposal to creditors, Orr asserted that Detroit's bus fares are "relatively low" and explicitly suggested hiking them to generate revenue while ignoring the impact this will have on the city's poorest residents, who are the most reliant on public transport. Although Detroit was once the global capital of car manufacturing, more than a fifth of households in the city today are unable to afford a car. As to quality, privatized services are primarily interested in making profits, not serving the public interest.[20]

Yet downtown and midtown investment in a 7.2-mile slice down Woodward Avenue is booming, with rental and commercial space nearing full occupancy. Even as Detroit's population shrank by 25 percent in the course of the last decade, downtown saw a 59 percent increase in the number of college-educated residents under the age of thirty-five.[21] This disparity suggests the creation of two different cities within Detroit, one a tiny thriving gentrified area of millennials and the other the devastated neighborhoods in most of the rest of Detroit, in a microcosm of the chasm of inequality nationwide.

A major player in this gentrification is multibillionaire Dan Gilbert of Quicken Loans, now the nation's largest online mortgage lender and third-largest residential mortgage lender. Although Gilbert has sought to distance Quicken Loans from predatory lending practices, the company was accused in a court suit by a group of former employees and customers of aggressive and improper sales tactics.[22] In a separate lawsuit in Ohio, Quicken was ordered by the state supreme court to pay $3.5 million to a defrauded homeowner.[23] Gilbert has bought up the equivalent of two square miles of downtown Detroit to sell to a variety of corporations for retail stores and cafes in the area. Buying skyscrapers to build a real estate empire, Gilbert and Rock Ventures, the umbrella group for more than eighty of his companies, currently own sixty properties that cover nine million square feet of real estate in downtown Detroit, including architectural treasures by Daniel Burnham, Minoru Yamasaki, and several by Albert Kahn.[24] Speculative entrepreneurs such as Gilbert seek monopoly rents, defined by David Harvey as monopoly claims based on criteria of "specialty, uniqueness, originality, and authenticity."[25] These qualities create a collective symbolic capital through branding, and the branding of cities has become big business even as their success, if they achieve it, leads to forms of homogenization and commercialization that undermine and erase originality and uniqueness. Collective symbolic capital in Detroit is built on its industrial and historic heritage and the vitality and aesthetics of its cultural production, including its distinctive music scene, food, arts institutions, sports teams, and signature downtown architecture (and even, ironically, its ruins, such as the Packard Plant and Michigan Central Station, which visitors to the city regularly drive by as part of their Detroit experience). Gilbert's monopoly rents attempt to control the commercial business corridor that capitalizes on the branding of the city.

The influx of coffee shops, bistros, art galleries, and upscale boutiques make parts of many cities increasingly appealing for young professionals (although many of these upstarts are still struggling and waiting for the revival to arrive), but they do not alter the everyday misery of working-class and poor urban neighborhoods. In cities across the nation, gentrification has raised property taxes, threatening working- and lower-middle-class homeowners. Newcomers to working-class areas such as the Mission District in San Francisco or the Shaw neighborhood in Washington, D.C., often do not plan to stay long and tend to move into new condos and lofts rather than existing houses, which is even more disruptive.[26] The cities of Boston, Philadelphia, Washington, D.C., and Pittsburgh have attempted to ameliorate the destructive process by introducing initiatives to reduce or freeze property taxes for threatened homeowners in order to stabilize neighborhoods and "provide a dividend of sorts to those who have stayed through years of high crime, population loss, and declining property values."[27] Even Mike Duggan announced plans to reduce property taxes in Detroit in order to more accurately reflect the value of homes in the city, which would encourage more home buyers and help reduce foreclosures. To reclaim our cities, however, these and other more far-reaching solutions must address the needs of the collective population and not just the interests of a small elite.

The "Creative Class"

There are those who imagine that Detroit is a blank slate waiting to be written on with niche market and artisanal entrepreneurial projects that will save the city and create the next Brooklyn or Berlin by attracting young urban pioneers—what urban planner Richard Florida calls the "creative class." Images of romantic ruination spur dreams of self-reinvention and economic resurgence and there are many young, mostly white, "creatives," in addition to artists, flocking to the city from around the world even as its longtime residents flee, suggesting that ruins and their representation create a mythos almost as appealing as it is appalling.

The creatives are the entrepreneurial adventurers who present themselves as fueling the city's comeback in what has been called "solutionism."[28] John Patrick Leary cites solutionism as a form of media-friendly utopian idealism combined with "the technocratic fantasy that systemic problems can be managed away with the right experts and right digital tools." He notes that the area of downtown Detroit controlled by Dan Gilbert, for example, provides no real solutions to such complex problems as urban unemployment or the funding of urban public schools. EM Kevyn Orr's suggestion that the city's huge financial debt is a function of "financial mismanagement," however, is an example of blaming the city by reframing the problem of city decline as local fiscal mismanagement, as if the city needs only some people with "better calculators and faster Internet connection."[29] Fundamental social change in Detroit requires more than "innovators" or individual solutions by members of the "creative class" and demands large-scale employment, civic infrastructure investment, and economic integration of the region.

Martha Rosler, an activist artist and culture critic, cautions that the public works of artists should not be confused with the projects of creatives. Rosler rejects Florida's conflation of the category of "artist" with the larger economic group of "creative class." Although artists have increasingly come to adapt the entrepreneurial strategies of creatives, many are committed and socially engaged, occupied with playing a role in social transformation. The public practices of others, however, may be entered into the creative class thesis in which, Rosler argues, they "transform cities, not by entering into transformative political struggle but rather to serve as unwitting assistants to upper-class rule."[30] It must be understood in this regard that culture is not necessarily viewed by the business and urban planning community as a "cultural good" in and of itself but as a "strategic asset" that may be instrumentalized to enhance the value of the urban business community. Entrepreneurial creatives, not to be confused with artists, are, at best, cut off from or blind to traditional forms of urban working-class organization; at worst, they are objectively antagonistic. "What often remains," writes Rosler, "is a nostalgic and romanticized version of city life in which labor is misperceived as little more than a covert service function, for the production of 'artisanal' goods, for example, and the creation of spaces of production and consumption alike (manufacturing lofts, workshops, bars, taverns, greasy spoons, barbershops) obscured by a nostalgic haze."[31]

Recent examples of companies who make expensive artisanal niche goods that construct a made-in-Detroit "brand" include Detroit Denim Co., which produces handmade jeans that sell for $250, and Shinola, which produces luxury watches, handmade bicycles, and leather goods. These companies present themselves as modest startups and promote the idea that buying something made in Detroit supports a distressed economy. The company behind Shinola, however, is Bedrock Brands, which was started by Tom Kartsotis, a founder of the Fossil brand of watches, making him, as the *New York Times* notes, "a mid-price watch mogul looking to go luxury under the cover of charitable business practices."[32] Shinola purchased its Tribeca flagship store for $14.5

million, which is not exactly what one would expect from a company that presents itself as a modest outpost of local craftsmanship. As Crain's *Detroit Business* reported in 2012, Kartsotis began the Detroit luxury brand after commissioning a study in which people were asked if they preferred pens made in China that cost $5, the United States at $10, or Detroit at $15, and the Detroit option was chosen even at the higher price.[33] Shinola plays on such liberal sympathies with portraits of its workers and even a "factory livecam" showing watchmakers at their work stations on its website. Like venture capitalists such as Dan Gilbert and his real estate empire in downtown Detroit, Shinola attempts to capitalize on Detroit's historic name brand in order to map the idea of Detroit's resurgence onto its own speculative investment and profits.

In a series of satiric videos, filmmaker Oren Goldenberg and friends lampoon the fixation of creatives on rescuing Detroit with their own invented genre called "hope porn." The short video "Save Detroit," for example, promoted an actual Kickstarter campaign for an online comedy series (until a private backer was found) and pitched a fake campaign to raise $500 million dollars to save Detroit (for $1, you get one ride on the People Mover; for $500, an abandoned house; for $20 million, the Water Department). In the summer of 2013 two more satirical video shorts were posted: "Detroit Pop-Up City" and "Detroit Diamond City," as part of the *Detroit (blank) City* series of send-ups where everyone is fair game, including urban farmers, local newscasters, Dan Gilbert, city mayoral candidates, and EM Kevyn Orr (see detroitblankcity.com). Among other targets, "Detroit Pop-Up City" parodies backyard farms as uncomfortably similar to the sharecropping past that the parents and grandparents of black Detroiters struggled to leave behind.[34] As Detroiter Paul Clemens witheringly notes, "No Parisian is as impatient with American mispronunciation, no New Yorker as disdainful of tourists needing directions, as is a born-and-bred Detroiter with the optimism of recent arrivals and their various schemes for the city's improvement."[35]

Privatizing Education

The narrow midtown and downtown boom also raises the question of how long young urban pioneers will stay once they start having children. In a further drive toward privatization, low-performing city public schools have been privatized, with some run by the state-created Educational Achievement Authority (EAA) and others by charter school operators or contracted private entities who manage school education at their own discretion. As a result, schools are showing an increased number of disciplinary incidents, including truancy and drug and firearm possessions, among other problems. According to a *Detroit News* report, the second quarter of the 2012–2013 school year showed 5,200 reported incidents in the 8,000-student district. The chancellor for the EAA,

John Covington, who received a four-year, $1.5-million contract, previously worked as the turnaround expert for failing schools in the Kansas City school system, which, under his watch, made no progress and lost its accreditation.[36]

Diane Ravitch, a former Bush administration official who is now the leading voice against school privatization, argues that public schools are in fact working very well for most students. She asserts that the leading factors in poor school performance are poverty and segregation, and she writes of corporate reformers:

> Though they speak of "reform," what they really mean is deregulation and privatization. When they speak of "accountability," what they really mean is a rigid reliance on standardized testing as both the means and the end of education. When they speak of "effective teachers," what they mean is teachers whose students produce higher scores on standardized tests every year, not teachers who inspire their students to love learning. When they speak of "innovation," they mean replacing teachers with technology to cut staffing costs. When they speak of "no excuses," they mean a boot-camp culture where students must obey orders and rules without question. . . . When they speak of "a successful school," they refer only to its test scores, not to a school that is the center of its community, with a great orchestra, an enthusiastic chorus, a hardworking chess team, a thriving robotics program, or teachers who have dedicated their lives to helping the students with the highest needs (and often the lowest scores).[37]

Governor Snyder, himself a multimillionaire former venture capitalist, has slashed hundreds of millions of dollars from public education to finance corporate tax cuts. In April 2013 secret meetings were revealed between Snyder administration officials, business leaders, and corporate public school "reformers" to circumvent the state's constitutional ban on subsidizing private schools in order to open the way for a vast expansion of corporate-run schools in Michigan using a voucher-like program.[38] The already dismal school system in Detroit is thus likely to get worse and will demotivate middle-class young couples with children who may be drawn to a gentrified midtown–downtown from staying in the city.

Corporate Subsidies

The state has played a critical role in Detroit's decline. Snyder has repeatedly said that the state will not "bail out" Detroit, and the federal government has echoed this sentiment. As former Michigan treasurer Robert Kleine argues, the state pushed policies that encouraged the city's failure, especially through cuts to revenue sharing that, he asserts, "doomed the city," including cutting business and income taxes in 2000 and then giving business yet another $1.8

billion tax break in 2011. This further eroded the tax base and contributed to the advancing decline of city services while doing little or nothing to create jobs.[39] A 2013 study by Good Jobs First shows that Michigan leads the nation in massive corporate tax breaks over the last thirty years.[40]

The kinds of bailouts that were available to the banks and auto companies during the 2008 economic crisis are clearly not available to the poor black city of Detroit. Those massive bailouts, which served to increase the profits of the banks and auto companies, were followed by plant closures and mass layoffs, clearing the way for investment in production facilities elsewhere in North America and the hiring of new and temporary workers at half the pay of senior workers. As David Harvey points out, it would be far better to reverse the politics of wage repression and to raise real wages in order to bolster consumer demand, but most capitalists are unwilling to contemplate such a solution. The Republicans in Congress blocked the initial plan to bail out the Detroit auto companies on the grounds that it did not reduce the wages and benefits of unionized labor low enough to match the nonunionized labor of Japanese and German auto companies located in the American South.[41] The negotiated bankruptcy of General Motors led to the creation of the two-tier system in which people joining the labor force are paid lower wages and benefits than those who are already employed. This two-tier system has spread throughout much of the United States, but the implementation of this plan only depressed consumer demand further.

The net global loss of jobs during the recession of 2007–2009 is estimated at 30 million, with three-quarters of those located in the advanced economies. The United States accounts for 7.5 million in newly unemployed, constituting a vast labor reserve that puts further downward pressure on wage rates and working conditions. Profits for corporations, however, have rapidly revived, helping to spark a recovery in the stock market as well as in the lavish lifestyles of corporate CEOs and Wall Street executives.[42] This corporate resurgence explains why the auto companies are thriving while Detroit continues to decline. City mismanagement, while real enough, has become a convenient scapegoat for the main perpetrators of Detroit's decline—the auto companies, who shut down the plants to pursue nonunion labor and higher profits elsewhere; the state, which delivered massive tax cuts to corporations while cutting education and social services; and the federal government, which has failed to support its cities while pressuring the auto companies to squeeze greater concessions from the labor force. As George Packer ruefully observes, some financial leaders who defended the banks, such as Henry Paulson or Timothy Geithner, "have suffered damaged reputations; a few have seen their net worth drop; none have had to hunt for food in garbage cans."[43]

To make matters worse, Republicans in the House of Representatives passed a farm bill that, if it had become law, would have slashed $20.5 billion from the Supplemental Nutrition Assistance Program over the next ten years, removing a total of 14 million people from what is known as the food stamp program and preventing school children from getting free lunches.[44] Instead the 2014 Farm Bill cut "only" $8.7 billion in food stamps, affecting 850, 000 households, about 1.7 million people, even as census data shows that nearly 47 million people live in poverty in this country. The federal poverty line, however, does not reflect the cost of living; if it included the cost of housing, transportation, and health care, researchers estimate that about 100 million Americans would qualify as poor.[45]

The loss of manufacturing jobs and jobs in related industries in the traditional manufacturing centers have also caused millions of home foreclosures, many of them based on bank fraud and deception. The situation was dire in Detroit. In 2007 nearly one hundred homes were foreclosed upon every day, with an estimated two thousand people moving out of the city each month. Crowds grew unruly when they could not get into overcrowded Cobo Hall job fairs, and ten thousand people lined up on the first day when one of the city's casinos advertised for new workers.[46] For decades, more buildings have been demolished than built in Detroit, a practice of "unbuilding" that has become the city's primary form of architectural activity.[47] The average price of homes dropped from $97,900 in 2003 to $12,400 in 2009.[48] The banks are also responsible for "zombie" properties, affecting thousands of people in Detroit and some three hundred thousand nationwide. These are created when banks start foreclosure proceedings but then decide not to finish the foreclosure process, walking away from vacant homes whose owners they have forced out. The banks are not required to notify the city or the borrower that they have abandoned the foreclosure process, leaving the owner legally and financially responsible for property tax payments, with tax bills sometimes arriving a year later, while the banks themselves avoid payment of city taxes.[49]

In 2014 the Detroit Blight Removal Task Force found that 84,641 homes and buildings across Detroit, 30 percent of the total stock, are dilapidated or heading that way, with 114,000 vacant lots and 559 big empty industrial buildings.[50] The task force, established by the Obama administration following the city's bankruptcy, is the most elaborate survey of the city, performed neighborhood by neighborhood. It recommends demolishing forty thousand derelict buildings but does not address what should become of the tens of thousands of empty lots left behind. Yet even vacant lots create voids that serve as counterparts to standing ruins, becoming "negative ruins," as graphically demonstrated by aerial photographs such as Julia Reyes Taubman's *East Grand Boulevard between Saint Paul and Agnes Streets* (figure 7).[51] The large structure near the top of the image is the seventy-three-apartment El Tovar Apartment Building, designed in the Spanish Moorish–Art Deco style. It was built in 1928 and represents a shift toward high-density housing at a time

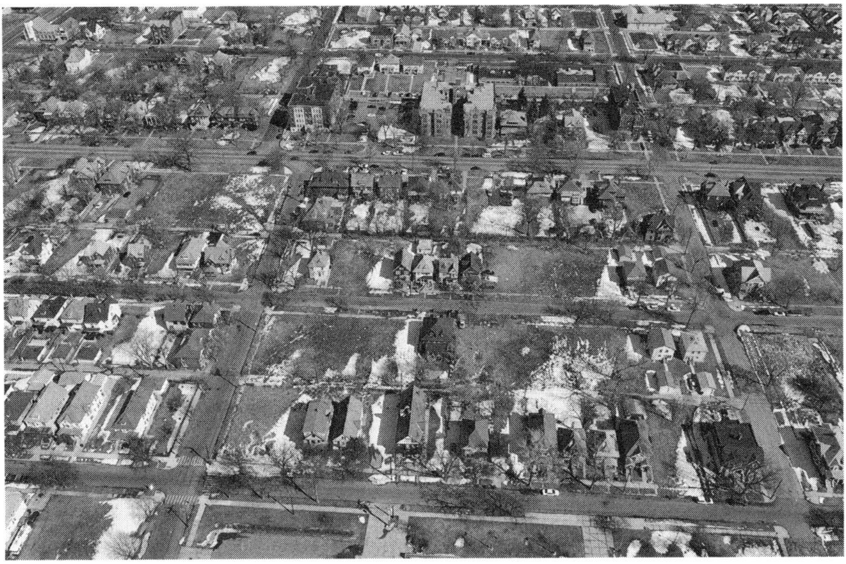

FIG. 7 Julia Reyes Taubman, *East Grand Boulevard between Saint Paul and Agnes Streets*, from *Detroit: 138 Square Miles*, 2011. Courtesy of the artist.

when Grand Boulevard was a prestigious address. Located near the Saint Paul Manor Apartments and Kingston Arms Apartments in the East Grand Boulevard Historic District, all three buildings face an increasingly depopulated area, with razed houses creating large empty spaces.

The power monopoly of the Big Three automakers of Ford, General Motors, and Chrysler was broken in the 1980s when the Japanese and Germans entered the American auto market. The auto companies, like capitalism itself, which initially developed within nation-state frameworks, had to become internationally competitive. This greater competition forced the use of labor-saving technologies as well as the use of state power to undermine organized labor and permit corporations to continue to make easy profits. Maximizing profit meant allocating surplus capital to wherever the profit rate was highest, which was not the traditional centers of production in the advanced industrial countries but in the poorest regions of the world, where labor and resources were cheap. Although Detroit has long functioned as a metonym for the auto companies, almost all of the auto plants have moved elsewhere, first to the suburbs and small towns, then to other parts of the country, North America, and overseas. The auto bailouts therefore did nothing to prevent Detroit's financial crisis; that is, it did nothing for the actual impoverished city as opposed to the fictive entity "Detroit," meaning the car companies.

As critical theorist Eric Cazdyn argues, we have entered a "new chronic mode" that maintains an acutely debilitated status quo in order to avoid the danger of sudden death. Cazdyn writes, "The maintenance of the status quo becomes, if not quite our ultimate goal, what we will settle for, and even fight for. If the system cannot be reformed (the cancer eradicated, the ocean cleaned, the corruption expunged), then the new chronic mode insists on maintaining the system and perpetually managing its constitutive crises, rather than confronting even a hint of the terminal, the system's (the body's, the planet's, capitalism's) own death."[52] Revolution, he suggests, becomes unthinkable as the chronic mode is managed and death held off. The present, despite its brutality, becomes naturalized, making it easier to choose the limits of the known than an unknown future that is difficult to imagine.

To maintain this chronic mode in Detroit, the state counts on the isolation of the city's poor, black population from the mainly white workforce in the rest of Michigan, and the rest of the country, in order to push through severe cuts against public sector employees that will then become the leading edge of an assault on all workers. The Detroit plan continues the battle by both Democratic and Republican parties against public employee unions, which now comprise about half of organized labor due to deindustrialization in the Midwest and Northeast and the precipitous decline of private-sector unions.[53] According to the Bureau of Labor Statistics, the total union membership rate in 2012 and 2013 was only 11.3 percent, or 14.5 million, down from 20.1 percent, or 17.7 million, in 1983, the first year for which comparable data was available.[54]

Ford's Empire

As early as the 1920s Henry Ford's disastrous attempt to extend his auto empire into the Amazonian jungle foreshadowed the decimation of Detroit today. Historian Greg Grandin relates the story of how Ford created Fordlandia, a rubber-producing company town in the jungle of Brazil with tennis courts, company square dances, and prohibition rules against drinking in accordance with Ford's own Puritanism. The Brazilian workers rebelled, and the Amazonian ecosystem did the rest. By insisting that his managers plant rubber trees in tight rows for greatest efficiency, like the factory machines in Detroit, Ford created the conditions for a massive insect infestation and blight that fed off rubber. Despite sinking millions of dollars into his jungle paradise, "The ruins of Fordlandia, in fact, look a lot like those in Highland Park," writes Grandin.[55] Ford's attempt to create a workers' utopia was in part a hubristic enterprise, in part a "civilizing mission," and in part a response to an American culture that spurned his social utopian visions in the service of modern industry. As Grandin observes, "Ford's frustrations with domestic politics and culture were legion: war, unions, Wall Street, energy monopolies, Jews, modern dance, cow's milk, the Roosevelts, cigarettes, alcohol, and creeping government intervention."[56] At the same time that Ford was pouring millions into trying to make his rubber plantation work and building the massive River Rouge complex in Dearborn, he was also collecting antiquarian Americana objects and building a model nineteenth-century American town at the Henry Ford Museum and Greenfield Village in Dearborn. Greenfield Village offered a self-serving narrative of technological progress ending in the assembly line, but it also created a nostalgic and idealized version of a vanished way of life whose demise Ford himself had helped bring about through automation.

Ford's spectacular failure in the Amazon did not undermine his overall imperialist success, which exported "Fordism" around the world. By breaking down the assembly process into small, repetitive tasks, parts and goods could be made virtually anywhere, without the need for employers to pay workers enough to buy the products they were ultimately helping to produce. Although Ford had once preached "high wages to create large markets," capitalist industrialization itself made this impossible to achieve, instead cutting labor costs to maintain an expanding rate of profit. "The result is a race to the bottom," writes Grandin, "a system of perpetual deindustrialization whereby corporations—including, most dramatically, the Ford Motor Company itself—bow before a global economy that they once mastered, moving manufacturing abroad in order to reduce labor costs just to survive."[57] It was not just international competition, which came much later, that led the Detroit auto companies to seek colonial labor regimes but also, well before that, the desire to avoid municipal oversight and union strength by seeking cheaper resources and labor.[58] But the destructive processes of Ford's industrial empire are often obscured as one finds streets and buildings named in his honor not only in Detroit, where he founded his company, but also in Mexico, Brazil, France, Germany, India, Canada, and other parts of the United States.[59]

Grandin also connects Detroit's deindustrialization to neoliberalism in Latin America where a number of multinational corporations, including Ford, Chrysler, Mercedes-Benz, Firestone, and Volkswagen, worked with brutally repressive regimes, helping to support the 1976-backed coup that broke the strong Argentine union movement and paved the way for the assault on unions that began in the United States under Ronald Reagan. These corporations supported the Latin American death squads from the 1960s to the 1980s. Ford, in particular, forged exclusive contracts with the Argentine security forces under the military junta, making the Ford Falcon an emblem of state terror against the thousands of "disappeared," the political dissidents and trade unionists murdered by the regime. That assault on the unions at home and abroad was part of the larger project of shifting the economic center of gravity in the United States from the industrial Northeast and Midwest to the open-shop South and other countries, hastening the transition to neoliberal globalization.[60] The readiness of the auto companies to exploit colonial labor and resources, and their willing alliance with murderous regimes to break strong union movements, has led directly to the ruination of Detroit and the traditional manufacturing centers. In this way the destruction of Detroit was built right into the capitalist project.

The Deindustrialization of Detroit

Kevin Boyle describes two narratives of Detroit's decline, one told by conservative whites, including Detroiters such as journalist Ze'ev Chafets in his lurid account, *Devil's Night and Other True Tales of Detroit*, and the other by historians. Chafets regards the 1940s and 1950s as a golden age when industry boomed and workers, both black and white, lived the good life. This was destroyed by the 1967 riots, which led to white flight from the city and resulted in a rapid shift to a black city with black rule. Exacerbated by the oil crisis of the 1970s and the subsequent collapse of the domestic auto industry, Detroit's decline accelerated. Boyle observes, "The popular story serves an obvious political purpose: black rioters and bad luck caused the city's decline; whites bear no responsibility for its problems."[61]

Historians, however, tell a very different story, tracing the city's decline not to the events of 1967 but to white rule in Detroit and the institutions they controlled. As Thomas Sugrue demonstrates in his seminal historical study, *The Origins of the Urban Crisis*, Detroit deindustrialization began immediately after World War II. Far from being a golden age, white rule of the city created and enforced segregation in the 1940s and 1950s that had devastating long-term effects on housing, jobs, and industry, well before the 1967 riots. Although there was a great housing shortage for blacks, the city's leadership, under Mayor Albert Cobo, opposed public housing because whites opposed building such housing in or near white areas. From 1950 to 1956 Detroit failed to take advantage of federal funds made available in the 1949 Housing Act, ranking eighteenth among the twenty-five largest cities in the ratio of low-rent starts to all housing starts. Detroit built less public housing in the 1950s than smaller cities such as Boston, Newark, Norfolk, St. Louis, and New Orleans.[62] At the same time, whites opposed black home ownership in white neighborhoods. Sugrue details the terror black families faced when they had the courage to move into all-white neighborhoods, including fire-bombing, shattered windows, and other forms of intimidation and violence.

In the auto plants, under Walter Reuther's leadership, the United Auto Workers union gave the corporations free rein to pursue policies regarding shop-floor discipline and privileges for white male workers that divided the workforce along racial lines. Blacks were the last hired and first fired; they were segregated at the bottom of the workforce, doing the dirtiest, most menial, and most dangerous work, and because they were concentrated in unskilled jobs, their jobs were the first to be eliminated through automation. Rather than laying off older workers, workforces were reduced by not hiring new employees, disproportionately affecting young black men. Between 1947 and 1963, Detroit lost 140,000 manufacturing jobs; by the end of the 1950s black job seekers in the city were already demoralized.

Meanwhile, white workers followed the factory relocations to the suburbs and to small cities in rural areas, or to the Sunbelt South. More affluent whites also left Detroit to follow investments in the suburbs. The process of racialized suburbanization was supported by government-funded highways and federally guaranteed mortgage loans that disproportionately favored white homebuyers. With blacks largely shut out of suburban housing as Detroit's depopulation began its unbroken slide, the city became increasingly poor and black. By 1960, the year in which Sugrue's study ends, Detroit was already dominated by abandoned factory buildings, surrounded by blocks of boarded-up stores and restaurants, as the loss of industry and jobs rippled through the entire local economy.[63] As Boyle notes, "White Detroiters thus reinforced African Americans' ghettoization, trapping them in the center of the city as it was being rapidly stripped of jobs. By so doing, they forced black Detroiters to bear the burden of deindustrialization."[64]

The factory zone that once surrounded the city, common to the model of a centralized metropolis, is a devastated brownfield, a zone of abandonment unparalleled by any in the nation, which runs right up to the northern border of the city at Eight Mile Road. The racial divide is stark, demonstrating the integral relationship between black oppression and capitalist exploitation. While Detroit is almost 83 percent black, the neighboring white working-class suburbs are less than 2 percent black.[65] With the departure of factories and white workers, in 1970 the three largest working-class suburbs of Dearborn, Livonia, and Warren, with a combined population of more than a hundred thousand people, had only eighty-six black residents.[66] Detroit never developed a rapid transit system centering on the downtown, nor does it have a unified bus system between the city and the suburbs. Although Detroit had streetcars at the beginning of the twentieth century, between 1936 and 1950 General Motors and other companies purchased and dismantled streetcar and electric train systems in forty-five cities.[67] Instead, a tight ring of expressways cut off downtown from the rest of the city. David Harvey explains the logic of this kind of reorganized urban infrastructure as alert to the control of restive populations, just as Georges-Eugène Haussmann's widening of Parisian boulevards made working-class barricade building more difficult: "The re-engineering of inner cities in the United States in the wake of the urban uprisings of the 1960s just happened to create major physical highway barriers—moats, in effect—between the citadels of high-value downtown property and impoverished inner-city neighborhoods."[68]

These expressways were also designed to channel traffic between the plants in Highland Park and Dearborn and the residential suburbs. Detroit's highway planners were careful to avoid disrupting white middle-class residential neighborhoods but felt no such compunction about destroying black neighborhoods, especially those closest to downtown.[69] Used as an excuse to "raze slums," the Chrysler Freeway cut through the neighborhood of Black Bottom, named for the richness of the soil from the former Savoyard River, and destroyed Hastings Street, known for its black-owned businesses, social institutions, and night clubs. With the adjacent black neighborhood of Paradise Valley, both east of downtown, the neighborhoods were especially known for their contributions to American music, including blues, big band, and jazz.

These intensified patterns of racial segregation and job loss that weighed disproportionately on the black population produced the extremity of Detroit's ruination in comparison to other deindustrialized cities and paved the way for the anger and frustration that exploded in the rebellion on Twelfth Street in 1967. Already suffering a housing shortage when Black Bottom was bulldozed, the Twelfth Street area became densely packed with apartments that were subdivided and had six to eight families living where two had lived before.[70] Commercial businesses in the area gave way to "pool halls, liquor stores, sleazy bars, pawn shops, and second-hand businesses."[71] The riot, which took place in the middle of a July heat wave, was triggered by the police who decided to arrest all 85 patrons of a "blind pig" (illegal drinking establishment) instead of the usual handful of owners and patrons. While waiting for reinforcements to arrive, a crowd of two hundred area residents gathered at 4 A.M., and by 8 P.M., the crowd had swelled to more than 3,000. It took 17,000 police, National Guardsmen, and federal troops to quell the riot after five days, leaving 43 people dead. Thirty of them were killed by police, including 25 African Americans. Over 7,200 people were arrested, more than 2,500 buildings burned, and over $36 million of insured property was lost, with much more uninsured property damaged.[72] Riots had broken out in 1943 as well, when thousands of white workers had arrived in Detroit from the South and, along with second-generation Poles, were generally hostile to black rights at a time when the city suffered an acute housing shortage. Comparing the 1967 rebellion to the 1943 riots, Dominic Capeci and Martha Wilkerson note, "Both disorders came at a time of rising expectations and blocked opportunities," especially in housing and employment; both also occurred during periods of strained community relations with a predominantly white, racist police force.[73]

The devastation and decentralization of Detroit's downtown resulting from city, federal, and corporate policies led to the urbanization of the suburbs, creating a proliferation of strip malls, shopping malls, and office parks and ultimately replacing Detroit's downtown with what the design critic Robert Fishman calls "a linear city" sixteen miles away on Big Beaver Road. Fishman observes that the "specialized engineering, design, procurement, marketing, public-relations, advertising, finance, accounting, and law firms that comprise the collective 'brains' of the industry" for the Big Three automakers are all found in the hundreds of office suites and technical facilities along Big Beaver Road.[74] The position of Big Beaver Road north of the metropolis inverts the traditional city design that locates the immigrant poor between the downtown and the factory zone, both of which should be accessible by public transit, and instead positions the wealthy residents of Troy, Birmingham, and Bloomfield Hills—among the wealthiest suburbs in the nation—closest to jobs and high-end shopping at the upscale Somerset Mall on Big Beaver Road, while the poor are the most isolated in the derelict city.[75] A version of this has occurred in many cities across the country; yet with the proximity of great wealth and devastating poverty, the extreme contradictions of class and race in America are writ large in Detroit.

The literature on Detroit generally fails to detail how federal and corporate policy in the 1970s and 1980s further promoted the city's deindustrialization through continued attacks on the working class and the continued gutting of public housing and transportation. But corporate policy emerges as the most significant factor in the unmaking of Detroit. By not updating their plants and instead stripping Detroit of the jobs that made it the Motor City, it was the corporations who turned one of the world's most productive manufacturing centers into the premier example of urban decay. As Boyle asserts, "The ruins of Detroit—the weed-choked lots where houses once stood, the shells of factories, the blocks of boarded-up storefronts—thus stand as symbols not of decay but of power, the power of the corporations to shape the rise and fall of a great American city."[76]

Nor was the city helped by its two-term mayor, Kwame Kilpatrick, and other officials, whose depth of corruption was staggering. Kilpatrick's appointed city treasurer, his ex-college frat brother, Jeffrey Beasley, for example, used Detroit pension funds to buy some California strip malls for $3.1 million, without transferring the title of those properties to the pension funds. Beasley is accused of taking bribes and kickbacks as he made bad investments that ultimately cost pension funds $84 million. Kilpatrick effectively ran the city as a criminal enterprise and in 2013 was convicted on twenty-four federal felony counts of racketeering, extortion, bribery, and fraud. The unrestrained corruption and lax oversight that allowed these actions suggest that corruption had been the norm through many administrations. A *Detroit Free Press* investigation estimates that corrupt and incompetent officials and appointees in Detroit over many years are responsible for almost half a billion dollars in wayward investments.[77]

Although decades in the making, Detroit's decline presages many more municipal failures across the country as well as credit downgrades, which raise borrowing costs for cities and put them deeper in debt. Since 2010 there have been at least thirty-six municipal bankruptcy filings, such as Jefferson County in Alabama, and Stockton, San Bernardino, and Vallejo in California. Cities are watching Detroit's bankruptcy proceedings, and one of the most dangerous precedents that may be set is the evasion of pension commitments, which until recently were considered legally protected. In two recent bankruptcies, one in Prichard, Alabama, and another in Central Falls, Rhode Island, pensions were cut by as much as 50 percent. Pension funds, a form of deferred wages that are supposed to be held in trust until they are needed, instead became pots of money for bankers and hedge fund managers in league with state pension plan managers to make some of their riskiest investments, burning the pension funds when these did not pan out. The refusal to cover the pension funds in a city as large as Detroit as well as the slashing or elimination of hard-won medical benefits could therefore have a major ripple effect across the United States, affecting tens of thousands of people who are counting on those benefits.

"Monetizing" the Detroit Institute of Arts

Even the art collection of the Detroit Institute of Arts (DIA) was considered a city asset by the EM and bond insurers in the event of bankruptcy. The collection includes works by Jan van Eyck, Fra Angelico, Bellini, Titian, Bronzino, Tintoretto, Rembrandt, Brueghel, Poussin, Cézanne, van Gogh, Frederic Church, Whistler, Degas, Picasso, Matisse, Kirchner, Kandinsky, Rothko, Warhol, Motherwell, the Detroit Industry frescoes by Diego Rivera, and many other works. Initially valued by local experts as worth between $10 billion and $15 billion, Orr said that he considered "monetizing" a half billion worth "reasonable."[78] "Creditors can really force the issue," said Orr's spokesman, Bill Nowling. "If you go into court, they can object and say, 'Hey, I'm taking a huge haircut, and you've got a billion dollars' worth of art sitting over there.'"[79] Estimated to be the fifth-largest encyclopedic museum in the nation, with a yearly attendance of nearly six hundred thousand visitors, this liquidationist view of the city's—and the region's—cultural wealth alarmed even the white suburbs and art world officials across the country. DIA director Graham Beal asserted the fundamental principle that the museum's collection is "held in the public trust"; Metropolitan Museum of Art director Thomas Campbell noted that selling off works of art would shock and outrage "the millions of people who admire the Detroit Institute of Arts and the entire cultural community who rightly believe that art is a permanent, rather than a liquid, community asset"; Sam Sachs, director of the DIA from 1985 to 1997, observed, "If you could sell off Detroit's hospitals and its universities, would you do that, too? If you do things like this, you're basically spelling the end of the city as an ongoing entity."[80]

In response, Nowling framed the issue as a choice between paying pensioners and maintaining an art collection: "It's hard to go to a pensioner on a fixed income and say 'We're going to cut 20 percent of your income or 30 percent or whatever the number is, but art is eternal.'"[81] This argument was taken at face value by Peter Schjeldahl, an art critic whose support for the sale of the DIA's art elicited a deluge of angry responses, including the question: "Would *New Yorker* art critic Peter Schjeldahl suggest that Greece sell the Parthenon to pay its crippling national debt?" Two days later, asserting a sounder grasp of the issues, Schjeldahl rescinded his endorsement.[82] Even the *Wall Street Journal* pointed out that the choice is not between pensions and paintings because the city will attempt to cut pensions in any case.[83]

Yet the "art for pensions" rhetoric was turned into an unusual "grand bargain" to save the art collection and "limit" pension cuts. Money raised by private foundations, the DIA, and the State of Michigan would be directed to the retiree pension fund, whose unfunded liabilities are estimated at $3.5 billion of the city's $18 billion in debts, while the DIA would be transferred to a charitable trust.[84] However, the bond insurers of Syncora Capital Assurance and the Financial Guaranty Insurance Company filed objections even to this deal, asserting that the proposal unfairly favors retirees over banks. As "creditors," the parasitic bond insurers, whose business it is to take financial risks for financial gain and who are already immensely wealthy, are hardly equivalent to the city's struggling retirees, who are not in the business of gambling with their pensions, which they earned as part of their labor contract.

The billionaire Koch brothers, through their right-wing organization Americans for Prosperity, also got involved to defend the bond insurers, condemning the grand bargain and announcing plans to contact ninety thousand conservatives around the state to build opposition to it.[85] The brothers have given millions of dollars to a conservative movement headed by the Tea Party in the U.S. Congress that ruthlessly cuts food stamps and denies welfare and daycare for millions of people living in poverty, even as they also fund medical philanthropy and the arts. We could see these attacks on the poor as forms of quiet violence. Slavoj Žižek points out in his book *Violence* that there are two kinds of violence: subjective violence, such as "crime and terror, civil unrest, international conflict," and objective violence, an unseen form of violence that is systemic and naturalized. Unseen, objective violence constitutes the zero-degree screen against which we perceive subjective violence. Proponents of what might be called "capitalists with a conscience," such as Bill Gates and George Soros and the CEOs of Google, IBM, Intel, and eBay, who present themselves as philanthropists first and businessmen second and who support humanitarian projects, help the smooth functioning of this unseen violence. As with the Koch brothers, such charity is no hardship, provides cover for the exploitation that is the source of their wealth, secures power and influence, and supports favored causes without disrupting the underlying logic of a violent system.[86]

The presumption of Orr, Nowling, Snyder, the bond insurers, and the Koch brothers seems to be that art and cultural patrimony, not to mention promised health care and pensions, are quite expendable but the sanctity of banks' and insurers' profits is indeed "eternal." Derek Donnelly, managing director of the Financial Guaranty Insurance Company, flatly stated, "The DIA or art is not an essential asset and especially not one that is essential to the delivery of services in the city."[87] Even as Michigan's attorney general, Bill Schuette, asserted that under the state's trust law and other laws, the collection was "held in trust for the public" and that "at no time have the people demanded their most precious cultural resources be sold in order to satisfy financial obligations," Snyder countered, "It's a bankruptcy judge that makes that determination."[88]

Orr hired the art auction house Christie's to formally assess the value of the most valuable works in the DIA collection, a contentious process that many saw as itself threatening to the integrity of the museum's collection. Orr instructed Christie's to evaluate 5 percent of the collection, which included only works bought with city funds, mostly between 1920 and 1930, when the city was most prosperous. Christie's returned an estimate of less than $1 billion, ranging between $454 million and $867 million. This estimate infuriated creditors such as Donnelly, who complained that Orr had unfairly excluded what experts believe is billions of dollars of city-owned art donated to the museum or bought with other funds that might include legal restrictions against selling. Eleven works accounted for 75 percent of the estimate, including Pieter Brueghel the Elder's *The Wedding Dance*; Vincent van Gogh's *Self-Portrait with Straw Hat*; Rembrandt's *The Visitation*; Henri Matisse's *Le guéridon*; Edgar Degas's *Danseuses au foyer*; Claude Monet's *Gladioli*; Michelangelo's *Scheme for the Decoration of the Ceiling of the Sistine Chapel*; Neri di Bicci's *The Palla Altarpiece: Tobias and Three Archangels*; Giovanni Bellini and Workshop's *Madonna and Child*; Frans Hals's *Portrait of Hendrik Swalmius*; and Michiel Sweerts's *In the Studio*.[89]

Creditors who think the assessment was lowballed and who regard the collection as a nonessential city asset that can and should be sold in times of financial distress petitioned the federal judge to establish, in Donnelly's words, "a committee made up of the city and all major creditor constituencies, using a fair and transparent process that considers a wide range of potential options" for valuing the art. Outrage was widespread, and protestors objecting to the sale of art held a rally and demonstration in front of the museum (figure 8).[90] Judge Rhodes denied the creditors' petition demanding the right to remove

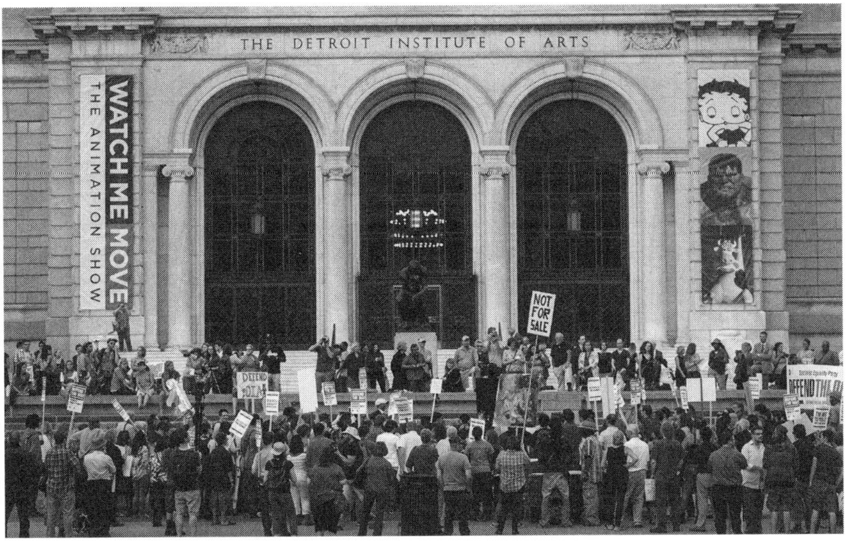

FIG. 8 Demonstration in front of the Detroit Institute of Arts protesting the projected sale of art by the Detroit emergency manager, October 4, 2013. Photo: James Fassinger.

artworks from the walls of the DIA in order to assess their value (telling them if they wanted to see the paintings to "buy a ticket"). However, he granted permission to evaluate all sixty-six thousand of the DIA's artworks. The city and the DIA jointly hired Artvest Partners, a New York art investment firm whose personnel could be called as expert witnesses against creditors trying to force a sale of art in court. Artvest valued the collection at $2.76 billion to $4.6 billion, noting the negative impact of releasing a large number of works onto the market at once and the recent declines in the value of auction sales. In response, Donnelly and Financial Guaranty Insurance Company hired Victor Wiener Associates of New York, which prepared another appraisal in just two weeks in order to meet a court deadline, coming in at $8.5 billion, about double that of Artvest. Weiner's fifty-page assessment relied on appraisals by Artvest and Christie's as well as its own appraisers, who never actually visited the DIA to inspect works of art.[91]

The proposal for a selloff came, ironically, after one of the few examples of regional cooperation, when the people of Detroit and surrounding suburbs in 2012 endorsed a tax initiative to fund the DIA, putting it on a secure financial footing for the first time in decades and giving residents of those counties free admission to the museum (the Museum of Modern Art in New York, by contrast, suggests an entry fee of $25). Wayne, Oakland, and Macomb Counties voted in favor of a ten-year commitment to a small increase in property taxes that would guarantee the DIA $23 million per year, roughly two-thirds of its annual operating budget. This tax vote would be automatically rescinded if the

DIA's art were sold to repay the city's debts (in addition to violating the city's own 1919 agreement with the institute).[92] The sale of any artworks would also mean that the museum could no longer attract donors; combined with the loss of operating revenue, this would lead to what the museum's director called a "nonprofit controlled liquidation" of the museum.[93]

In his initial essay, Schjeldahl suggested that auctioned works would be bought by other American institutions, implying that the country as a whole would still remain in control of its "image wealth."[94] Given the value of many of these major works, however, the buyers most likely able to afford them, as the DIA's chief operating officer, Annmarie Erickson, notes, would be private collectors from Russia, China, or the Middle East.[95] A selloff of major works would be the equivalent of looting the museum—not unlike the looting that took place in Baghdad during the American invasion of Iraq—and a significant loss of cultural capital. As one of the city's greatest institutions, moreover, the decline of the DIA would not only *not* solve the city's problems in any fundamental way, it would further weaken the city through cultural impoverishment, affecting real estate values and donations to other cultural institutions, which in turn would pave the way for further financial failure down the road. At the same time it would promote the widening separation of art and culture from everyday life, a condition already reflected in the fact that art and music programs have been drastically cut in public schools across the nation.[96]

The blithe talk about selling or monetizing works of art from the DIA collection not only represents an utter disregard for the effects such an event would have on the city but also combines naked greed with the anti-intellectual bias of the corporate business elite and their political spokesmen. On a smaller scale, this sort of narrow-minded indifference is echoed by the unceremonious dumping of a historic book collection in Highland Park. The collection consisted of ten thousand black history volumes, films, videos, and other artifacts, with many of the publications now out of print. Paul Lee, a historian who originally helped put the collection together in the 1960s, was able to rescue one thousand of the books from a Dumpster, while parents and others in the school district erupted in outrage.[97] Angry residents held a public protest in which they blocked traffic, wielded megaphones, and displayed picket signs with slogans like "21st Century Hitler Burning Books" and "Dump the EM, Not the Books," referring to the Highland Park EM, Donald Weatherspoon. While claiming it was "an accident," Weatherspoon asserted in the same breath that the school district could not afford to preserve the collection. The second-floor library that had housed the collection had been cleared out to make room for district officials' offices.[98]

The willingness to plunder Detroit's cultural assets goes hand in hand with the assaults on unions and on higher education. After Snyder signed legislation establishing a "right-to-work" state, the state legislature expected Michigan universities to substantially weaken their faculty unions, and Wayne State University attempted to do so during extended contract negotiations that began in 2012. A show of strength from the union, however, helped keep the Board of Governors from backing down under threats from the legislature to slash the school's state funding by $27.5 million in retaliation for passing an eight-year contract (instead of the usual three years) in response to the anti-union "right-to-work" law that was about to go into effect. The University of Michigan was threatened with a $47.3 million cut at its three state campuses. It is no accident that as union power has waned in the United States, income inequality has grown, middle-class incomes have stagnated, and blue-collar jobs are less secure, lower-paying, and have fewer benefits. Inequality is greatest in right-to-work states, and unions—where they exist—too often use their resources trying to influence elections instead of confronting employers directly and defending the rights of workers through social struggle.[99] The fact that the legislature backed down on their threats against the universities in this case was a victory for teachers and students, but the blatant disregard for the potential undermining of higher education suggests that legislative priorities lie elsewhere.[100] The indifference to higher education and the potential looting of Detroit's cultural and intellectual assets is not simply a matter of greed, although it is certainly that, but a view of neoliberal values. The willingness to severely undermine arts and educational institutions in the service of profits not only contributes to the financial ruin of the city but to the ruin of democracy and civil society.

Can Detroit Be Saved?

The problems of Detroit are in part problems of national policy that has allowed cities to fall to the bottom of the priority list for the last forty years. Following a burst of spending on community development and social services in the 1960s and early 1970s, federal urban spending steadily fell as President Gerald Ford told cities to "drop dead," Jimmy Carter focused on an anti-inflation agenda, Ronald Reagan reduced federal urban spending from 12 percent to 3 percent of the budget, and the George H. W. Bush, Bill Clinton, George W. Bush, and Barack Obama administrations followed suit by doing little to create new jobs or to support impoverished neighborhoods.[101]

Any strategy for solving Detroit's problems, however, requires the integration of city resources with the affluent surrounding suburbs in a form of regional reorganization and centralized planning that would serve the needs of all. *Remapping Debate*, a bimonthly online publication on public policy, devoted four issues to Detroit in 2011–2012, analyzing proposals since the 1970s that deal with the city's ongoing and accelerating crisis of a shrinking population and eroding tax base. Its author, Mike Alberti, forcefully argues that any solution has to address the suburbs as well as the city.[102] Steadily declining for the last half century, Detroit's 2010 population of 713,000 is the lowest since 1910 and less than half the mid-century high point of 1.85 million in 1950. Interim census estimates indicate that this figure has already shrunk by 26,000, to 687,000.[103] According to the U.S. Census Bureau, Detroit's population fell by 25 percent between 2000 and 2010 alone, the largest decline in any large American city except for New Orleans after Hurricane Katrina. Even the dead are exhumed from Detroit cemeteries and relocated at a rate of three hundred bodies per year. Of the nearly 83 percent of black Detroit residents, a quarter are unemployed, less than 12 percent of adults have a bachelor's degree, and the 40 percent who live below the poverty level represent the highest percentage among the nation's seventy-seven largest cities.[104] Detroit has the lowest per capita income in the nation, at just over $15,000, while the median household income in the wealthy northern suburb of Bloomfield Hills is more than $125,000.[105] Based on FBI statistics released in September 2013, Detroit also has the nation's highest crime rate among cities of two hundred thousand or more, followed by Oakland, St. Louis, Memphis, Stockton, Birmingham, Baltimore, Cleveland, Atlanta, and Milwaukee.[106]

The result is that property taxes are continually raised as the tax base declines along with the taxable value of those properties. At the same time, the state has dramatically reduced funding to the city while the need for services, such as police, fire, trash pickup, maintenance, and lighting, in all 139 square miles of the city, continues. The primary way in which Detroit has grappled with its deficit is by issuing bonds, which are below investment grade and have high borrowing and debt-service costs. "Right-sizing" has been one of the proposed solutions, which would uproot, dispossess, and consolidate the city's residents. A study from the Equality of Opportunity Project led by economists at Harvard and Berkeley suggests that America has more of an entrenched class system than other advanced nations, finding a strong correlation between high or low social mobility and residential segregation by class—that is, where different social classes live far apart, the ability of the poor to rise is significantly limited. City sprawl and ineffective public transportation simply strands workers without cars and families without multiple cars, while compact centers with access to public transit promote equality of opportunity. However, right-sizing, if it were to occur, must be done with the needs and interests of residents foremost, making it an expensive undertaking that would require improved housing for displaced residents. Moreover, it would need to be combined with reforms that would integrate Detroit into the regional economy, including the creation of a regional transit system. Otherwise, consolidation would run the risk of isolating the city even more while further oppressing its citizens.[107]

Although cities such as Indianapolis, Portland, Louisville, Nashville, and Minneapolis–St. Paul have successfully put in place some form of regional government or regional tax sharing, strong resistance from both suburban and city officials in the Detroit metro area has prevented any kind of tax-sharing plan. This makes Detroit one of the most polarized regions in the country, segregated by race and class. A regional master plan, first proposed in the 1970s, would have been especially beneficial for housing and transportation policy; with an economic and land-use plan, it could have arrested the deindustrialization of the city by incorporating the new factories built in the suburbs after the war. Instead, investment went to the richer part of the region, making those suburbs wealthy while poverty in Detroit greatly intensified.[108]

Moreover, from the 1930s onward, public schools were segregated, and federal housing and transportation policies encouraged white home owners and employers to defend neighborhood segregation. To address the effects of desegregation, in 1972 the National Association for the Advancement of Colored People (NAACP) sued the state and the school board in federal district court in a case entitled *Milliken v. Bradley*, arguing that the state and school board had deliberately kept the school system segregated. While the district court found in favor of the NAACP, the Supreme Court reversed the ruling on appeal, perversely arguing that there were no housing segregation violations in segregated communities, while integrated communities faced mandatory desegregation. One justice even asserted that housing segregation was caused by "unknown and unknowable causes."[109]

The effect was enormous, making it nearly impossible to desegregate northern white metropolitan areas, which, by keeping blacks out, avoided mandatory desegregation of schools. The ruling instead provided incentive for white families to leave Detroit and many whites abandoned the city for the suburbs to avoid integration. John Mogk, a law professor at Wayne State University, asserts, "Everybody thinks that it was the riots that caused the white families to leave. Some people were leaving at that time but, really, it was after *Milliken* that you saw mass flight to the suburbs."[110] After that, positions became hardened and there was little advocacy or appetite for a regional tax-base sharing system, which could have pooled new revenue for use in the entire region. Such a system would not have prevented industry from moving to the open-shop South, but it would have mitigated the structural problems of the city, including loss of taxes and city services, segregation in housing and schools, and the resulting decline in quality of life, while encouraging diversification and decreased reliance on the auto industry.[111] Neoliberal capitalism, which established itself in the 1970s, exacerbates problems that began long before.

The separate city and suburban narratives settled into opposing perspectives, which Alberti succinctly summarizes: "Historically, both Detroit and its suburbs have viewed efforts at regional cooperation with hostility: the suburbs have long been wary of regional tax policy proposals, because they see them as attempts to use suburban money to subsidize Detroit; the city, on the other hand, has tended to see proposals for regional governance as schemes aimed at diluting its political power."[112] However, a regional tax policy could be based on new growth only; it could take the form of a percentage of revenue from taxes on new growth from each municipality; in this way, growth anywhere in the region would benefit the entire region. It would also require the lingering segregation barriers to come down and a regional transportation system to be built so that people could get to jobs anywhere in the region. The alternative of further cutting labor costs and reducing services only contributes to the downward spiral of the city.[113]

As most cities and states face huge deficits, they are legally prohibited from deficit spending, increasing the miseries of city and state populations. To make matters worse, the tax on employers to pay jobless benefits has fallen by 40 percent due to tax-cut policies supported by business lobbies and state governments competing for investments. This means that states are increasingly unable to pay jobless benefits, requiring cash infusions from the federal government while exposing the increasing irrationality of the entire system and the increasingly meaningless separation between city and suburb. Following this path, the prognosis for Detroit and other declining cities, such as Laredo, Camden, Dayton, Miami, and Cincinnati, looks grim, with chronic economic crises, at best, as the operative status quo even as the corporations and banks grow wealthier. Without major political and economic transformations, the ruination of Detroit may serve as the bellwether for the economic health of cities across the nation because the devastating effects of deindustrialization and privatization, racism, poverty, and the continuing explosive growth of social inequality cannot be resolved under the current economic system but only managed as a series of continuing crises in an attempt to avoid total collapse.

A successfully reorganized economy based on central planning ultimately would have to be calibrated on a national scale. In *Rebel Cities: From the Right to the City to Urban Revolution*, David Harvey asserts the need to "claim the right to the city" (following Henri Lefebvre) as an important demand in its own right and as a political way station on the road to a much broader anticapitalist movement.[114] Historically, the city functions as the critical site of political action and revolt—from the Paris Commune of 1871 and the 1937 sit-down strike in Flint (supported by the unemployed and neighborhood organizations) to Tahrir Square in Cairo; Madison, Wisconsin; Plaza del Sol in Madrid; and Syntagma Square in Athens as a few recent examples. These are the cracks in the system that offer moments of opportunity for revolutionary organizing. Unless spontaneous protest movements are organized on an anticapitalist platform, however, they will quickly fade away or be reabsorbed into dominant capitalist practices, and a tiny elite will continue to shape the city according to its own needs and desires, protecting its assets while subjecting the collective to the ongoing urban processes of displacement, decline, and dispossession. And unless an anticapitalist drive is consolidated at a general scale, it will lapse back at the state level into constitutional reformism that can do little more than reconstitute capitalist competition under regimes that may be as bad or even worse than before (as we have seen, for example, in Egypt). Claiming the right to the city begins with the reasonable demands for decent housing, jobs, food security, transportation, and access to education and health care, but realizing just these basic demands will ultimately require systemic reorganization.

3

Urban Exploration

Beauty in Decay

As both the birthplace of Fordism and now the unrivaled center of urban decay, Detroit exerts a seductive power. It has become a thriving destination for artists, urban explorers, academics, and other curious travelers and researchers who want to experience for themselves industrial, civic, and residential abandonment on a massive scale. Not surprisingly, so-called ruin tours have become a burgeoning enterprise, providing a useful service for those unfamiliar with the ruins. These can be dangerous places that are structurally unsound, with crumbling or collapsing floors, stairs, ceilings, and vanished safety rails, as well as isolated sites for carjackers and thieves who target tourists with expensive camera equipment. Other hazards include conflicts with scrappers, who strip anything of value from buildings, as well as scavengers, drunks, vagrants, and dogs. In addition, entering abandoned buildings is illegal. For these reasons, many tours start early in the morning and require waivers that acknowledge the possibility of fines and agreement not to sue in case of injury or death. The Detroit police hardly have the resources to patrol all the sites but give $225 tickets for trespassing in abandoned schools. These drawbacks have not stopped hundreds of people from all over the world from exploring Detroit's ruins. Even television personality Anthony Bourdain toured abandoned buildings as part of his CNN food show *Parts Unknown*, saying, "It's hard to look away from the ruin, to not find beauty in the decay."[1]

Few of us are immune to the appeal of urban ruins and their complex affects. Urban explorer groups, however, explicitly devote themselves to investigating and photographing urban ruins. The urban explorer movement regards urban exploration as invaluable personal experience and the ruins as beautiful structures that should be left to decay naturally without human intervention. Urban explorers publish picture books and post thousands of photographs onto hundreds of websites. The emphasis on subjective experience engages an aesthetic strategy for surviving in a depressed environment; at the same time, it often leads to an embrace of decline that regards it as not only historically inevitable but even desirable.

The Thrill of Trespass

The urban explorer movement, also known as urbex and UE, emerged in the mid-1990s in Toronto around Jeff Chapman, code-named "Ninjalicious," who is considered the "spiritual father" of urbex. Ninjalicious founded the zine and website *Infiltration*, which urges thousands of young people to "go places you're not supposed to go." His book *Access All Areas: A User's Guide to the Art of Urban Exploration* was released in 2005, after his death. Ninjalicious coined the term "urban exploration" and spawned a global movement that he estimated included up to 350 urban explorer groups worldwide, which often specialize in particular kinds of sites such as abandoned buildings, buildings in use, catacombs, sewers and storm drains, and tunnels. The website and others like it illustrate ruin explorations and recount what urban explorers see and feel as they penetrate abandoned industrial sites, most of them professing to abide by the ethical dictum "Take only pictures, leave only footprints" advocated by Ninjalicious, which was originally the slogan of forest preservationists in the United States and Canada.[2] Ninjalicious asserts that urban explorers have only respect for the sites they explore: "Genuine urban explorers never vandalize, steal or damage anything—we don't even litter. We're in it for the thrill of discovery and a few nice pictures, and probably have more respect for and appreciation of our cities' hidden spaces than most of the people who think we're naughty. We don't harm the places we explore. We *love* the places we explore."[3] In this sense, urbex may be seen as a productive and educational form of play or leisure activity. The code of conduct that Ninjalicious insists upon is meant not only to preserve sites but also to differentiate the urban explorer from destructive trespassers.

Other urban explorers suggest that the hobby is more than just thrill-seeking; they assert that it preserves history and memory through the photographs of abandoned buildings taken before they are demolished or repurposed. "Urban Exploration could be seen as a huge spontaneous Archiving Project," claim the authors of the urbex photo book *Beauty in Decay*. "Before sites like Ninjalicious' Infiltration, Urbexers were not a community at all but rather a few scattered individuals. Now, bearing in mind that the internet is basically a huge multi-user filing system, Urbex is effectively creating an enormous database of images documenting abandoned buildings and urban decay. Almost by accident, the adventure has become a historical conservation project."[4] Yet this form of documentation hardly conforms to any recognized standard of historical conservation. Rather, it is presented as "an experiential, subjective vision of what history is."[5] Since it is experiential and subjective, the actual location and history of the ruin sites do not seem to matter, and therefore the photographs in *Beauty in Decay* provide minimal information. Thumbnail images at the back of the book offer the photographer's name and the location of the image by city or country or type of building (e.g., "France," or "Asylum, UK"). In addition, they offer the type of camera used and the personal website and e-mail address of the photographer.

The focus of urbex is thus on individual experience and building the urbex community, and the sense of history pursued refers to an imagined personal connection to the past and its anonymous inhabitants.[6] This subjective concept of history is articulated as "history unmediated, in its raw pure form" as experienced by the urban explorer: "This encounter between the living and the dead is the source of the stories that we tell to make sense of being alive, and to be that explorer at that moment is to be given back the power to tell those stories for yourself. We don't want to be passive consumers of History with a capital H, neither spoon fed to us by the Discovery Channel or intellectualized beyond our reach in the lecture halls."[7] The target audience is disaffected youth, many with at least some college education. They are primarily male, as generally confirmed by the assertion that solving the thrilling puzzle of getting into a derelict building "requires balls, great hairy swinging balls."[8] As a dangerous and thrilling experience—thrilling *because* it's dangerous—ruin exploration appeals primarily to white middle-class men, offering a landscape of collapsed boundaries and liberating forms of transgression that include not only trespass and discovery but also secret spaces for raves, sex, drugs, games, and other activities free from bourgeois convention, public surveillance, and normative regulations.

A key focus is on the gear, the type of cameras employed, the settings used for different lighting conditions, and the software through which the images are processed and posted online. The inclusion of personal websites and e-mail addresses emphasizes the creation of an online urbex community that shares the transgressive thrill of defying authority by going where they are "not supposed to go." Urbex becomes a way of escaping from the drudgery of life by engaging in the illegal and the forbidden: "Your moment of peace, outside the everyday world and far from the thundering of life toward death, is only a NO ENTRY sign away," and "UE is about doing the forbidden, the not-allowed and its forbidden nature is a key part of its attraction."[9] The pleasure of transgression is both explicitly stated and central to the appeal. Focusing on subjective experience, most urban explorers are unconcerned with when or why factories closed; instead, former sites of production become deindustrial playgrounds.[10] The dehistoricized ruins of *Beauty in Decay* fetishize decay for its own sake and the pleasure it provides, not only in search of escape and adventure but as a way of coping with everyday life and, for many, creating a photographic practice.

Urban explorers are on a perpetual mission to recapture the thrill of childhood discovery. *Beauty in Decay* urges, "Think back to your childhood for a moment and it all begins to make sense. Do you remember the terrifying yet seductive draw of the archetypal haunted house? Every neighborhood and every childhood has one."[11] Urbex evokes the thrill of ghosts in addition to the lure of nature, discovery, forbidden trespass, and escape from the mundane and depressing world. "And for most of us, leading lives of quiet desperation, the milestones of our lives pass by in a blur. Always we live with the feeling that life is elsewhere."[12] Invoking Thoreau's famous rejection of the values and practices of an industrial, commercial society, the authors of *Beauty in Decay* appeal to those who feel socially alienated with a melancholic nostalgia for an imagined idealized "elsewhere" located in the past.

Another urbex publication, *Jinx Magazine*, describes the difference between a trespasser and explorer in rather disturbing terms: "With *Infiltration* magazine, then, the urban explorer truly parted company with the mundane trespasser. Ninjalicious became an explorer when he faithfully published his observations and enriched posterity by them. The trespasser, by contrast, always consigned his story to silence; he, like the base Indian, threw a pearl away richer than all his tribe."[13] In addition to the racist analogy of the "base Indian," the category of "mundane trespassers" possibly implies those who live in the vicinity of ruins, that is, the working-class sons and daughters of those who may have once toiled in the abandoned factories but who may not write blogs and create websites. In *Corporate Wasteland*, Steven High and David Lewis declare the explorer/trespasser dichotomy to be an invention meant "to distance middle class explorers from working class trespassers."[14] They suggest that part of the lure for urban explorers is not so much the traveling of great physical distances but "great social distances" in which the industrial past seems to be a realm of primitive otherness separated from the more civilized postindustrial present; at its worst, the very notion of the modern "explorer" recalls a colonialist pretension imbued with the rhetoric of class and race.[15]

We might see the uncanny pleasure of ruin exploration and its representation as suggesting two simultaneous and seemingly opposed perspectives. On one hand, the contemplation of ruins provides a sense of superiority and comfort for having "survived the collapse of past dreams of the future," as art critic Brian Dillon observes; on the other, urbex paradoxically produces a sense of being cast forward into "the future ruin of our own present."[16] From both perspectives, the urban explorer is an intrepid survivor of collapse, both past and future. Ruin exploration is thus an exciting and pleasurable way of containing and controlling the anxiety of decline and the cultural pessimism it produces.

Urbexers explore abandoned auto plants, schools, libraries, hotels, theaters, and other building ruins in a search for extreme experience that defers or avoids historicity, instead seeking immersive sensual pleasure that is suspended in time and space or allows an unfolding of ambiguous time that moves backward and forward simultaneously. As *Beauty in Decay* urges, "Go find the nether places between the day and the night where the walls are thin and you can for a moment step outside of time."[17] This suspended sense of time and history creates a feeling of freedom from ordinary social constraints and anxieties, of having survived the trauma of past and future decay. Both senses of survival offer the temporal and mental distance necessary for the experience of ruination to be enjoyably aestheticized. One dwells in and on the ruins as a way of mastering the anxieties of survival itself, while the thousands of images posted online and published in books expand the shared experience of the deindustrial sublime.

Robert Smithson, an artist who toured Passaic, New Jersey, in 1967, also wrote about the ambiguous unfolding of time when regarding building construction along the banks of the Passaic River. Artificial craters and pipes seemed to create a "zero panorama" of "*ruins in reverse*, that is—all the new construction that would eventually be built. This is the opposite of the 'romantic ruin' because the buildings don't *fall* into ruin *after* they are built but rather rise into ruin before they are built. . . . Those holes in a sense are the monumental vacancies that define, without trying, the memory-traces of an abandoned set of futures."[18] Smithson gestures toward a failed set of futures that are already built into the system even as new corporate buildings take form. His observation also reminds us that buildings abandoned partway through the construction process—of which there are many since the 2008 financial crisis—are just as much ruins as buildings that have fallen into decay. Even the negative ruins of vacant lots make the effort to ward off ruination through incessant demolition self-defeating.[19] Whether rising into ruination or demolished through neglect, these "monumental vacancies" suggest the exhaustion of both the future and the past in the present.

The urbex focus on exotic discovery approaches ruins as sites of unregulated space and sensual materiality that displace the rational and the ordered with the formless and disordered.[20] In contrast to Georg Simmel's notions of unity and symmetry, urbex images that convey a sense of the deindustrial sublime through beauty in decay no longer privilege the "higher" status of culture but the "lower" pull of nature in a climate of cultural pessimism that naturalizes decline and reifies the urban "explorer" as possessing a privileged gaze.

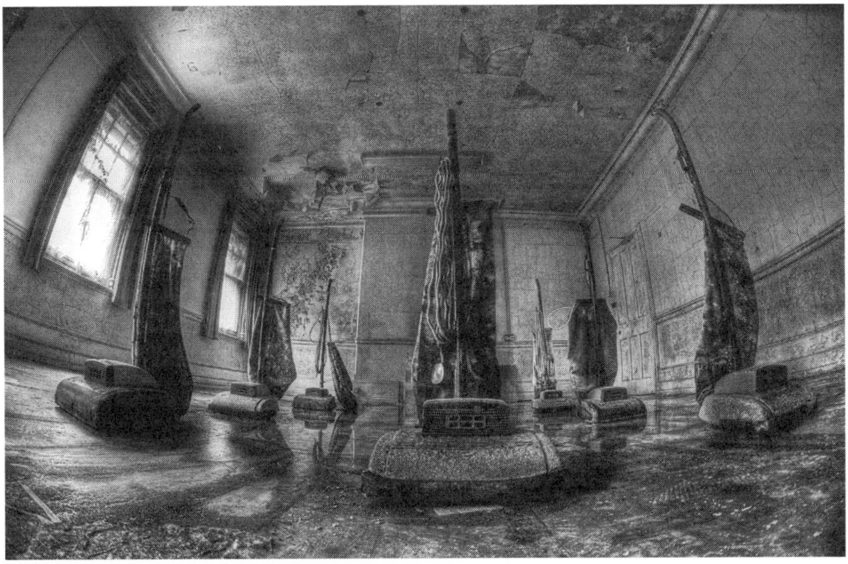

FIG. 9 RomanyWG, *Hoover Squadron*, abandoned asylum, UK, from *Beauty in Decay*, 2010. Courtesy of the artist.

These sensual spaces offer a kind of freedom from everyday life, although privileging aesthetic pleasure and transgressive experience over historical specificity comes at the price of historical understanding.

Urbex images often have a distorted, hyperdigital look, produced by the HDR digital postproduction technique that takes several shots of the same scene and blends them together with the best information from each shot. In *Beauty in Decay*, RomanyWG's *Hoover Squadron*, taken at an abandoned asylum somewhere in the United Kingdom, provides an example in which HDR gives the cleaning machines a kind of animate and even menacing quality (figure 9).[21] The authors note that these HDR photographs are controversial because they take on the artificial look and theatrical feel of video game images. Other urbex photos are dramatically staged, featuring objects that have been introduced by the photographer, or live figures in deliberately mysterious postures, sometimes wearing *commedia dell 'arte* masks or gas masks, as in Martino Zegwaard's *The Lost Philosopher*, of a wandering figure who seems traumatized by dreams of gas attacks (figure 10). This staging and technical manipulation suggests that the fictive and fantasized mood and atmosphere produced in the urbex photograph is at least as important as documenting the space itself. A niche genre has developed among female artists who photograph themselves nude in industrial settings, such as Kristine Diven, who moved to Detroit from Brooklyn in 2010 and who poses naked in abandoned buildings, or New York–based Miru Kim, who makes photographs and videos

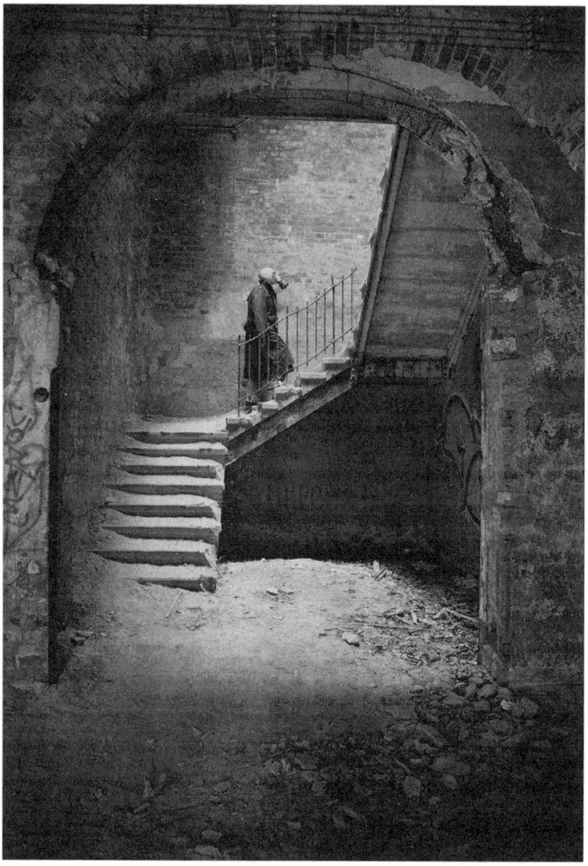

FIG. 10 Martino Zegwaard, *The Lost Philosopher*, hospital, Germany, from *Beauty in Decay*, 2010. Courtesy of the artist (www.flickr.com/photos/martino).

of herself nude amid the ruins of the catacombs beneath Paris, abandoned buildings in Istanbul, or industrial ruins in New York City.[22]

Many video game designers are also inspired by ruins, creating games such as *Silent Hill*, which is set in an abandoned town in the mountains. The role-player creeps around derelict schools, shops, and industrial buildings while fending off knife-wielding zombie babies. After first-person shooter video games, such role-playing games, or RPGs, are the second-most-popular category in video games. The top-rated games and most popular RPGs all contain an extensive use of ruins. The Elder Scrolls games *Oblivion* and *Fallout 3*, for example, which have sold over 16.6 million copies worldwide, demonstrate the wide range of fictive ruins employed. *Oblivion* is set in fantastical classical-style ruins with vaguely medieval architecture while *Fallout 3* is set in the imagined future ruins of Washington, D.C., and the area surrounding the nation's capital after it has been devastated by nuclear war.[23] Such fantasized scenarios extend the ruin imaginary into fresh media spheres and encourage the participation of a new generation in exploring the projected sensual spaces of ruination while aesthetically mediating the anxiety of decline.

More than two centuries ago, Giovanni Battista Piranesi produced imagined ruins in his invented prison etchings, the *Carceri.* As Andreas Huyssen observes, Piranesi's etchings create uncanny spaces that seem to grow out of the earth and defy Euclidian rules of geometry; they bend light, confuse spatial arrangements, and contain architectural features such as staircases, passages, and hallways that seem to lead in all directions yet lack spatial logic or closure; they produce a sense of darkness even as they open into infinity, refusing to give the viewer a fixed perspective or safe distance from which to contemplate these terrifying spaces (figure 11).[24] Such illogical and sinister space is

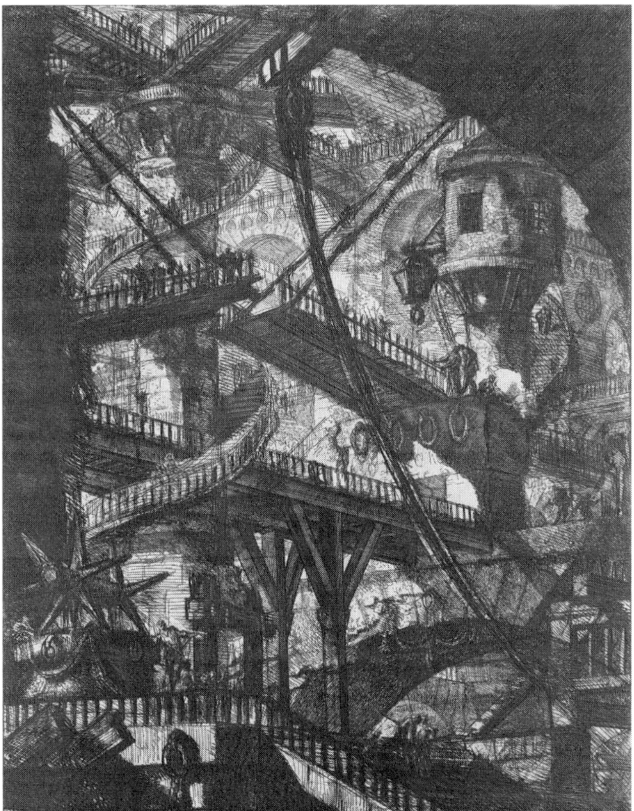

FIG. 11 Giovanni Battista Piranesi, *The Drawbridge*, plate VII from *Carceri d'Invenzione.* 1745. Cooper-Hewitt, National Design Museum, Smithsonian Institution / Art Resource, NY.

the opposite of Simmel's romantic reconciliation of spirit and nature. Instead the aura of these ruins is threatening and oppressive as space and time remain indefinable. Produced in the eighteenth century, in contrast to Enlightenment optimism, "Piranesi's prisons and ruins," writes Huyssen, "can be read as allegories of a modernity whose utopia of freedom and progress and of linear time and geometric space they not only question but cancel out."[25] Although Piranesi thoroughly explored the classical architecture of Roman ruins, an architecture that dominated the era of the Enlightenment, his was a ruin imaginary that also focused on the terror of ruins, asserting a critical consciousness in regard to the modernist present that, Huyssen suggests, accompanied the Enlightenment from its inception.

The debates about ruins and ruin imagery among contemporary urban explorers and historians focus broadly either on the ontological value of ruins or on their cultural and historical significance. Urban explorers defend ruins as having intrinsic value, the exploration and contemplation of which constitutes significant personal experience that produces valuable knowledge. Ruins, they assert, should therefore be left alone. The other side, represented by High and Lewis, regards the fetishizing of ruins as indulging corporate waste and squandered resources while obscuring ruined lives. They feel that the emphasis on personal experience and the knowledge it produces ignores or undermines an understanding of the larger social and political implications of ruination. The emphasis on individualism itself may be regarded as a typical aspect of capitalism.

Space and Materiality

The British geographer Tim Edensor, who has explored industrial ruins for thirty years, is a leading voice in defense of urbex and ruins as valuable sites. In *Industrial Ruins: Space, Aesthetics and Materiality* Edensor's central argument is that ordinary urban space, which is constrained and regulated, breeds the desire and need for the unregulated, the transgressive, and the disordered space represented by ruins. He rejects the view of ruins as places of absence and waste that are always potentially available for exploitation and utilization. For Edensor, ruins are a welcome and necessary challenge to the overrationalization of space and regimes of surveillance in city life. The disordered, unregulated spaces of ruins and the vitality of the unconventional activities they allow, which are marginalized or forbidden elsewhere, provide an important sense of freedom. This freedom resists commodification and the dominant aesthetic order, creating new ways of thinking about space and materiality that are spontaneous and unfixed.[26] Edensor differentiates his perspective on ruins from both romantic nostalgia and a gothic aesthetics of gloom in order to posit a "celebratory" view of ruins. For Edensor, ruins play a positive and upbeat role in society as spaces that are beautiful, useful, and pleasurable primarily because of the numerous liberating activities they enable.

Edensor also argues that ruins provide useful unofficial ways of remembering the past. While important critiques have been made of official commemorative or heritage sites, the alternative of decomposing ruins presents its own practical dangers and conceptual problems, as demonstrated by the ahistorical approach most urban explorers assume toward these sites.[27] This aspect of Edensor's argument therefore seems to be more of an afterthought in his defense of ruins, whose potential as sites of pleasurable exploration and unconstrained activity is his primary focus. High and Lewis critique industrial heritage tourism as part of the larger phenomenon of "dark tourism" in which the postmodern tourist, traveler, or explorer visits trauma sites of death and disaster such as Nazi death camps, former battlegrounds, sites of national catastrophe, and deindustrial ruins. But their condemnatory perspective does not sufficiently account for the intense appeal of such sites and what they may teach us.

Like the authors of *Beauty in Decay*, Edensor emphasizes the happy resonance of ruin exploration with childhood memories. Ruins have become so pervasive that most people in the last two or three generations are all too likely to have experience exploring abandoned factories and mills or other empty buildings in their hometowns, or to have experienced war ruins, especially in post–World War II Europe or in many places in the Middle East, North Africa, and elsewhere today. Seeing the inner workings of architectural structures that were never meant to be seen and going into spaces never meant to be public may indeed produce new perceptions that open imaginative pathways not as readily accessible to those who grow up in well-ordered and rationalized spaces. Seeing the hidden infrastructure of a city may provide insight into the social order, especially when it is a result of war. In this regard, Lebbeus Woods, architect and author of *War and Architecture*, observes, "[The form of ruins] must be respected as integrity, embodying a history that must not be denied. In their damaged states they suggest new forms of thought and comprehension, and suggest new conceptions of space that confirm the potential of the human to integrate itself, to be whole and free outside of any predetermined totalizing system. There is an ethical and moral commitment in such an existence and therefore a basis for community."[28] For Woods, as for Edensor, the ability to escape a totalizing system of regulated space offers a form of freedom that is central to the fascination with and respect for modern ruins.

Yet the "history that must not be denied" that Woods finds in war ruins is hardly critical for Edensor or other contemporary urban explorers. On the contrary, Edensor refuses to even identify the locations of the ruins pictured in *Industrial Ruins*, offering this explanation: "The particular geographical locations of the ruins featured here are . . . not important to this endeavour, for assumptions about their embeddedness in imaginary geographies are likely to provide unwelcome interference with the more generic points I wish to make. That is why none of the photographs are labeled, for it is my wish that they evoke individual responses amongst readers without their being contextualized by surplus information."[29] Edensor plainly privileges the sensual immanence of the ruin and the subjective individual response and deliberately avoids "distracting" the reader with any social, political, or historical context. He also lists twenty-seven towns and cities where he has personally encountered industrial ruins but informs the reader that "this is the last time I shall refer to their location, for the argument of the book would be less pertinent if they were accompanied by this superfluous geographical information."[30] By generalizing and mythologizing ruins, Edensor avoids examining the ruin's relationship to the present and evades any meaningful connections to history, let alone to any "history that must not be denied." As High and Lewis observe, "In universalizing his gaze, Edensor strips these former industrial sites of their history and their geography just as surely as the departing companies, entrepreneurs, and trophy hunters stripped the sites of their assets."[31] History itself becomes "surplus information."

In making his case for the liberating and noncommercial uses of ruined spaces, Edensor includes activities such as "plundering" (the stripping of machinery, furniture, copper wire, architectural details, and other assets by "strippers" for profit) and "home-making" (ruins as shelter for the homeless) as well as adventurous play and the use of space by drug users, rave-goers, sex workers, and those who enjoy smashing things. He notes the pleasure of exploring architecture for its "adventuresome physicality" and "the thrill of the risk entailed"; the taking of photographs and writing of blogs; the mundane leisure practices, such as walking a dog, "tethering grazing ponies," growing vegetables and fruit, cultivating marijuana plants, dumping rubbish, and using the space as a free car park; and the use of the space by graffiti artists, artists using found materials, and filmmakers. In Edensor's elaboration of all the liberating, creative, playful, and social things one can do in ruins, it is more than a little disquieting when he includes on his list "lawless pursuits" such as sorting out stolen goods. Since one of the prime virtues of ruins is that they exist away from the prying eyes of conventional society, Edensor recognizes this as a common activity and writes approvingly:

> Ruins are ideal places to empty the contents of stolen handbags and safes. More evidently, they are sites to which stolen cars and motorbikes can be taken. At once, the goods yards and factory floors provide an environment where cars can be driven and the layout of obstacles can serve as improvised circuits for adventurous forms of joyriding. Wooden doors can be driven through in emulation of spectacular actions from television and cinema, adjacent objects can be

collided with and sent flying, and vehicles can be skidded, turned over, set alight and detonated.[32]

Moving seamlessly from dumping the contents of stolen handbags to joyriding in stolen cars around factory floors, Edensor describes these activities as forms of high-spirited fun without critical pause. He seems exuberant over ruins as "ideal places" for assessing stolen booty or acting out "spectacular actions from television and cinema" and apparently has no concern for those whose handbags, safes—presumably acquired as a result of home invasion—cars, and motorcycles have been so blithely stolen, or for the ethics of such theft. These issues appear to be too insignificant for Edensor to even mention in comparison to the giddy excitement that release from bourgeois constraints provides; instead, theft is valorized and included as part of the "possible alternative eco-centric, artistic and social futures in the city" that ruins can provide.[33] Yet such a lawless future resonates not with happy childhood memories and aspirations of creative freedom but with postapocalyptic survival scenarios in which constant menace and threat are the rule. Indeed, ruins and abandoned structures are not only "ideal places" for enjoying stolen goods but also for people to be dragged into and raped, beaten, robbed, and murdered, events which occur all too often. Such an irresponsible attitude and unethical perspective deeply undermines Edensor's more serious arguments. Dangers such as these are represented in Curtis Hanson's 2002 film *8 Mile*, which is set in Detroit. The lead character, played by Eminem, and his friends identify a vacant home as the source of neighborhood problems, including a rape, and burn it down to prevent future occurrences. A similar event takes place in the 2012 documentary *Burn: One Year on the Front Lines of the Battle to Save Detroit*, directed by Tom Putnam and Brenna Sanchez, about Detroit firefighters and the challenges they face.

While Edensor's ethics are at best fuzzy, his understanding that ruins provide unregulated and unpoliced space free from bourgeois convention is key to what thousands of urbexers find so appealing. But it must be understood that this view of ruins, although patently ahistorical, is not apolitical. While Edensor is cognizant of the destabilizing effects of economic decline, he nonetheless regards decline itself as historically inevitable and cyclical: "Industrial ruins deride the pretensions of governments and local authorities to maintain economic prosperity and hence social stability, and give the lie to those myths of endless progress. . . . Instead, ruins demonstrate that these processes are inexorably cyclical, whereby the new is rapidly and inevitably transformed into the archaic; what was vibrant is suddenly inert."[34]

Edensor attributes the myth of "endless progress" and the boom-and-bust cycle not to capitalism itself but to the pretensions of government and local authorities who obscure the true nature of unchangeable economic processes.

This political perspective explains the "celebratory" nature of Edensor's view of ruins because he regards them as part of a natural process, which cannot be helped or hindered. Ruins are fun and even capable of gesturing toward a utopian future that is distinguished from the present only by greater individual freedom within the ruins of the present system. This is utopian indeed, as all evidence points to greater surveillance and control under the present system, with the growth of ruins suggesting greater impoverishment, not greater freedom. The dichotomy Edensor sets up is not between freedom and capitalism, which cannot support the populations it rules, but between individual rights and government authorities, a middle-class form of personal rebellion. Defending ruins as havens and countersites to the normative bourgeois order thus assumes and reifies this order even as it justifies lawless practices as a rejection of authority. The logic of Edensor's argument suggests not only a mythologizing and romanticizing of ruins but the active preservation of ruins in the sense that they should be left to decay on their own. Edensor hesitates to make this case only briefly, on the grounds that "it seems cranky to argue that decay should be succoured," before concluding, "There is a case for a politics which allows them [ruins] to remain, to crumble at their own pace."[35]

Nothingness and the Aesthetics of Decay

The other leading voice for urbex, British philosopher Dylan Trigg, also argues for such a politics but for different reasons. In *The Aesthetics of Decay: Nothingness, Nostalgia, and the Absence of Reason*, Trigg takes a more long-term philosophical view and argues that the decline of reason, embodied in ruins, enables a critique of progress that puts to rest the theory of ongoing and inevitable progress that has prevailed in developed countries for more than two hundred years. At the same time he defends the ontological value of modern ruins because they help us to see the truth of our current reality. This reality is not a cycle of growth and decline, as Edensor suggests, but a downward spiral of ongoing decline that cannot be stopped. Noting that Walter Benjamin in *The Arcades Project* analyzes ruins in terms of the socioeconomic mechanisms that determine the logic of capitalism, Trigg distinguishes his own defense of ruins from Benjamin's perspective: "My focus is not on the social significance of decay and waste, which reduces them [ruins] to a utilitarian purpose, but rather the ontological value of that decay. Whereas decay and ruin have predominately been employed in a transformative guise, conferring a supposed legitimacy upon them, in my consideration they require no further justification. In their incompletion, they are already complete."[36] Ruins are thus stripped of their social significance and valued for their own sake while helping us to see the truth of an approaching systemic collapse.

In explaining the aesthetic value of ruins, Trigg provides a compelling explanation for the mentality that finds beauty in decay as a form of "decadent consciousness" that aestheticizes its own decline. He writes, "As rationality is disrupted by decline, the aestheticizing of that decline ensues, so establishing the decadent consciousness, a trait evident in urban exploration and romanticism. Because of this temporal proximity between culture and aesthetics, the ruin is able to be elevated from its initial disregard. The strangeness of treating present ruins aesthetically is peculiar to decadence. Rome exemplifies this and nineteenth century romanticism mirrors it."[37]

But Trigg distinguishes the contemporary ruin from other kinds of ruins. The classical ruin has reached its absolute form and serves to affirm the identity of the present, whereas industrial ruins do the opposite: they erode a sense of contemporary identity. The war ruin has an alleged purpose in justifying an end result, which allows the war ruin to evade the charge of "aestheticism" because of its humanitarian component. No such imperative exists in regard to postindustrial ruins, which allows ruination to become detached from reason.[38] This failure of reason and technology, already evident by the end of the nineteenth century, has led to an irreversible cultural pessimism in which the collective has given way to subjective individualism, and reason has given way to emotion. Writes Trigg: "What this pessimism signifies is recognition of the gradual collapse of environmental, economic, political and sociological factors, whereby faith in progress is disillusioned by historical experience. Cultural pessimism marks the end of rational faith in history and collective politics as apathy and cynicism replace harmony and trust. Withdrawal from the collective means that success is replaced by subjectivism and individualism."[39] This form of cultural pessimism as apathy and cynicism clearly defines the urbex movement, which abandons history and collective politics for subjective individualism.

But in pointing to the cultural pessimism generated by gradual collapse, Trigg's assumed "apathy and cynicism" and "withdrawal from the collective" is too categorical and fatalistic. The recent and continuing rebellions and uprisings across North Africa, the Middle East, Europe, North and South America, from Tahrir Square to Tacsim Square, Athens to Wall Street to Rio de Janeiro, inchoate though many of these uprisings may be and despite their problematic outcomes, suggest otherwise. In Trigg's pessimistic view, what he calls the postindustrial sublime of ruination inverts the concept of the Kantian sublime as a taming of the terrible, constituting not the transcendence of the human over the external but descent and despair. Sweeping away any sense of balance between nature and culture, Trigg's postindustrial sublime "pulls us beneath nature so that the preservation of the self is undermined as boundaries become ambiguous."[40]

Like Edensor, however, Trigg suggests that what is affirming about the ruin is its capacity for critical resistance to the enforcement of spatial rationality. For Trigg this resistance is based not on the activities that might take place within the ruin but on its structural formlessness, ultimately leading to total collapse. He defines this collapse as a new category of post-sublime aesthetics that he names "the dissolute," the point at which the object vanishes completely. As decline becomes more evident, leading from the beautiful to the sublime to the dissolute, cultural pessimism intensifies, and this leads Trigg to the very bottom of a philosophical abyss:

> We witness the shape of history, from the canonization of reason to its successive failures and thence to its gradual demise unfolding in spatial form. We see the correlation between solidity and progress give way to disintegration, rot, and erosion. We are at home among the debris. The ruin soothes us through reinforcing what was already present, albeit latently. By embodying the pathway from incipience to extinction, the ruin theatrically reenacts the structure of our age. After modernity and postmodernity, the ruin mirrors the gathering of closures. The final movement of the ruin is a rebirth that will exist only in the absence of its being. For us, tending to its disappearance is enough. The ruin as a home is realized the nearer we hold out into the Nothing. In the process of internalizing what the ruin symbolizes, we recognize the drive toward collapse. The "hard cold facts of late life" have been placed upon us. Ours is an age whose virtue is our nearness to the end.[41]

Trigg accepts the inevitability of our "nearness to the end" and "the ruin as a home." In a form of elegant but total nihilism, he is unable to imagine an alternative to the capitalist decline he describes; his thesis therefore explicitly dismisses a social and political analysis of ruins since he sees no possibility, even theoretically, for collective political action in response to the loss of rationality inherent to capitalism. Instead, he argues for an active embrace of the resulting cultural pessimism and of a future that inexorably descends into dissolution and collapse. This is a future that ends not with an apocalyptic bang but with the quiet whoosh of a structure gradually and irresistibly falling in on itself. In case we have not grasped this, he adds, "From the viewpoint of the present work, decline is not something to be resisted."[42]

While Edensor celebrates the unregulated "space, aesthetics and materiality" of ruins as a necessary balance to overregulated urban space and regards this balance as part of a naturalized cycle of ongoing growth and decline, Trigg recognizes the failure of capitalism and foresees progress without reason as a future descending into decline—but with no mitigating intervention through human agency possible. For Trigg, ruination permanently confirms "the downward direction of progress." Contemporary ruins, then, must be appreciated for their intrinsic "aesthetics of decay" as they progress toward the dissolute, reflecting the central fact of contemporary reality: the Nothingness that embodies the absence of reason. While Edensor takes an ahistorical view based on the imagined natural cycle of creation through destruction, Trigg views the descent into the void as the result of an unstoppable historical decline. Although coming from different perspectives, both arrive at similar conclusions, which must be understood as political: while taking pleasure in the immanent sensuous nature of ruins, both counsel against any attempts to combat the progress of ruination—Edensor because he enjoys the liberation found within the ruins; Trigg because he is convinced that the future has already been written. These are the key inspirational voices for urbex today.

But there are other possibilities. Although reason is indeed absent from the global system of capitalist accumulation, it is not absent as a thinkable category applied to the logics of an emancipatory political program. While historical and philosophical pessimists have lost faith in the possibility of reason as a guide to collective agency, counseling others to abandon hope is not a neutral position but capitulates to the very system that has brought about decline and helps to ensure its morbid success. Put another way, subjective individualism is guaranteed to fail in effecting social change. Trigg not only diagnoses individualism as a problem but fully embodies it, insists on it. By counseling against any attempt at social change, he dismisses the impulse for social struggle, instead fostering a slide into hopeless melancholy, while Edensor's more hedonistic perspective tends toward amoralism. This helps to explain why the ethos of urban exploration emphasizes subjective experience while ignoring historical or political inquiry. Trigg's definition of decadent consciousness as the aestheticizing of one's own decline is a useful concept for understanding urban exploration, but it is not a productive political vision for the future.

The aestheticization of decay must be understood as a constituent element of the deindustrial sublime that can easily lull us into complacency. Yet ruin images cannot help but picture the violence and breaking quality at their center, the recognition of which admits the possibility of collective agency and political action even as it signals the need to contain and control the anxiety of social breakdown and cultural pessimism. To behold the descent of contemporary society into collapse and to find it pleasurable and beautiful without, at the same time, finding it politically troubling and contingent is to succumb to the profound demoralization effected by a capitalist system that has nearly suffocated the idea of an emancipated society based on equality instead of class privilege. This despairing view of an exhausted future recalls the famous assertion first put forward by Fredric Jameson in the early 1990s, that it is easier to imagine the end of the world than it is to imagine the end of capitalism.[43] Disaster capitalism will truly triumph if we surrender to a despairing vision that counsels powerlessness and encourages hopelessness, with no possibility of collective social struggle.

4

Detit Ruin Images

Where Are the People?

A romantic fetishization of the relationship between nature and culture lies at the heart of ruin imagery and is central to what makes it appealing. Ruin images tend to picture derelict architecture in the process of being reclaimed by animals and vegetation. This suggests a "timeless" struggle between nature and culture that either places nature in the ascendancy over ruined culture as part of a downward spiral or, conversely, asserts the redemption of social ruin through signs of new life in nature. Yet for the poor population, no matter how haunting or strangely beautiful ruins may be, they are not romantic artifacts but reminders of jobs and homes lost, neighborhoods destroyed, and lives derailed. Photography that focuses only on the aesthetics of decay in architecture offers a narrative that distances and obscures the ongoing crisis of poverty and unemployment.

The invisibility to photographers of the black populace in Detroit, moreover, reflects and reinforces their invisibility to the corporations and policy makers that are the real agents of decline, those who helped create the patterns of ghettoized, racialized poverty that have long obtained in the city. The visual narrative of the empty, unpeopled city returning to nature has helped to justify and legitimize continued austerity measures and official indifference. Yet even as typical ruin photography suggests a retrogressive "return to nature" or an eternal cycle of growth and decay, it also inevitably reveals the contradictions of the ruin discourse that constructs Detroit as both representative of urban decline and uniquely responsible for its own deterioration.

Nature versus Culture

There is a third way to think about the presence of nature in the city, which is neither critical nor celebratory. Nate Millington, an urban geographer, asserts that plants and animals are always part of urban space, despite their wrongly assumed absence, so that nature does not "return to the city," as the rhetoric of ruination suggests, but is always present and important to the production of urban environments. The more visible incursions of nature into the city of Detroit should be understood, argues Millington, as helping to create new urban ecologies. Because biophysical processes and human intent and knowledge are co-constitutive, "understanding nature and the city as distinct conceptual categories renders them both opaque."[1] Consequently, the intertwining of nature with urban space may be seen not as representing lack or regression but as constructing new urban spaces. Rather than view nature as a dystopian signifier, it may be seen as a way for ecology and community to intersect in new hybrid forms.

Conceiving of nature as helping to create new urban ecologies, however, does not adequately address the still evolving urban crisis in Detroit. More significant than the actual functions of nature in the city are the political repercussions of representations of nature as part of the architecturally decaying landscape. Millington argues that the metaphor of nature reclaiming the city, whether used in negative or redemptive terms, neutralizes the actual processes that have a destructive impact on a city, such as the virulent racism, antiunionism, and industrial disinvestment that are the critical factors in Detroit.[2] This is important for understanding why Detroit ruin imagery contains a notable absence of people and why many observers often do not realize there are still almost seven hundred thousand residents in the city. The racist and moralizing narrative that Detroit is a poor black city that has only itself to blame for its problems is paradoxically reinforced by the general invisibility of the city's residents. By largely "disappearing" the victims of the city's decline, the discourse of ruination remains focused on architecture and the "reclamation" of the city by nature. This suggests either a return to a preindustrial state or a new ecological idyll—but it does not suggest a need to focus on the city's impoverished population. Presenting a landscape that is empty and open, regressing to the past or waiting for new creative uses, displaces the discourse about people and the effects of abandonment and decay on their lives. To claim that the deindustrialization of Detroit is part of a natural cycle of history, a timeless struggle between nature and culture, ignores the real and specific political and economic factors leading to the city's decline, which, as Millington observes, are far from "natural."

The context of ruin photos is also critical. Reinforcing the discourse of the unpeopled city, the front page of a print edition of the *New York Times*, for

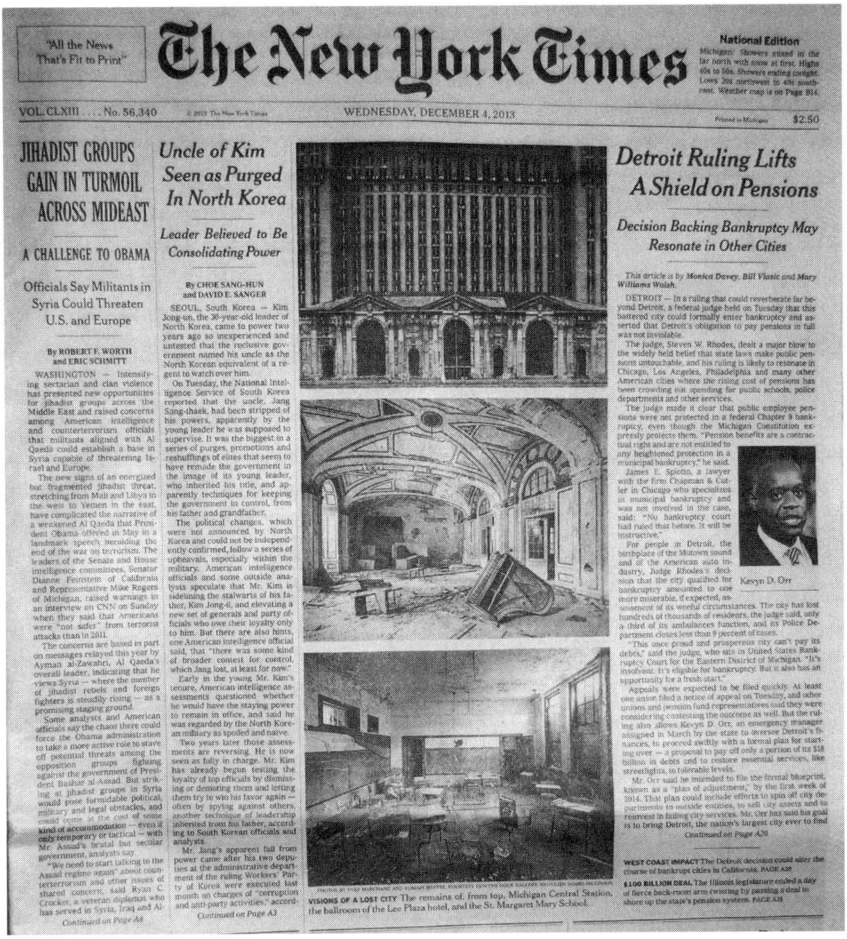

"All the News That's Fit to Print"

The New York Times

National Edition

Michigan: Showers mixed in the far north with snow at first. Highs 40s to 50s. Showers ending tonight. Lows 20s northwest to 40s southeast. Weather map is on Page B14.

VOL. CLXIII . . . No. 56,340 — © 2013 The New York Times — WEDNESDAY, DECEMBER 4, 2013 — Printed in Michigan — $2.50

JIHADIST GROUPS GAIN IN TURMOIL ACROSS MIDEAST

A CHALLENGE TO OBAMA

Officials Say Militants in Syria Could Threaten U.S. and Europe

By ROBERT F. WORTH and ERIC SCHMITT

WASHINGTON — Intensifying sectarian and clan violence has presented new opportunities for jihadist groups across the Middle East and raised concerns among American intelligence and counterterrorism officials that militants aligned with Al Qaeda could establish a base in Syria capable of threatening Israel and Europe.

The new signs of an energized but fragmented jihadist threat, stretching from Mali and Libya in the west to Yemen in the east, have complicated the narrative of a weakened Al Qaeda that President Obama offered in May in a landmark speech heralding the end of the war on terrorism. The leaders of the Senate and House intelligence committees, Senator Dianne Feinstein of California and Representative Mike Rogers of Michigan, raised warnings in an interview on CNN on Sunday when they said that Americans were "not safer" from terrorist attacks than in 2011.

The concerns are based in part on messages relayed this year by Ayman al-Zawahri, Al Qaeda's overall leader, indicating that he views Syria — where the number of jihadist rebels and foreign fighters is steadily rising — as a promising staging ground.

Some analysts and American officials say the chaos there could force the Obama administration to take a more active role to stave off potential threats among the opposition groups fighting against the government of President Bashar al-Assad. But striking at jihadist groups in Syria would pose formidable political, military and legal obstacles, and could come at the cost of some kind of accommodation — even if only temporary or tactical — with Mr. Assad's brutal but secular government, analysts say.

"We need to start talking to the Assad regime again" about counterterrorism and other issues of shared concern, said Ryan C. Crocker, a veteran diplomat who has served in Syria, Iraq and Af-

Continued on Page A8

Uncle of Kim Seen as Purged In North Korea

Leader Believed to Be Consolidating Power

By CHOE SANG-HUN and DAVID E. SANGER

SEOUL, South Korea — Kim Jong-un, the 30-year-old leader of North Korea, came to power two years ago so inexperienced and untested that the reclusive government named his uncle as the North Korean equivalent of a regent to watch over him.

On Tuesday, the National Intelligence Service of South Korea reported that the uncle, Jang Song-thaek, had been stripped of his powers, apparently by the young leader he was supposed to supervise. It was the biggest in a series of purges, promotions and reshufflings of elites that seem to have remade the government in the image of its young leader, who inherited his title, and apparently techniques for keeping the government in control, from his father and grandfather.

The political changes, which were not announced by North Korea and could not be independently confirmed, follow a series of upheavals, especially within the military. American intelligence officials and some outside analysts speculate that Mr. Kim is sidelining the stalwarts of his father, Kim Jong-il, and elevating a new set of generals and party officials who owe their loyalty only to him. But there are also hints, one American intelligence official said, that "there was some kind of broader contest for control, which Jang lost, at least for now."

Early in the young Mr. Kim's tenure, American intelligence assessments questioned whether he would have the staying power to remain in office, and said he was regarded by the North Korean military as spoiled and naive.

Two years later those assessments are reversing. He is now seen as fully in charge. Mr. Kim has already begun testing the loyalty of top officials by dismissing or demoting them and letting them try to win his favor again — often by spying against others, another technique of leadership inherited from his father, according to South Korean officials and analysts.

Mr. Jang's apparent fall from power came after his two deputies at the administrative department of the ruling Workers' Party of Korea were executed last month on charges of "corruption and anti-party activities," accord-

Continued on Page A3

VISIONS OF A LOST CITY The remains of, from top, Michigan Central Station, the ballroom of the Lee Plaza hotel, and the St. Margaret Mary School.

Detroit Ruling Lifts A Shield on Pensions

Decision Backing Bankruptcy May Resonate in Other Cities

This article is by Monica Davey, Bill Vlasic and Mary Williams Walsh.

DETROIT — In a ruling that could reverberate far beyond Detroit, a federal judge held on Tuesday that this battered city could formally enter bankruptcy and asserted that Detroit's obligation to pay pensions in full was not inviolable.

The judge, Steven W. Rhodes, dealt a major blow to the widely held belief that state laws make public pensions untouchable, and his ruling is likely to resonate in Chicago, Los Angeles, Philadelphia and many other American cities where the rising cost of pensions has been crowding out spending for public schools, police departments and other services.

The judge made it clear that public employee pensions were not protected in a federal Chapter 9 bankruptcy, even though the Michigan Constitution expressly protects them. "Pension benefits are a contractual right and are not entitled to any heightened protection in a municipal bankruptcy," he said.

James E. Spiotto, a lawyer with the firm Chapman & Cutler in Chicago who specializes in municipal bankruptcy and was not involved in the case, said: "No bankruptcy court had ruled that before. It will be instructive."

Kevyn D. Orr

For people in Detroit, the birthplace of the Motown sound and of the American auto industry, Judge Rhodes's decision that the city qualified for bankruptcy amounted to one more miserable, if expected, assessment of its woeful circumstances. The city has lost hundreds of thousands of residents, the judge said, only a third of its ambulances function, and its Police Department closes less than 9 percent of cases.

"This once proud and prosperous city can't pay its debts," said the judge, who sits in United States Bankruptcy Court for the Eastern District of Michigan. "It's insolvent. It's eligible for bankruptcy. But it also has an opportunity for a fresh start."

Appeals were expected to be filed quickly. At least one union filed a notice of appeal on Tuesday, and other unions and pension fund representatives said they were considering contesting the outcome as well. But the ruling also allows Kevyn D. Orr, an emergency manager assigned in March by the state to oversee Detroit's finances, to proceed swiftly with a formal plan for starting over — a proposal to pay off only a portion of its $18 billion in debts and to restore essential services, like streetlights, to tolerable levels.

Mr. Orr said he intended to file the formal blueprint, known as a "plan of adjustment," by the first week of 2014. That plan could include efforts to spin off city departments to outside entities, to sell city assets and to reinvest in failing city services. Mr. Orr has said his goal is to bring Detroit, the nation's largest city ever to find

Continued on Page A20

WEST COAST IMPACT The Detroit decision could alter the course of bankrupt cities in California. PAGE A20

$100 BILLION DEAL The Illinois legislature ended a day of fierce back-room arm-twisting by passing a deal to shore up the state's pension system. PAGE A18

FIG. 12 *New York Times* front page, "Detroit Ruling Lifts a Shield on Pensions," with three photos of abandoned sites by Yves Marchand and Romain Meffre, December 4, 2013.

example, used three Detroit ruin photos to accompany the article "Detroit Ruling Lifts a Shield on Pensions," announcing a federal judge's ruling that Detroit was formally qualified to enter bankruptcy without protections for city pensions.[3] Illustrating the story with a trio of photos above the fold, the top photo, taken by the French team of Yves Marchand and Romain Meffre, represents the iconic Michigan Central Station, an abandoned grand civic structure that has come to serve as a symbol of city failure. Below that are two more color images by Marchand and Meffre: the ballroom of the Lee Plaza Hotel with its overturned and crippled grand piano below a beautifully painted ceiling, and a water-damaged classroom at the former Saint Margaret Mary School, with peeling paint and a few desks randomly scattered about. From these photos one might imagine that Detroit was already a ghost town (figure 12).

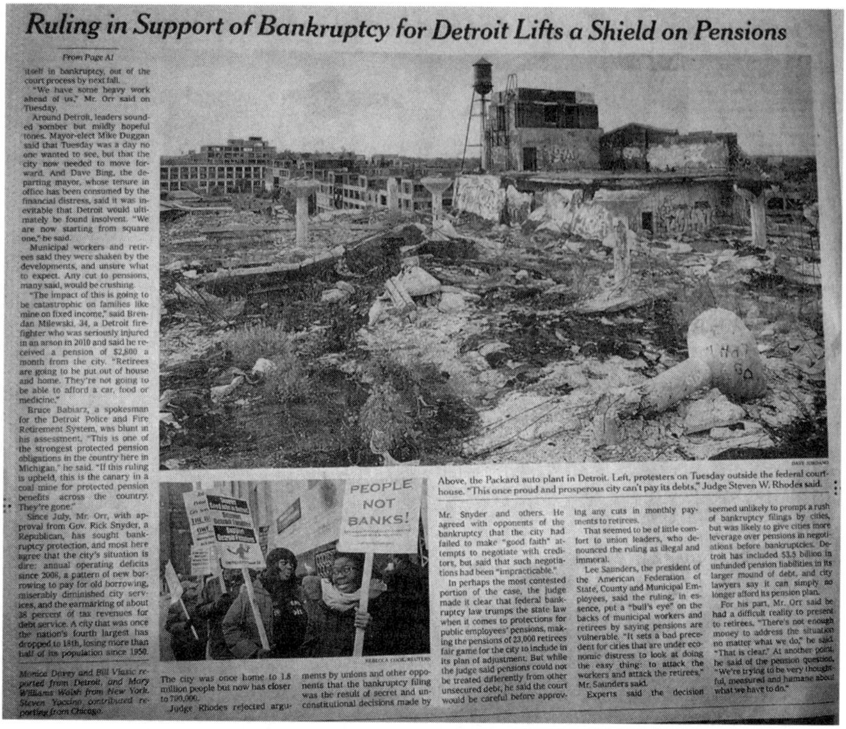

Ruling in Support of Bankruptcy for Detroit Lifts a Shield on Pensions

From Page A1

itself in bankruptcy, out of the court process by next fall.

"We have some heavy work ahead of us," Mr. Orr said on Tuesday.

Around Detroit, leaders sounded somber but mildly hopeful tones. Mayor-elect Mike Duggan said that Tuesday was a day no one wanted to see, but that the city now needed to move forward. And Dave Bing, the departing mayor, whose tenure in office has been consumed by the financial distress, said it was inevitable that Detroit would ultimately be found insolvent. "We are now starting from square one," he said.

Municipal workers and retirees said they were shaken by the developments, and unsure what to expect. Any cut to pensions, many said, would be crushing.

"The impact of this is going to be catastrophic on families like mine on fixed income," said Brendan Milewski, 34, a Detroit firefighter who was seriously injured in an arson in 2010 and said he received a pension of $2,800 a month from the city. "Retirees are going to be put out of house and home. They're not going to be able to afford a car, food or medicine."

Bruce Babiarz, a spokesman for the Detroit Police and Fire Retirement System, was blunt in his assessment. "This is one of the strongest protected pension obligations in the country here in Michigan," he said. "If this ruling is upheld, this is the canary in a coal mine for protected pension benefits across the country. They're gone."

Since July, Mr. Orr, with approval from Gov. Rick Snyder, a Republican, has sought bankruptcy protection, and most here agree that the city's situation is dire: annual operating deficits since 2008, a pattern of new borrowing to pay for old borrowing, miserably diminished city services, and the earmarking of about 38 percent of tax revenues for debt service. A city that was once the nation's fourth largest has dropped to 18th, losing more than half of its population since 1950.

Monica Davey and Bill Vlasic reported from Detroit, and Mary Williams Walsh from New York. Steven Yaccino contributed reporting from Chicago.

DAVE JORDANO

REBECCA COOK/REUTERS

Above, the Packard auto plant in Detroit. Left, protesters on Tuesday outside the federal courthouse. "This once proud and prosperous city can't pay its debts," Judge Steven W. Rhodes said.

The city was once home to 1.8 million people but now has closer to 700,000.

Judge Rhodes rejected arguments by unions and other opponents that the bankruptcy filing was the result of secret and unconstitutional decisions made by Mr. Snyder and others. He agreed with opponents of the bankruptcy that the city had failed to make "good faith" attempts to negotiate with creditors, but said that such negotiations had been "impracticable."

In perhaps the most contested portion of the case, the judge made it clear that federal bankruptcy law trumps the state law when it comes to protections for public employees' pensions, making the pensions of 23,000 retirees fair game for the city to include in its plan of adjustment. But while the judge said pensions could not be treated differently from other unsecured debt, he said the court would be careful before approving any cuts in monthly payments to retirees.

That seemed to be of little comfort to union leaders, who denounced the ruling as illegal and immoral.

Lee Saunders, the president of the American Federation of State, County and Municipal Employees, said the ruling, in essence, put a "bull's eye" on the backs of municipal workers and retirees by saying pensions are vulnerable. "It sets a bad precedent for cities that are under economic distress to look at doing the easy thing: to attack the workers and attack the retirees," Mr. Saunders said.

Experts said the decision seemed unlikely to prompt a rush of bankruptcy filings by cities, but was likely to give cities more leverage over pensions in negotiations before bankruptcies. Detroit has included $3.5 billion in unfunded pension liabilities in its larger mound of debt, and city lawyers say it can simply no longer afford its pension plan.

For his part, Mr. Orr said he had a difficult reality to present to retirees. "There's not enough money to address the situation no matter what we do," he said. "That is clear." At another point, he said of the pension question, "We're trying to be very thoughtful, measured and humane about what we have to do."

FIG. 13 *New York Times*, continuation on page 20 of "Detroit Ruling Lifts a Shield on Pensions," with photos of Packard Plant by Dave Jordano and courthouse demonstration by Rebecca Cook/Reuters, December 4, 2013.

Inside on page 20 is a huge black-and-white photo of the Packard Plant, in all its crumbling decrepitude. Beneath it is a much smaller photo of a demonstration outside the federal courthouse where black protesters carry signs saying "People not Banks!" and "Support Good Jobs in Detroit; Support Detroit Families; Support Detroit Pensions" (figure 13). Minimizing the active human presence and combative local response to the judge's ruling, the front-page trio of ruin photos—representing the failed civic monument, the opulent architecture of a once prosperous heyday, and the dashed hopes for the next generation—suggest an already dead and mummified city. This morbid view is reinforced by the boldface caption, "Visions of a Lost City." The immediate effect is to provide ideological support for the cutting of city pensions even as those cuts are contested by the pictured protesters on the inside page. If the city is already lost, the struggle of a few workers to preserve their meager incomes is rendered insignificant and futile, if also poignant.

The larger effect is to isolate Detroit as the nation's repository for urban nightmares. The small picture of protesters makes it clear that the "lost city" is a black city. Yet pushing through pension cuts and slashing the health benefits of city employees in Detroit will establish a precedent for public workers everywhere, so that the images also serve a disciplinary purpose. While implicitly contrasting the unpeopled city on the front page with the living cities inhabited by readers of the *New York Times*, these photos nonetheless reiterate key icons of the American landscape—the dilapidated civic institutions, former hotels, abandoned schools, and derelict factories found in declining towns and cities across the nation. These cities and towns are also in the process of imposing further austerities on their own impoverished populations, and seeking to cut pensions for public employees (a *New York Times* front-page headline the very next day announced, "Chicago Pursues Deal to Change Pension Funding"). Thus we may see the dual role of the Detroit ruin imaginary, in which the images serve as warnings of the extreme conditions to which many cities are vulnerable, thereby preparing them for their own fiscal austerities, while also presenting Detroit as an isolated example of a racialized city that is responsible for its own disastrous decline. These are flip sides of the same coin; by extension, every declining city will be blamed for its own decline, thereby justifying placing the burden of debt not on the banks and corporations but on the city's workers.

A Contemporary Pompeii?

Artist and sociologist Camilo José Vergara has been among the most systematic photographers, returning to the city over the course of decades to rephotograph sites and document transformations over time, building by building and block by block.[4] Vergara was criticized in the mid-1990s, however, for suggesting that contemporary icons of decay be turned into classical-style objects of aesthetic contemplation, most notoriously for his proposal to preserve Detroit's abandoned 1920s-era skyscrapers. On the one hand, Vergara hoped to preserve buildings designed by nationally known architects such as Daniel Burnham, George Post, Albert Kahn, and McKim, Mead & White from the wrecking ball; on the other hand, he felt they possessed an Athenian splendor redolent of a lost civilization. Thus his suggestion that a "skyscraper park" in downtown Detroit be stabilized as an "American Acropolis" and a "memorial to a disappearing civilization" evoked a firestorm of controversy by seeming to give up hope for revitalization and renewal.[5] Vergara, however, is not insensitive to the history of the city or the effects of ruination on the city's inhabitants in the sometimes poetic writing that accompanies his photography. He observes, for example: "The spasms of the millennium are being felt in the city of Henry Ford, Rosa Parks, Diego Rivera, 'Raw Dog,' 'Ghetto Killer,' and 'The Beast 666.' One wonders about the meanings of the scrawlings found on the walls of different floors in Detroit's abandoned train station: 'Today's Menu: Wombat Dick Stew' 'Today's Menu: Orangutan Asshole.' 'Today's Menu:

Afterbirth cooked in its own juices.' To me this seems like the right language to deal with the disrupted lives, the lack of future, the city's destruction."[6]

The photography team of Yves Marchand and Romain Meffre, both born in the Parisian suburbs, embarked on a five-year collaboration on Detroit ruins starting in 2005 (when they were twenty-four and eighteen years old, respectively), which resulted in the book *The Ruins of Detroit* that includes a foreword by Robert Polidori and an essay by Thomas Sugrue. Their own introductory text sets out their perspective, which naturalizes Detroit's decline as a vaguely inevitable historical process, "the volatile result of a change of era and the fall of empires," and a "natural and sublime demonstration of our human destinies and of their paradoxes, a dramatization of our creative and self-destructive vanities." They refer to Detroit as "that contemporary Pompeii, with all the archetypal buildings of an American city in a state of mummification." For them the city is indeed already dead and mummified, no less than the ancient city of Pompeii, whose inhabitants were expunged in one fell swoop by a volcanic force of nature.

This view is confirmed by their photographs, as the *New York Times* understood. The images are taken in darkly overcast and cool light conditions, conveying the lost beauty of the past in compositions both chilling and compelling as well as devoid of people. The captions identify the sites, and each section of the book includes text that provides more information or a brief history, making visible and legible the waste and destruction and shedding light on the past. Unlike the urbex ethos found in *Beauty in Decay*, Marchand and Meffre are more historically specific. Their images include photos of grand old mansions, abandoned hotels, schools, theaters, apartment buildings, administrative buildings, a decaying dentist's office, and the Packard Plant, among other images.[7] Reinforcing the view that Detroit is already a lost city, however, only two images in the book's nearly 230 pages feature recognizable humans, and these are seen from a distance. One of these is the very last photo, which pictures the photographers themselves as two tiny silhouettes walking down an alley amid the derelict buildings of the Packard Plant (facing the acknowledgments page).[8] As a farewell image, the alley appears to be an empty street and the desolate plant a metonym for the city which by implication is also empty and abandoned (figure 14). The image appeared on the cover of *Time* in October 2009 in their special report, "The Tragedy of Detroit," which reasserted a narrative that blamed the 1967 riots; Coleman Young, Detroit's mayor from 1974 to 1994; and foreign automobile competition for Detroit's decline.[9]

In a series of photos of the former Highland Park Police Station, a tiny municipality surrounded by Detroit and even more impoverished, Marchand and Meffre convey the official dysfunction exposed by sudden abandonment. *Highland Park Police Station* portrays the chaotic mess of photographic and forensic evidence left behind when the police station was closed in 2001

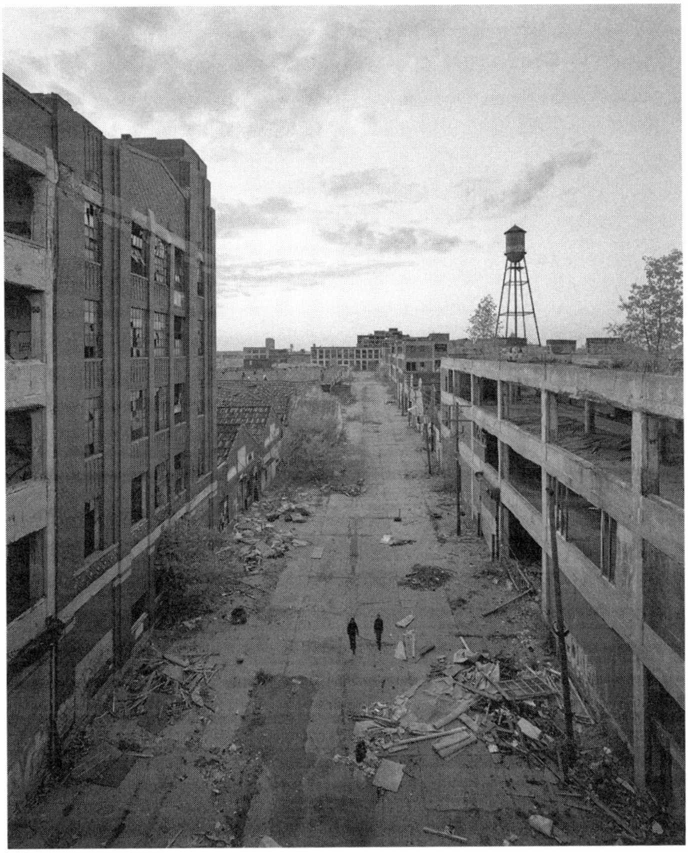

FIG. 14 Yves Marchand and Romain Meffre, *Southern Part, Packard Motors Plant*, 2009, from *The Ruins of Detroit*, 2010. Courtesy of the artists.

(figure 15). Desks and file cabinets are haphazardly shoved together, their drawers emptied of the evidence, now strewn on the floor. The forensic samples in some of the photos in this series (including hair and blood samples), relate to the case of Benjamin Atkins, who raped and murdered eleven women between 1991 and 1992 and dumped their bodies in abandoned buildings between Detroit and Highland Park. Convicted in 1992, Atkins died of AIDS in prison four years later.[10] The scope of underfunded investigations for rape, however, was revealed in 2009, when prosecutors in Detroit discovered more than eleven thousand boxes of potential evidence in rape cases left completely unprocessed; the rape kits had sat untouched on shelves for years, with no DNA evidence extracted. This turns out to be true of many cities where "hundreds of thousands" of rape kits lay untested on storeroom shelves for years and are only now, in some cases, being tested and used to solve rape cases.[11] The eleven thousand rape kits in Detroit rival the eleven thousand unsolved

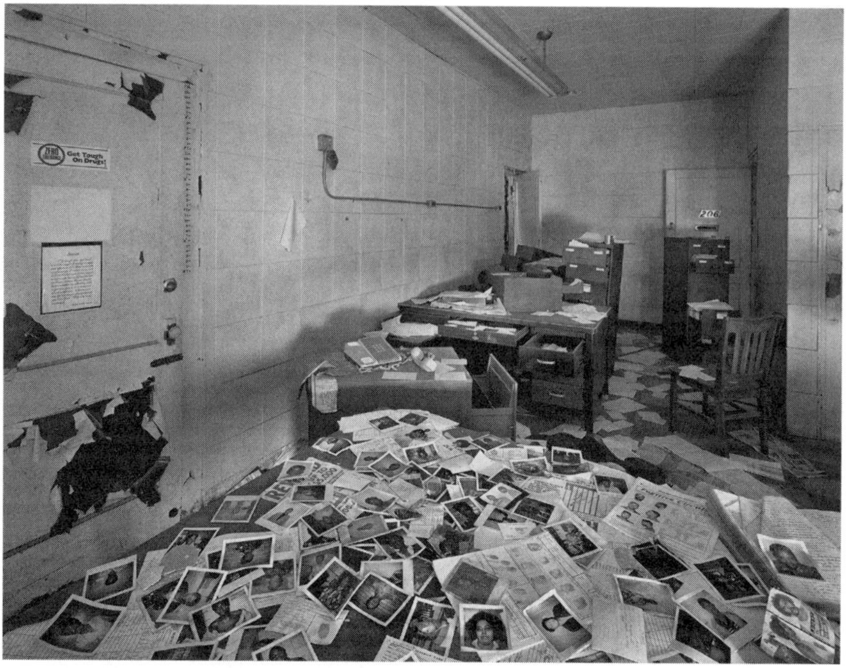

FIG. 15 Yves Marchand and Romain Meffre, *Highland Park Police Station*, 2007, from *The Ruins of Detroit*, 2010. Courtesy of the artists.

city homicides, dating back to 1960, reported in Charlie LeDuff's *Detroit: An American Autopsy.*

The Michigan Central Station (MCS), pictured by the *New York Times*, has become *the* iconic image and is de rigueur for all photographers of Detroit ruins—a magnificent structure whose many broken windows allow the spectator, from the right position, to see right through the building. Marchand and Meffre put this image on the cover of their book, tightly framing it to allow no space outside the cool gray tones of the structure itself so that we are drawn through the broken windows toward the interior darkness (figure 16). Such bravura city monuments are important to city-building, helping to construct communal identity and civic pride. For Detroit, the MCS became the single most awe-inspiring civic structure, a Beaux Arts building that opened in 1913 as the tallest railroad station in the world. It consists of a three-story train depot with a lavish waiting room of terrazzo floors and fifty-four foot ceilings modeled on the Roman Baths of Caracalla as well as an eighteen-story office tower. The MCS was built by the architects Warren & Wetmore of New York and Reed and Stem of St. Paul, Minnesota, who had previously collaborated to design New York's Grand Central Terminal. The MCS was itself a subsidiary of the New York Central Railroad owned by railroad baron William

Vanderbilt. It was built near the entrance to an underwater railway tunnel in southwest Detroit, at a distance from the downtown. Acquiring the approximately fifty acres for the station and the park it was meant to include meant buying or condemning about three hundred homes. Opening on short notice and ahead of schedule when the old train station burned down, the MCS was hailed by the *Detroit Tribune* in December 1913 as "a sentinel of progress."[12]

In the period following World War II, passenger trains faced stiff competition from government-subsidized highways and intercity airline traffic. The station's location far from downtown, the lack of parking, the high cost of maintenance due to the structure's massive size, and the decline of the city's population led to a further decline in use. In 1971 the federal government formed Amtrak, which took over the MCS, and in 1975 the MCS was added to the National Register of Historic Places. It was sold in 1985 to Kaybee Corporation and was sold again in 1989 to real estate developer Mark Longton Jr., who hoped to turn it into a casino, but city voters opposed casinos until 1996, long after Longton had given up. The MCS was open to trespass and looting throughout the 1990s and was bought in 1995 by Controlled Terminals Inc., owned by billionaire Manuel "Matty" Moroun, Michigan's largest private property owner, who also owns the Ambassador Bridge between Detroit and

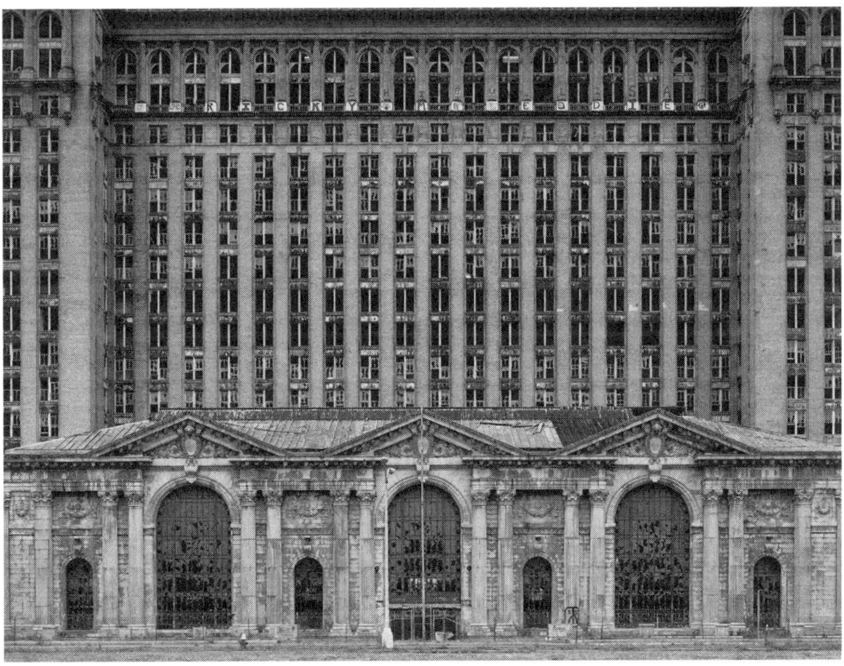

FIG. 16 Yves Marchand and Romain Meffre, *Michigan Central Station*, 2007, from *The Ruins of Detroit*, 2010. Courtesy of the artists.

Canada and a network of trucking companies. The Ambassador Bridge is the only major border crossing in the country that is privately owned, through which 25 percent of U.S.-Canada truck freight passes, and brings in a daily toll take of $156,000. Moroun's motives for buying the MCS are not certain, but he owns property in nearby blighted neighborhoods in both Detroit and Windsor in the apparent hope of building a second span.[13] Moroun left the MCS untouched for years, allowing it to decay beyond repair. Various plans to turn the MCS into the city's new police headquarters, a hotel–office complex, or a Homeland Security and Customs and Border Protection headquarters have all been stymied by the multimillion-dollar costs of renovation. In 2009 the Detroit City Council passed a resolution, at the instigation of Detroit City Council member Barbara-Rose Collins, to demolish the MCS at Moroun's expense.[14] At a projected cost of $5 million to $10 million, this measure also failed and caused an outcry from residents who wish to preserve the station despite the embarrassment it causes the City Council, which regards the once towering sentinel of progress as a monumental symbol of decay. "Monuments become anti-monuments," observes Dylan Trigg, "as soon as their symbolic association has been subverted."[15] As an anti-monument, the MCS figures the body of the city in radically destabilized form, undermining it as fragmentary and broken.

Radically destabilized form became a design strategy for Coop Himmelblau and Gordon Matta-Clark, who deliberately decentered the classical aesthetic of the humanist tradition. Coop Himmelblau, a leading avant-garde architectural design firm for more than two decades, calls for an "architecture of desolation" that refuses notions of a safe and comfortable city and reflects a perceived sense of loss. Matta-Clark (who died in 1978) engaged with dismembered architecture by slicing into empty suburban houses and abandoned buildings with a power saw to produce strange and disquieting voids and fissures, calling attention to issues of gentrification and urban decay. Both Coop Himmelblau's and Matta-Clark's projects reflect declining confidence in humanist progress and the state of urban development.[16]

Yet the MCS remains impressive and imposing both for its design and for its uncontested dominance of the urban landscape. It embodies both the grandiosity of capitalist ambition and the terror of capitalist decline. As *Detroit Free Press* reporter Bill McGraw observes, the city's inability to restore the MCS "reflects its inability to control its image and destiny."[17] This was amply demonstrated by the leading front-page position of the MCS photo in the *New York Times* as a "vision of a lost city."

As the largest ruin in the country, the Packard Plant is the second-most-iconic monument in Detroit after the MCS. Designed by Albert Kahn and built by the Packard brothers in 1903, it was the first modern automobile factory and includes forty-seven buildings spread over more than forty acres on Detroit's east side. In the 1950s, the turning point for Detroit's economy, the city suffered four major recessions, and auto manufacturers and suppliers began to reduce their workforces, close plants, and relocate to other parts of the country that were white and nonunion. As an independent producer, Packard was unable to compete with the Big Three auto companies of Ford, General Motors, and Chrysler; Packard closed its doors in 1956.[18]

Although it has been extensively stripped, the Packard Plant has served as a haven for small businesses, artists and graffiti artists, urban explorers, paintball battles, techno parties, raves, fashion shoots, auto scrappers, and the homeless. Allan Hill, a semiretired auto-body worker, for example, has lived in the ruined plant since 2008 and serves as its on-site historian and foremost guide.[19] That people live in the ruins is a sad commentary on homelessness and poverty in Detroit. Others romanticize the ruins so that even wedding couples have themselves photographed at the plant.[20] Calls for the Packard Plant's demolition have been stymied by cost estimates of $20 million, including asbestos removal, while fervid hopes for its renovation appeared unlikely until the plant was purchased by Fernando Palazuelo of Lima, Peru, for $405,000 in a tax-foreclosure sale at the end of 2013. Palazuelo hired twenty-four-hour security patrols and is trying to raise $350 million to redevelop the site as a mixed-use project over a period of ten to fifteen years or more, saving some of the old buildings and building new ones. His long-term plan includes retail, residential, and cultural components.[21]

A political controversy erupted in February 2013 when letter placards spelling out the Nazi slogan "Arbeit macht frei" were placed in the windows of the East Grand Boulevard Bridge at the plant (figure 17). Complaints of racism and antisemitism were immediately raised by Jewish community groups, prompting community volunteers to hastily remove the placards. But this interpretation of their meaning misses the point of the heavily ironic slogan in the context of the Packard Plant. The assertion that "work sets you free" metaphorically likens the tens of thousands of Detroit's auto workers to the ruined lives of the Jews in Auschwitz. Both were treated as expendable human populations while the ugly truth was disguised with empty high-flown phrases. Of course the abandonment of the workers in Detroit is not same as the genocide of the Jews, but figuring the destructive effects on one in terms of the catastrophe of the other is meant to underscore not only the tragic conditions that industrial abandonment has wrought but also the disillusionment that has come with it—the death of the American dream and the belief that hard work brings prosperity and well-being.

Despite their captions, Marchand and Meffre's texts in *Ruins of Detroit* sometimes elide important aspects of the complex history they attempt to engage. One such caption suggests that school desegregation busing "proved counterproductive" and led to white flight to the suburbs, implicitly placing

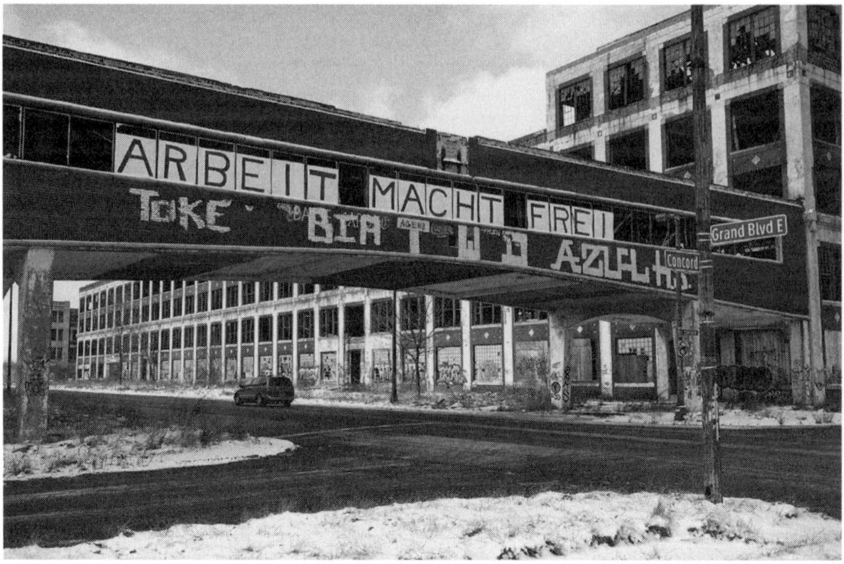

FIG. 17 Packard Plant with placards spelling *Arbeit macht Frei*, 2013. Photo: James Fassinger.

the blame on the desegregation attempt itself rather than on the implementation of a court ruling. In this case, the Supreme Court decision in *Milliken v. Bradley* blocked busing in those suburbs, deliberately isolating African Americans in Detroit.[22] This distinction is significant because it demonstrates that different policies could have led to different outcomes.

In another example, the text on the Lee Plaza Hotel explains the structure's original purpose as a luxury residential hotel when it was completed in 1929, on the eve of the Great Depression, causing the authors to muse: "Today one wonders which disaster wiped away the elegance of the sumptuous hotel. Its permanent residents seem to have vanished in a nuclear catastrophe."[23] This is followed by a series of ten ghostly images, some hinting at the vanished Gilded Age but most conveying a spare and impoverished existence. In *Room 1504, Lee Plaza Hotel*, among the water-damaged ceiling and walls, peeling paint, the cabinet about to fall, and chairs with disintegrating fabric covers, a small television sits in the middle of a kitchen table, facing what was likely once the most comfortable chair in the apartment, surrounded by several jars, perhaps the last repast of a frugal and circumscribed existence (figure 18). The authors' dramatic statement sweeps away the decades leading to the hotel's closure in 2010. In its longest reincarnation, from 1969 to 1997, it served as a subsidized assisted living facility for low-income senior citizens.[24] What happened to the seniors when the building was abandoned? The "nuclear catastrophe" for them was the prosaic event of city budget cuts.[25] An important difference between Detroit and Pompeii is that the people affected by that earlier catastrophe were long dead when that city was rediscovered and excavated many centuries later; in Detroit, there are hundreds of thousands of people still searching for ways to survive.

Trained at Princeton with photographer Emmet Gowin, New York–based photographer Andrew Moore covers similar territory to that of Marchand and Meffre, who invited the older photographer, known for his images of ruins in countries such as Cuba and post-Soviet Russia, to join them in 2008, introducing Moore to Detroit. Moore and the French photographers often shot the same subjects but with subtle differences. In an interview with *National Geographic*, Moore acknowledges the French team's likening of Detroit to Pompeii but rejects this analogy because Pompeii must be seen as a dead city whereas Moore sees Detroit as continuing to evolve. *Detroit Disassembled* is his vision of the city's regeneration, which is based on its reclamation by nature, a view

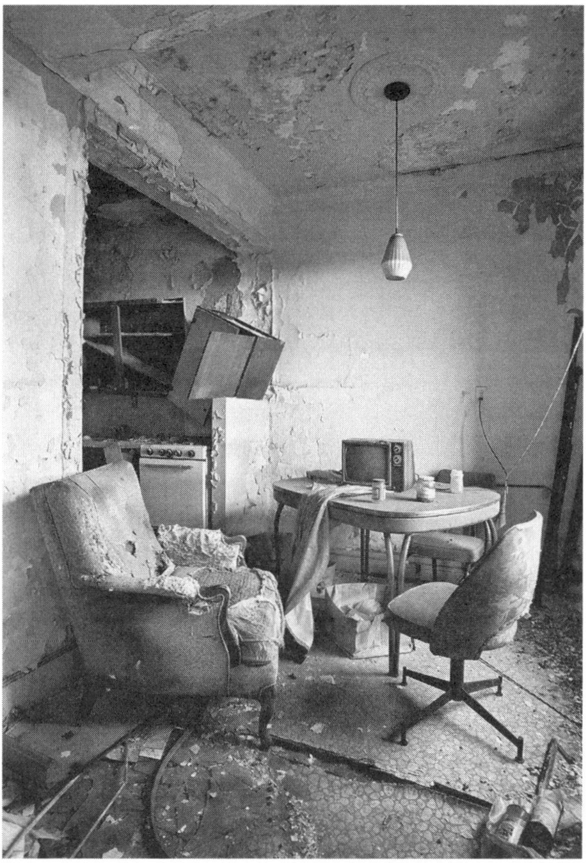

FIG. 18 Yves Marchand and Romain Meffre, *Room 1504, Lee Plaza Hotel*, 2005, from *The Ruins of Detroit*, 2010. Courtesy of the artists.

that also naturalizes and romanticizes Detroit's decline: "With its shuttered factories, schools, homes, and theaters, Detroit is an obvious symbol of America's slow industrial decline. But where others see an end, I see a beginning. The potent forces of nature and entropy are starting to reclaim and transform the Motor City. These pictures are my attempt to elegize the past by documenting the emerging landscape. . . . At first glance it seems like a modern Pompeii. But look closer at the ruins. In some places man's work is yielding to green, as at this East Detroit house. Elsewhere urban prairies and farming collectives are taking root. No one knows what will become of Detroit. But decay isn't static. And this city's story isn't over."[26] This is still an architectural story, however; unlike Moore's photos of Havana and Russia, which sometimes feature the inhabitants as primary subjects, his pictures of Detroit tend to emphasize the relationship of nature and culture, with nature in the ascendancy, as in *House on Walden Street, East Side* (figure 19). The greenery creates a living, breathing, if windowless, façade, as if the home were deliberately subsuming itself, while the blue garage door and blue-painted curb echo the sky to invoke a tropical idyll.

For Moore, "nature is a metaphor of resurrection." This suggests a redemptive role for nature, which might have been a religious truth or revelation in

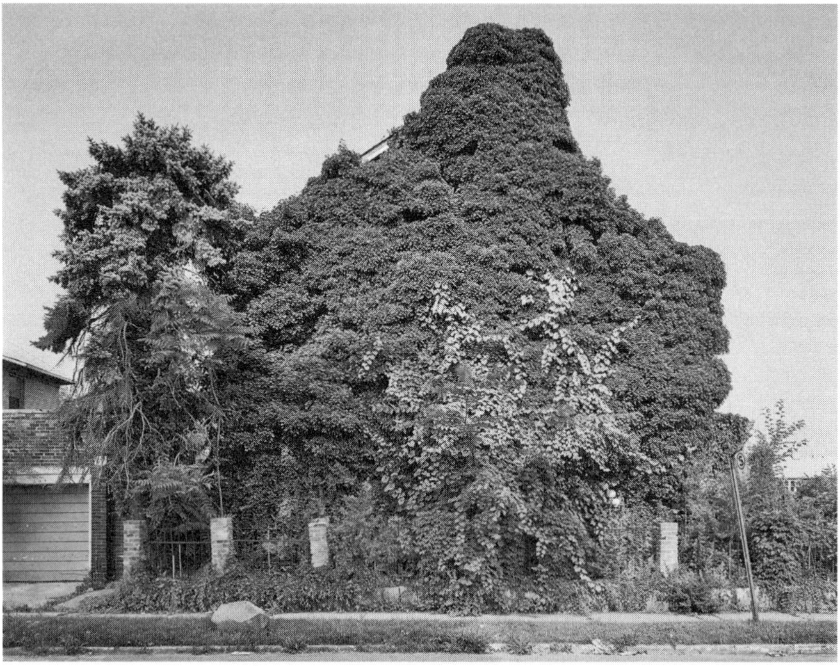

FIG. 19 Andrew Moore, *House on Walden Street, East Side*, from *Detroit Disassembled*, 2010. © Andrew Moore.

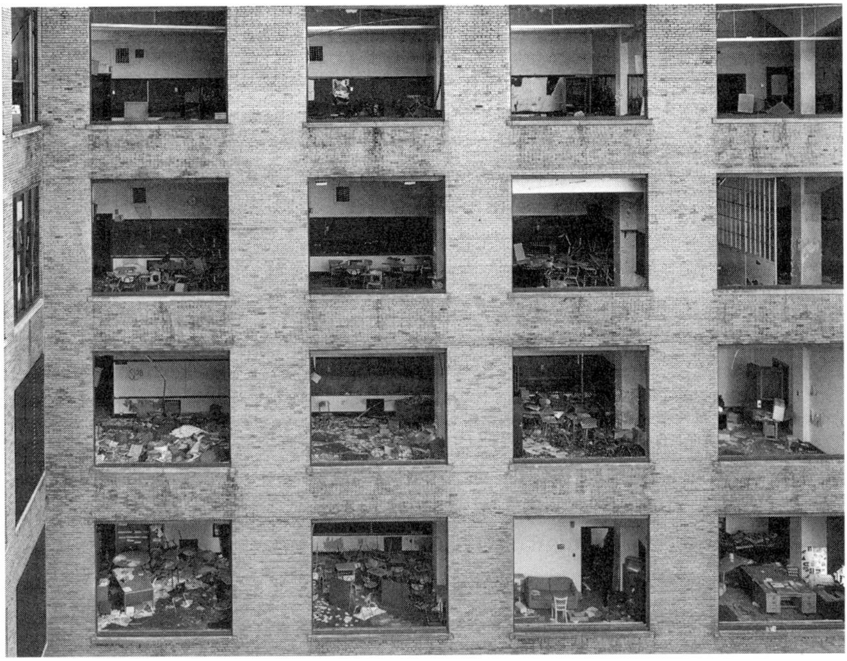

FIG. 20 Andrew Moore, *Courtyard, Former Cass Technical High School Building*, from *Detroit Disassembled*, 2010. © Andrew Moore.

the past but operates in secular guise today.[27] Either way, however, the notion of nature as redemptive obscures or neutralizes the political forces of decline. Focusing on the natural forces of entropy as unstoppable, Moore frankly describes the basis of his aesthetic as a "romantic sense of horror and beauty" and lists as foremost among his photographic concerns the forces of entropy, color, and detail, and the drama of light and weather. Accordingly, his lush, color-saturated prints evoke the romantic paintings of Caspar David Friedrich and Frederic Edwin Church, both of whom he admires.[28]

Like Marchand and Meffre, Moore captures the sense of sudden wholesale abandonment that seems to have occurred in Detroit. As with the former Highland Park Police Station, where the inhabitants appear to have simply walked away, Moore photographs a view into Cass Tech High School (also photographed by Marchand and Meffre and now demolished), which had been abandoned five years earlier when a new school was built nearby. Exposed and windowless classrooms appear to have been vacated only the day before, with school supplies and equipment scattered on counters and strewn about on the floor, leaving the viewer to wonder why these supplies weren't donated or recycled (figure 20). The grid of abandoned classrooms seems like a metonym for the city grids of abandoned homes and apartment buildings. Similarly,

Marchand and Meffre photographed the Mark Twain Public Library, a branch of the Detroit Public Library, built in 1940 and closed in 1998 for renovations that were never completed. Now on a list of buildings to be demolished, the library is still filled with books and looks freshly abandoned. This image contrasts sharply with the former Detroit Public Schools Book Depository, pictured by Marchand and Meffre as well as Moore, where trees grow out of masses of rotting books, completing an uncanny cycle of trees to books and back to trees (see figure 6). We move backward and forward in time in such images, imagining the past before it became the ruined future. Other images juxtapose heavily ironic spray-painted phrases with ruined spaces: "God Has Left Detroit," in an abandoned nursing home photographed by Moore, or "And you shall say that God did it," in the abandoned East Grand Boulevard Methodist Church photographed by both sets of photographers.

Overall, Marchand and Meffre and Andrew Moore offer seemingly opposite yet parallel approaches: Marchand and Meffre's somber photographs, cool and drained of life, suggest a lamentation for a state of irreversible decline and mortal rigor, while Moore's photographs, warm and vibrant with color, offer a commemorative tribute to the beauty of decay and the resurgence of nature. These are flip sides of the same aesthetic strategy. One laments city decline as a deindustrialized wasteland yet finds beauty in decay; the other engages in romanticized reveries on the struggle between nature and culture in order to find beauty in decay. These approaches are integral to the ruin imaginary and the worldwide urban explorer movement.

Julia Reyes Taubman spent six years and took more than thirty-five thousand photos of Detroit, from which she culled over four hundred images for *Detroit: 138 Square Miles*, her homage to the city with a foreword by Elmore Leonard (the fiction writer and a neighbor of Taubman's until his death in 2013).[29] The book includes images of local denizens—at hockey games, an Eminem/Jay Z concert, cafes and bars, the Detroit Autorama hot rod show, a motorcycle club—as well as many aerial shots providing broad views of the desolate landscape, impoverished neighborhoods, and decaying industrial buildings, most in a cool, flattened color palette. In the back is a "Guide to the Photographs" next to grouped thumbnail images for many of them, consisting of brief explanatory texts produced with the help of Robert Fishman and Michael McCulloch, professors at the University of Michigan.

Jerry Herron provides an introductory essay. As in most of his writing, Herron's pique is aroused by those who seem ignorant of or who trivialize Detroit's history. In an earlier essay, he likens himself to Petrarch encountering the city of Rome, as evoked by Edward Gibbon in *The Decline and Fall of the Roman Empire*. Petrarch "was astonished at the supine indifference of the Romans themselves" and felt that he, a stranger, "was more conversant with these antiquities than the nobles and natives of the metropolis." Writes Herron, "I feel like Gibbon's Petrarch, then: astonished at the seeming indifference of the local citizenry to Detroit's monumental fragments, humbled at the discovery that after 30 years in the city I seem to know more about its crumbling relics than the natives do—many of them, at least." The larger rant, however, is against ruin imagery that aestheticizes decline, based on the mistaken assumption that it is possible for imagery to do otherwise. Although he finds the photographs of Andrew Moore's *Detroit Disassembled*, which he saw at the Akron Art Museum, to be "truly amazing, transformative even," he nonetheless dismisses the work as "ruin porn" and, just as damningly, as "art" that stalks the usual sites and "mystifies into 'poetic' inconsequence and remoteness the past that is represented by Detroit."[30]

In "Living with Detroit," his essay for Taubman's book, in which Taubman has photographs of some of the very same sites as Moore, Herron also criticizes outsiders and "their urge for drive-by solutions" while praising Taubman's photographs: "There's nothing one-off or drive-by about them; they're an insider's view of what it feels like and looks like to live with this place."[31] This statement raises the question of how one distinguishes between a photo that is "drive-by" and one that is not, but Herron offers few clues. His praise for one set of images over the other is based on his perception that it *feels* like "an insider's view," made by someone who cares enough "to live with this place" rather than someone who visits in order to leave again. "There *is* something uniquely arresting here," writes Herron, "that much I'll give the drive-by opportunists. But Detroit is not a sight simply to be gawked and groped, and then walked away from." And what does it feel like to live with Detroit? "Truth to tell, it is not *like* anything," writes Herron. "It just is, and that's the mystery of it, and the wonder. And that's the wonder of the images in this book."[32] Herron is understandably hard pressed to describe the difference in visual terms and thus offers his own mystifying description of it.

The critique of images by "outsiders" is perhaps driven by a sense of powerlessness at the inability to act against the ruination. The images evoke the affects of anger and resentment—not necessarily at the conditions of the city directly but against the pictures that convey them and seem to make those conditions worse simply by publicizing them, making the city seem alien and pathetic and, perhaps worst of all, provoking pity as a depersonalized response to "distant suffering," akin to seeing pictures of starving children in Africa. Anger and resentment are common affects provoked by "outsider" images, existing in a state of tension with a more stricken sense of empathy and intimate identification.[33] And this is why the visual imagery itself is glossed over in vague terms, or dismissed even if "amazing" and "transformative," because ultimately it is the real or imagined subject positions of the photographers and their presumed commitment to the city rather than the images themselves that are at issue.

Taubman, however, unlike Herron, does not actually live in Detroit either but in the northern suburb of Bloomfield Hills, one of the wealthiest communities in the nation. She has demonstrated her commitment to the arts in Detroit and the surrounding area through her support for Cranbrook Academy of Art and Art Museum, and as chair of the board of the noncollecting Museum of Contemporary Art Detroit (MoCAD), which she helped found in 2006. MoCAD is located in a converted former auto dealership, which was designed as a raw museum space by architect Andrew Zago, and one of its first exhibitions was *Shrinking Cities*, done in collaboration with Cranbrook Art Museum, a largely conceptual exhibition dealing with population loss and shifting urban concentrations in several cities around the world, with Detroit as a main focus.

Taubman herself disdains photography by outsiders as "ruin porn," thereby making a proprietary claim to the city, while her detractors suggest that her wealth and class position make her work problematic, giving her the influence and clout to hire police escorts for photo shoots, engage low-flying planes for panoramic shots, and have book parties at the Whitney Museum of American Art in New York. Chicago art critic Pedro Vélez refers to this criticism when he notes, "Nine years ago she arrived in Detroit's high society via her marriage to mall magnate Robert Taubman (son of former Sotheby's chairman A. Alfred Taubman)" but dismisses this critique of her privileged position on the grounds that "You can tell she cares."[34] Vélez is right that Taubman's wealth and class position are not the issue, but he fails to explain, like Herron, how "caring" may be visually distinguished from not caring enough.

Like other urban explorers, however, Taubman is not interested in stopping the forces of entropy; on the contrary, she is firmly opposed to it. In an interview with *Vogue* magazine, Taubman said, "If the book is 'about' anything, it's about these buildings as monuments. No one should tear these buildings down, but no one should rehabilitate them, either." Accordingly, she signed copies of her book at the Whitney book party "Rust in Peace."[35] We might ask how this view is fundamentally different from Vergara's suggestion of an "American Acropolis" that outraged so many, or how such a position can be justified when most cities, provided they have the resources, restore or rebuild their ruins. Perhaps fifteen years of accelerated decline is the difference between outrage and acceptance. Or perhaps nostalgia for the ruins that have become integral to the city's urban fabric has become more fully embedded. The ruins incorporate different layers of the city's history and create alternatives spaces that could potentially coexist with other kinds of urban development—something akin to Tacheles in Berlin, a ruined department store taken over by up to eighty artists that existed for twenty-two years before artists were evicted for capitalist redevelopment.

Whether constructing negative or redemptive narratives of the struggle between nature and culture, all of these bodies of photography engage with the aesthetic pleasures and terrors of deindustrial ruins as an inescapably powerful attraction in today's world. Aside from judgments based on aesthetic taste and sensibility, what is interesting about such bodies of photography is how they operate affectively and politically, how they work within the social field and connect to everyday life, and how they conjure an understanding of Detroit ruination.

The work of Taubman, Moore, and Marchand and Meffre visually intensifies the realities of economic and cultural deterioration. By making their devastating and moving effects starkly visible in carefully composed portraits of ruination, they evoke a variety of affects, from pleasure to unease. Like late romantic art and literature that critiqued the imperial pretentions of its own empire, contemporary ruin imagery also functions as an implicit critique of our domestic status quo because the aesthetics of decay serve as a warning of imperial decline. Yet, like the work of other urban photographers, the images participate, wittingly or not, in constructing the dominant narrative of Detroit as a story about an eternal romantic struggle between culture and nature, or a natural downward spiral of historical progress. This romantic narrative is precisely, perversely, what yields the pleasure of the deindustrial sublime, containing and controlling the anxiety of decline provoked by the images through the safety and distance of representation. This mental mastery of the terrifying is the nature of the ruin imaginary. Even as it makes evident the disastrous decline of modernity, the more aesthetically refined and pleasing the photograph, the more effective the distancing.

The fact that Detroit was once the preeminent manufacturing city and is now a failing *black* city also allows the anxiety of decline in the rest of the country and abroad to be more easily mastered. By safely consigning the excesses of decline to a city regarded as a racialized alien zone, Detroit is seen as ultimately responsible for its own urban decay. The city thus appears as representative and unique at the same time, emblematic of the widespread destructive effects of decline yet singular in causing its own degeneration. This isolation of the city evokes a sense of safety for those who feel disconnected from the everyday effects of urban decline.

The extended visual narratives of the photography books as well as exhibitions of ruin images may be understood as attempts to complicate perceptions of and relationships to the city, and to insert the bodies of photography themselves into the ongoing narratives about the city. Exhibitions such as *Cities in Transition* at the Grand Rapids Art Museum, a suite of four shows in the summer of 2012 that included *Detroit Disassembled: Photographs by Andrew Moore*, were followed by the Detroit Institute of Arts exhibition *Detroit Revealed: Photographs, 2000–2010*, which featured works by eight photographers, including an image of operations within the Ford River Rouge Complex in Dearborn by Detroit-based Michelle Andonian from her sleek black-and-white series *Reinvention: Rouge Photographs* (2004).[36] In homage to Charles Sheeler, Andonian focuses on the changeover of manufacturing operations and automobile models as well as on modernization initiatives at the plant. The exhibition also included the video *Four Stories* (2003–2004), featuring ethnically diverse teens from Detroit's now-closed Chadsey High School produced by Chicago-based Dawoud Bey; the photo series *Beyond Borders: Latino Immigrants and Southwest Detroit* (2010), presenting the lovingly decorated religious shrines in the yards of the Latino community along with portraits of Latino immigrants by Detroit-based Carlos Diaz; photographs of neighbors, alternative urban lifestyles, and street culture from the series *Your Town Tomorrow* (2010) by Detroit-based Corine Vermeulen; and photos by Scott Hocking, Ari Marcopoulos, and Alec Soth.[37] Combining photographers based outside the city with Detroit-based artists, both "outsiders" and "insiders" elevate and legitimize each other's work or render the distinctions moot.

Also included was Andrew Moore's color photo *Shelter, Engine Works, Detroit Dry Dock Company, Rivertown Neighborhood* (2009) in which a makeshift living space in an abandoned building dominates the composition, with a barely noticeable homeless man tucked away in the corner behind a protective plastic sheet (figure 21). Oscillating between the horrifying and the poetic, the slow exposure of the large-scale image in the darkened space transforms the long tarp draped over the living area into an indoor waterfall that opens onto a pool of refuse in the foreground. As Moore observes, the Detroit Dry Dock building, a remarkable late-nineteenth-century structure with a steel frame on the inside, was once used to build propellers for the boats that plied the Great Lakes. It was also where a young Henry Ford worked as an apprentice and was first introduced to the combustion engine. Although the metal stairs to the second floor are cut away, Moore speculates that the homeless man, who appeared to be a longtime resident, "somehow must have figured out how to climb up there and hang up that sheet. And he's the only person that could have been motivated to do it. There's no other explanation."[38] The plastic curtain suggests a desire for privacy that may be violated by the photograph, yet the image provides a telling portrait of a long-term homeless encampment in an abandoned Detroit building.

Among other follow-up exhibitions, the Detroit Institute of Arts mounted *Motor City Muse: Detroit Photographs, Then and Now* (2013), which included works by Henri Cartier-Bresson, who photographed a 1940s wedding on Belle

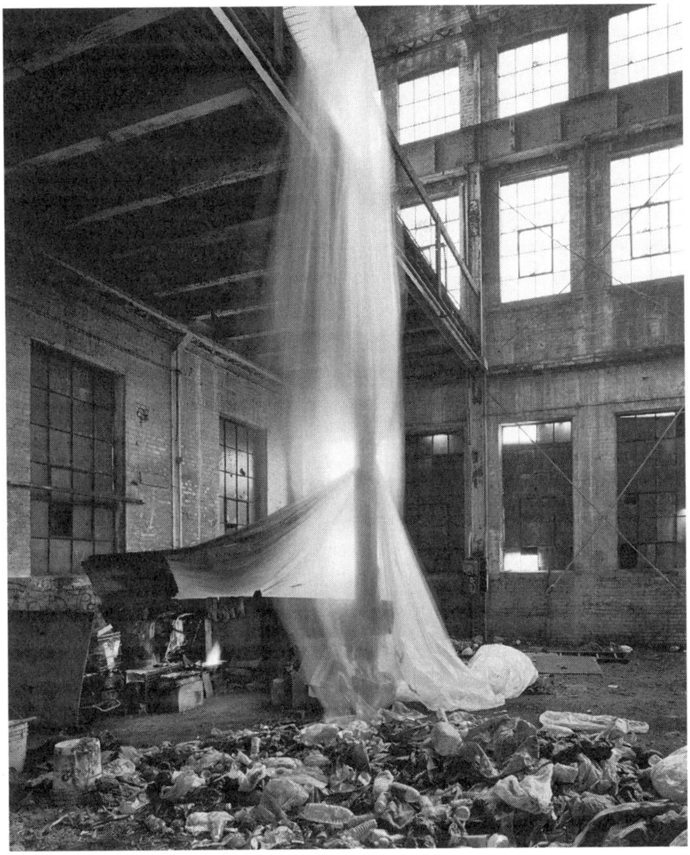

FIG. 21 Andrew Moore, *Shelter, Engine Works, Detroit Dry Docks*, from *Detroit Disassembled*, 2010. © Andrew Moore.

Isle, an island park in the Detroit River; Bill Rauhauser and Dave Jordano, both Detroit-based photographers who have shot the city for decades; Robert Frank, who photographed in Detroit for his series *The Americans*; Nicola Kuperus; Russ Marshall; and Karin Jobst.[39] In New York, *Another Look at Detroit* opened in 2014 as a joint project between Marianne Boesky Gallery and Marlborough Chelsea, focusing on the city as a creative center for the last 150 years. Such exhibitions seek to intervene in the flow of negative affect created by news media representations of Detroit's decline by presenting images that multiply connections between ruination and ongoing life in the city. They create more complex collective enunciations about Detroit that reorder or at least enrich perceptions of it while themselves becoming part its ongoing life. They activate connections between artworks, extend the city's history backward, and suggest possible new ways of being part of the still unfolding events.

Nostalgia for the "Golden Age"

Lowell Boileau, a Detroit artist and unofficial city historian, chronicles the decline of the city in his "Fabulous Ruins of Detroit" website and picture tour, now part of a larger website called "DetroitYES!" His mission is to provide a "sympathetic telling" of the story of Detroit's decline. Not unlike Vergara, Boileau positions Detroit's ruins as akin to the grand ruins of the ancient world. In his website introduction, he writes, "Zimbabwe, Ephesus, El Tajin, Athens, Rome. Now, as for centuries, tourists behold those ruins with awe and wonder. Yet today, a vast and history laden ruin site passes unnoticed, even despised, into oblivion. Come, travel with me, as I guide you on a tour through the fabulous and vanishing ruins of my beloved Detroit." Boileau's mission statement is accompanied by a photograph of the flagship J. L. Hudson department store building in mid-implosion, a traumatic event for many Detroiters (figure 22). Located at the center of downtown, on Woodward Avenue, with twenty-eight stories and four levels of basements, it was second only to Macy's in New York City in size and, at its busiest in the 1950s employed a staff of twelve thousand. It stood empty from the time of its closing in 1983 until its implosion in 1998, when thousands came downtown to watch.[40] Boileau evokes the classical humanist aesthetic that relates architecture to the body when he likens the demolition of Hudson's to an execution, repeatedly invoking an embodied vocabulary of pain ("wounded," "gutted") to describe "the proud tower" as it fell. The fragmentation and disintegration at the core of the modern deindustrial sublime must be understood as not only a mental but an embodied affect.

The sites documented on Boileau's "fabulous tour" are divided into categories based on their type or location, including industrial ruins, downtown ruins, neighborhood ruins, and Gilded Age ruins. In a section called "The City Rises" Boileau describes successful preservation, restoration, and more recent construction projects such as the Renaissance Center, designed by John Portman, although it was heavily critiqued as a corporate fortress when it was built during the administration of Coleman Young. Meant to revitalize Detroit as a thriving urban center and wipe out Detroit's decay, as with the later building of gambling casinos, it instead reflected the desperate and misguided hope that Detroit would become a playground for the wealthy and boost the economy through low-wage service jobs.

While "The Fabulous Ruins of Detroit" overlaps with the motives and interests of urban exploration, unlike urbex, Boileau's website supports preservation and restoration and pursues ongoing historical inquiry and information-sharing on its interactive forums and discussions about the ruins. Sites with personal significance to Boileau are given more attention, such as Tiger Stadium before its demolition, with plans to build what is now Comerica Park

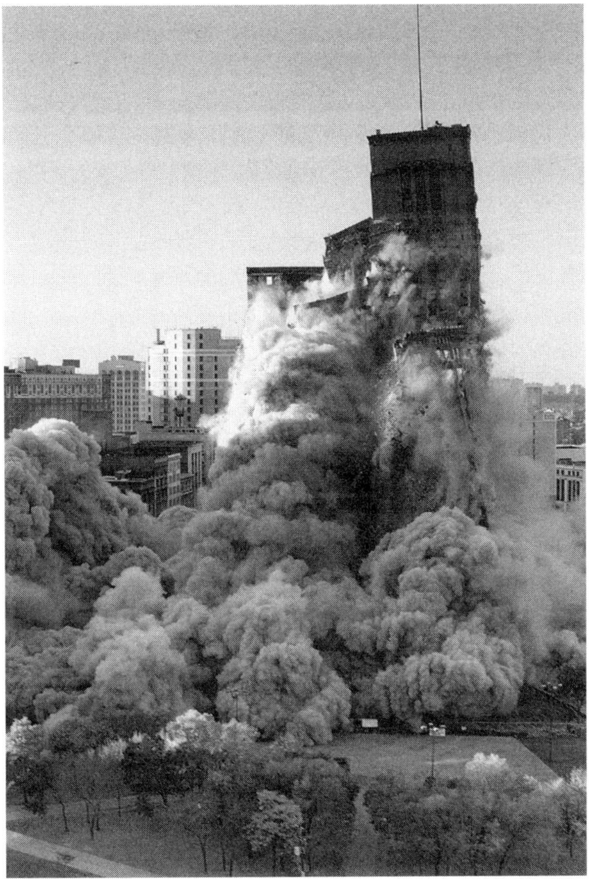

FIG. 22 Lowell Boileau, *The Proud Tower*, from *Requiem for Hudson's Suite*, 1998. © Lowell Boileau, DetroitYES.com.

decisively condemned. As an artist, Boileau includes a section about art in the city in which he documents well-known projects such as the Heidelberg Project and various sites of anonymous street art as well as a section that allows viewers to buy Boileau's own artworks. He also includes a section in which he recounts his travels to ancient sites such as Athens, Rome, and Zimbabwe, establishing his ruin explorer credentials as a worldwide traveler, while hinting at a nostalgic longing for Detroit's glorious past.

Although engaging and extending Detroit's history, such nostalgia may also obscure the fact that until the 1970s, including its imagined "golden age" in the 1920s, Detroit was subject to white rule and patterns of racial discrimination in housing and jobs that greatly contributed to the processes of black ghettoization and deindustrialization. In the late 1940s and 1950s, long before the

1967 riots that are typically blamed for the city's decline, these processes were already well under way. The 1920s were, however, a time of massive wealth and growth, with more than half a million people arriving in Detroit, land annexations adding to the size of the city, and skyscrapers rising downtown. It was the era of factory growth, with Henry Ford's River Rouge in Dearborn, southwest of Detroit, becoming the largest plant in the world; at its peak, the Rouge had ninety-three buildings and constituted the first vertical production process that began with raw materials and ended with a finished car.

Ford's policy toward black employment was deeply discriminatory. Under pressure from black ministers, he moved black workers from the Highland Park Ford Plant to the Rouge. But he employed few blacks elsewhere and disproportionately assigned them the dirtiest, hottest, and least desirable jobs while keeping them out of the higher-paying skilled trades. After 1921 other companies had caught up to Ford's wages, and the company instituted a regime of speedup and continual insecurity. Ford exercised a monopoly of power over the company's black workers because other companies would not hire them.[41] He established a paternalistic relationship as well, isolating black workers in the segregated town of Inkster, where he gave money to black churches and, in return, used those same loyal black ministers to screen job applicants for their antiunionism. While Ford's paper, the *Dearborn Independent*, portrayed black people as beneficiaries of the "white man's civilization," they lived in poor bungalows with little access to basic services or decent schools. As Greg Grandin notes, "The Great Depression finally forced Ford to spend tens of thousands of dollars to rehabilitate Inkster. But it was too little, too late and served only to reinforce segregation in Dearborn, which the Ford Motor Company never contested and which lasted well into the 1970s."[42] Following the victory of the 1941 Ford River Rouge strike, which brought ten thousand black workers into the United Auto Workers (UAW) union, Ford cut off money to Inkster and instituted an anti-black-hiring policy at his plants. The UAW leadership, for its part, did not fight to upgrade black workers to better jobs or fight the racism that remained in its own ranks.

Black oppression in the 1920s was also enforced by the Ku Klux Klan, which grew to more than three million members nationally, with its primary support in the Midwest. Michigan had eighty thousand Klan members in the mid-1920s, mostly Protestant whites uncomfortable with Catholic and multiracial populations in the city.[43] New homes built in Detroit after the 1920s came with deed restrictions, assigned by real estate developers, which prevented black families from buying property. An attempt by Ossian Sweet and his family to move into a Polish American neighborhood in 1925 was met with a mob of more than one thousand whites who pelted the Sweet home with rocks and bottles. Sweet defended his home and fired two shots, killing one white man. A trial ensued, in which Sweet was defended by a team headed by famed lawyer Clarence Darrow. Eventually Sweet was acquitted, but housing remained segregated nonetheless.

A secretive, antiunion, antisemitic, white supremacist organization known as the Black Legion also began forming in 1925 across Ohio, Indiana, Illinois, and Michigan, with tens of thousands of members, including many who were active in Detroit. The Black Legion was responsible for a series of beatings, kidnappings, and murders.[44] At the same time, Father Charles Coughlin, a Roman Catholic priest at the Shrine of the Little Flower church on Woodward Avenue (north of Detroit in Royal Oak), became one of the nation's most popular radio broadcasters. Coughlin grew increasingly antisemitic and proto-fascist, echoing the racist and antigovernment sentiments of Henry Ford. If this was a "golden age," it was for whites only.

Likewise the 1940s, often considered a period of prosperity because of wartime production, was rife with racial tensions. A series of reactionary "hate strikes" erupted in the early 1940s in the auto plants, including a walkout by twenty-five thousand white workers protesting the upgrade of three black workers to the assembly line at the Packard Plant, where the Klan had a presence. The UAW leadership, facing a threat to the union's existence and backed by federal officials, announced that all workers who struck against black labor would be expelled from the union and fired. This led to the dismissal of thirty whites just weeks before the 1943 riots erupted.[45]

While the photographs on Boileau's website offer the opportunity for greater inquiry and dialogue, and the photos in high-end photography books such as *The Ruins of Detroit*, *Detroit Disassembled*, and *Detroit: 138 Square Miles* are often powerful, compelling, and intriguing, in aggregate these photographers reinforce the perspective of urban explorers for whom the industrial past often seems like another country visited from the postindustrial present. Absorbed by the romanticized horror and beauty of grand and "fabulous" ruins, beautiful decay is usually held to be inviolate, even sacralized, by a contemporary decadent consciousness that aestheticizes its own decline. The idea of preserving history becomes subordinated to the personal and subjective experience of ruin exploration—the sense of suspended time; the thrill of trespass; the drama of color, light, and weather; the scale and magnitude of industrial dereliction—fetishizing the beauty of decay while containing and controlling the anxiety of decline. As a reviewer of Taubman's book enthusiastically exclaimed, "The imagination is stirred by the contemplation of ruins as we cast ourselves inside the post-apocalyptic future of the present."[46]

While these bodies of photography may draw sympathy and support for the city, the ruin imaginary they help to construct also isolates the seeming end of history in the dying former manufacturing center at the heart of the nation, reinforcing the effect of an "alien nation" within, even as the images make the disturbing effects of deindustrialization visible. These dual roles of ruin images thus may be seen as circumscribing the terrifying otherness of a city that already seems beyond revival while at the same time enshrining it as America's most "fabulous" site of ruin and decay. The pained contradiction of this position is evident in the anger at the ruin tourism that is its natural outcome, the resentment aimed at "drive-by" photographers who come to gawk at the fabulous ruins but do not have to live with their everyday effects.

Ours is an age in which we are all seduced by ruins. Although they have been integral to the modern era since its beginning, how we perceive them has changed significantly from the ruins of classical antiquity to the ruins of war to the ruins of shrinking deindustrialized cities. The contemporary ruin imaginary, even as it continues to be romanticized, is nonetheless deeply imbued with the apocalyptic imagination. Its grip on contemporary consciousness is growing, not abating, as confidence in the state and the capitalist system continues to erode. Conveying "the haunting knowledge of decline," ruin imagery has become pervasive, meditating on the collapse of past dreams of the future and suggesting the future ruin of our own present.[47] Ruin imagery makes visible the effects of capitalist deindustrialization in ways that might otherwise remain invisible, even if the causes of deindustrialization are too complex to easily convey. As Dylan Trigg suggests, ruins reveal something about the time in which we live, and their decay signifies a great deal more than the abandonment of industry, shops, and houses; they also embody the steady erosion of faith in progress.

Ruin images can lament, elegize, or celebrate; they can embrace the effects of ruination as beautiful or melancholic, or they can make connections to ongoing life in the city. But they cannot disguise the halt in progress that ruins represent. This halt in progress, which evokes an eroding faith in a better future, drives the desire for the aesthetic mediation of ruination through representation. Ruin images are meant to soothe and domesticate the sense of brokenness, fragmentation, and violence at the core of ruination, producing the pleasure of the deindustrial sublime. By taking pleasure in the safely circumscribed beauty of ruins, we establish the mental distance that allows us to contain the threat of being overwhelmed, even as the growing scope of ruination is made visible. And by consigning that threat to one major city in which the scale of decay is mitigated by the seeming absence of a population, the rest of the country may be relieved of concern over that invisible population's fate. Detroit ruin imagery thus performs a doubly reassuring function, suggesting either that the city is to blame for its own conditions or that this state of affairs is historically inevitable and no one is to blame. Either way, the dominant forces of capital as the real agents of decline become naturalized and the threat of fiscal austerities for many other towns and cities hidden from view.

Creative Interventions and Public Projects

Artists who attempt to effect social transformation through public projects can be important agents of political agitation, cultural critique, and resistance, although the pressures of the art world, if they wish to succeed in it, and the struggle for mere survival often work against them.[48] The architectural project *Ice House Detroit*, defying initial reactions of local incomprehension and unexpected expense, asserts a critique of the national housing crisis and its destructive effects in Detroit. Photographer Gregory Holm and architect Matthew Radune encased an entire abandoned house in ice during the winter of 2009–10 by pouring gallons and gallons of water over it and letting it freeze while filming and photographing the process (figure 23). They worked in twenty-four hour shifts for several weeks during the coldest part of winter, using a fire hose to build up the ice in layers. Neighborhood residents came to have their photos taken in front of the house and served as community liaisons.[49] The work conveys the simultaneous sense of collapsed or suspended time and continuous dissolution in the gradually dissolving form of an ice house. The light emanating from a home in the background makes the hermetically sealed ice house appear all the more chilling, evoking frozen assets, hell frozen over, and a long winter of discontent. Although *Ice House Detroit* creates a sense of being frozen in time, it exists within an animate landscape, suggesting both

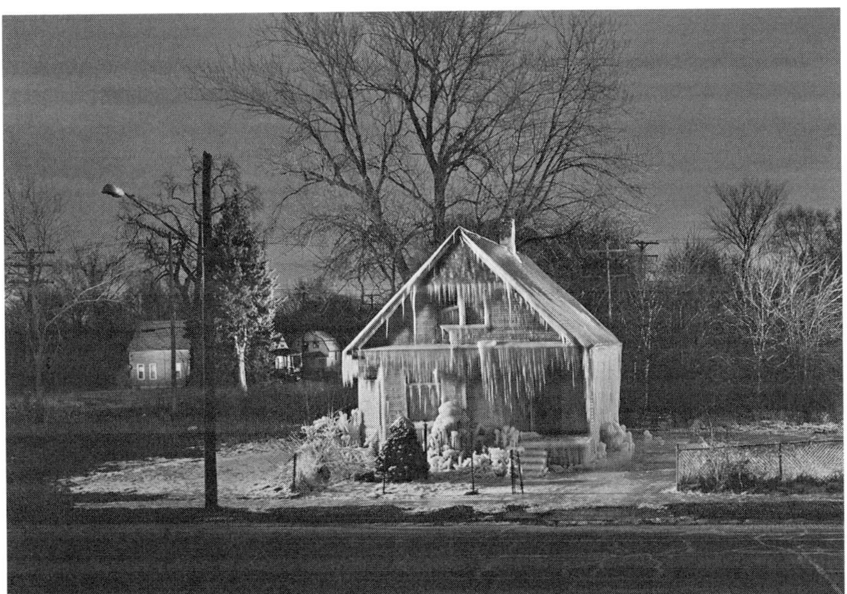

FIG. 23 Gregory Holm and Mathew Radune, *Ice House Detroit*, 2009–2010. Courtesy Gregory Holm.

immobility and inexorable devolution. The sense of a future that is already past suggests the shrinking possibilities in the lives of those whose hopes and dreams have been lost to the endless rounds of privatization and austerity that are the foundation of capitalist neoliberalism since the 1970s. And yet the stark beauty of the image is darkly compelling even as it reflects a loss of faith in the ideals of reason, order, and progress that are foundational to modernity. By drawing on the aesthetic of the deindustrial sublime to create an object of uncanny beauty, *Ice House Detroit* allegorizes the contradictions of capitalism and its effects on people. This construction of ruination confronts us with a haunting vision of a foreclosed future that contains within it a cold and terrible violence.

The ice house project was meant to draw attention to the mortgage foreclosure crisis, which disproportionately hit areas where most residents are black, Latino, or Asian, as well as the elderly who live on fixed incomes. According to RealtyTrac, by 2007 Detroit had the highest rate of home foreclosures in the United States (followed by Stockton, California, and Las Vegas, Nevada).[50] In 2011 it was estimated that approximately 3.5 million people in the country were homeless (many of them veterans) while, at the same time, 18.5 million homes were vacant in the country, enough for each homeless person to have several; in addition, the 2010 census figures revealed that "1 in 2 Americans" had fallen into poverty or were struggling to live on low incomes.[51]

Holm and Radune acquired the use of the abandoned house from the Michigan State Land Bank Fast Track Authority (the public authority devoted to economic development of blighted and tax-reverted properties). Their fee went toward the purchase and rehabilitation of another property owned by the land bank, which helped a single mother and her children move into it, and helped fund the deconstruction and recycling of materials from the ice house property for which the land bank retained ownership. Holm and Radune engaged in homeless relief activism while working on the project and used the press to promote local groups dedicated to social good and urban farming in the city.[52] Nonetheless, the project had strong detractors who "saw two Brooklyn artists coming to the city of Detroit to do a public art project one day and leave the next."[53] In reality, Holm, a Detroit native, was living in both cities, owns property in Detroit, and has a longstanding relationship to the arts in the city. The need to insist upon these facts, however, speaks to the insider's resentment of the outsider's gaze of privileged fascination. The power of the work, however, offers a compelling critique of modern ruination apart from the extracurricular advocacy work or residential preferences of its producers. Of course it is always important to suspend one's preconceptions and complicate one's understanding of and relationship to a city by patiently listening and allowing oneself to be transformed by the people and stories of the city, especially before considering political or ethical action.[54] Yet it is also useful to be open to the perceptions of those who see through fresh eyes from a more dispassionate perspective.

By addressing the issue of home foreclosure, *Ice House Detroit* also evokes the continuing problem of homelessness in Detroit, where police have invented a novel, if illegal, way of keeping the homeless from marring the pleasure of suburban tourists who visit downtown night spots such as Greektown, with its casino, restaurants, and other entertainments. In April 2013 it was reported that police were taking the homeless off the streets and dumping them outside city limits. In a city as large as Detroit, this often meant driving them for half an hour to get them outside the city, so that it would take many hours for the homeless to find their way back. There are almost twenty thousand chronically homeless people in Detroit, with poverty levels continuing to rise. The number of homeless children across the state has surged by an astounding 66 percent over four years, with more than 37,500 homeless students reported during the 2011–2012 school year. The number of homeless students nationwide is more than one million, and many are members of homeless families.[55] Despite the alleged recovery since the economic crisis of 2008, income gains from economic growth have accrued almost exclusively to the top 1 percent of earners while unemployment and poverty remain widespread; instead of job creation and programs to subsidize education and cut student debt, there is continuing pressure from the financial elite to reduce programs that aid the homeless, the unemployed, and students. *Ice House Detroit* thus gives visual form to deep disillusionment, a central characteristic of the network of ruin imagery to which it contributes. It evokes the disruptive brokenness and disaster that precedes ruined lives and suggests that the right to decent housing is a political demand that is not merely an individual but a collective right.

Mitch Cope's seven black-and-white photographs from the series *Zen and the Art of Garbage Hunting and the Protectors of the Refuse* also evoke disrupted lives by documenting the piles of rubbish that litter the neighborhood in which Cope lives. Using heaps of debris often found in abandoned garages, back alleys, and even along the sidewalks, Cope's work transforms the lowly status of garbage by the addition of totems. In *Eddy's Pile*, for example, a totem dominates the chaotic heap of broken furniture and goods of an emptied home, including a shopping cart with vacuum parts, various jeep car parts, three black sofas, a cushy chair, a stool, a dresser, two baby mattresses, a playpen, assorted garbage, boys' and girls' clothing, various plastic bins, paperwork, miscellaneous VHS tapes, several yogurt cups, a television, and a child's plastic push car with its steering wheel on the ground (figure 24). The fantastical apparition hovers above the wreckage like a protective spirit and guardian of memory. Many of these refuse heaps were put out for bulk pickup day but

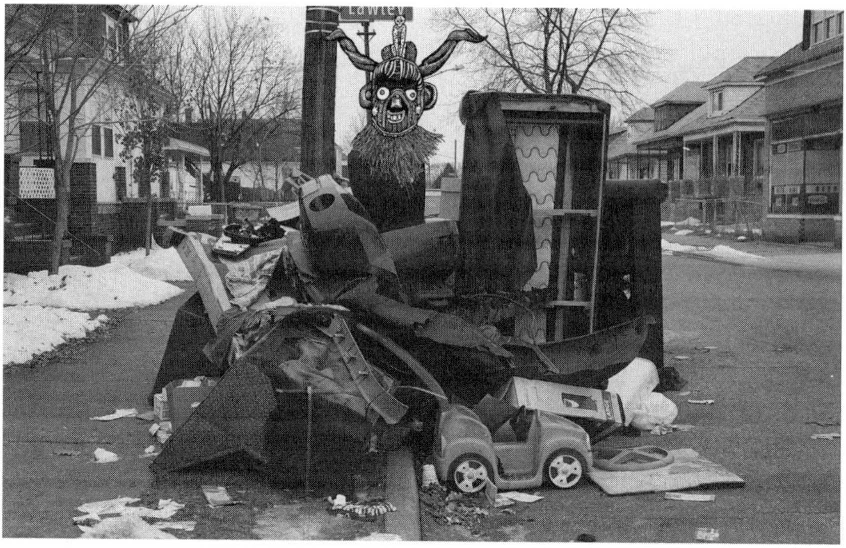

FIG. 24 Mitch Cope, *Eddy's Pile*, from *Zen and the Art of Garbage Hunting and the Protectors of the Refuse*, 2014. Courtesy of the artist.

were left uncollected by the city due to a blizzard; the piles then became larger as they sat waiting for the next bulk pickup day three months later, the last free pickup before the city garbage services in Hamtramck were privatized.[56]

Brooklyn-based Detroit native Sandra Osip also conjures with memories soiled by depressing realities. Her six-foot sculpture *Beautiful Homes and Gardens* from the series *Broken Dreams* conveys the destruction of an entire neighborhood through a literal pile-up of broken and derelict houses (figure 25). On a return visit to Detroit, Osip was shocked to find her childhood home, those of friends, and local shops razed and surrounded by empty lots strewn with garbage; she was further appalled to learn that at least a dozen bodies had been found in the previous twelve months in this neglected part of the city on the east side of Detroit. The destruction of the neighborhood and sense of place where she and her friends had come of age became the driving force of Osip's work. Osip based *Beautiful Homes and Gardens* on photos of destroyed and burned out houses surrounding her former high school as well as photos of houses near Warren and Mack Avenues, where she lived when she attended Cranbrook Academy of Art.[57] The jumble of abandoned and decaying homes, some decorated with graffiti, convey a sense of the ruined past and its memories piled up like a heap of trash. Yet, like Mitch Cope's photograph, it remains resonant with the echoes of lived experience.

Some Detroit-based artists offer a more redemptive view of decline. Scott Hocking, who has posted photographs of some three dozen bodies of work in the city on his website, has produced sculptural interventions in Detroit's abandoned auto plants that allude to ancient geometric forms among the ruins and suggest a timeless cycle of creation and destruction. These include works such as *The Egg and the MCTS # 4718* at the Michigan Central Train Station, *Ziggurat* at Fisher Body Plant 21, and *Garden of the Gods* at the Packard Plant. His site-specific installations are constructed using materials found on site and create mysterious and mythic forms, such as eggs and pyramids, within the ruined environment. *The Egg and the MCTS* was created using thousands of sheet marble fragments that had once lined the walls of the building's corridors and invokes the egg as a symbol of rebirth as well as the stacked stones of the cairn symbolic of tomb markers (figure 26). Reinforcing the idea of an inevitable historical cycle, Hocking asserts that his project will end with the work's destruction: "Beginning with a photo project in 2007, the egg was built over the course of 18 months, and the series will culminate with photos of the site once the sculpture is destroyed by forces of nature or man."[58] Outside the plants he has created works such as *Tire Pyramid*, a sculptural installation

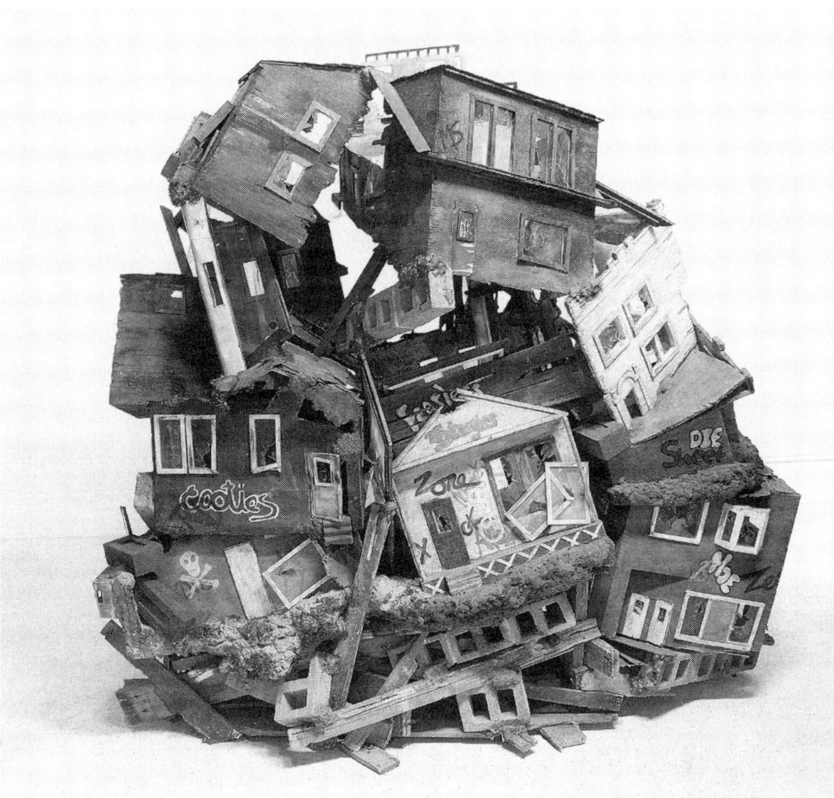

FIG. 25 Sandra Osip, *Beautiful Homes and Gardens*, 2014, mixed media sculpture, 2014, from *Broken Dreams.* Courtesy of the artist.

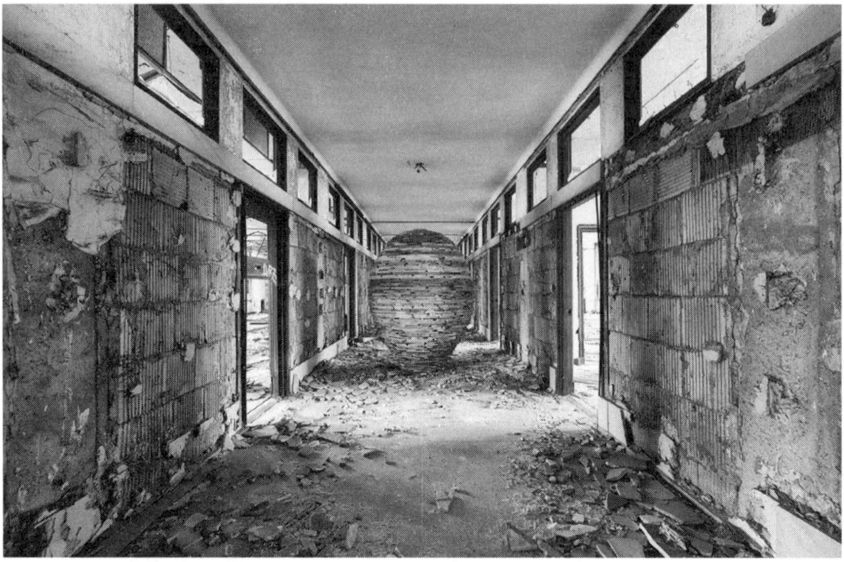

FIG. 26 Scott Hocking, *The Egg and MCTS #4718*, 2012, from *The Egg and the Michigan Central Train Station*, 2007–2013. Courtesy of the artist and Susanne Hilberry Gallery.

made from 2,109 tires illegally dumped throughout Detroit neighborhoods and abandoned sites that were gathered over the course of a week and installed on the front lawn of Julia Taubman's home in Bloomfield Hills for two weeks, then removed for recycling at a cost of two dollars per tire, drawing attention to the most commonly dumped object in the city.

Hocking's 2013 installation, *The End of the World* at the Susanne Hilberry Gallery in Ferndale, just outside the city limits, included over two hundred books on destruction mythologies as well as a wall of taxidermy birds that looked upon the decrepit remains of a 1955 Mercury Monterey parked atop a pile of rock salt as a stand-in for the ancient Greek god Mercury. Mercury was "a messenger between planes, and the transporter of souls to the afterlife" just as the birds are winged messengers, suggesting transformation rather than death.[59] The exhibition included the photography series *Detroit Nights* (2007–12), portraying a variety of haunting and abandoned nocturnally lit architectural structures and landscapes. By deliberately positioning Detroit's decline as part of a natural cosmic process, Hocking removes the city from its historical specificity and maps its ruination onto ancient mythologies of transformation through destruction and creation. This dehistoricizing approach attempts to sublimate the terror of ruination by producing a sense of timeless inevitability and mythic distance from the ruins.

Inspired by the crisis of decline more than a quarter century ago, Tyree Guyton's Heidelberg Project (begun in 1986) is the most renowned public art project in Detroit and the city's third-most-popular tourist destination after the Detroit Institute of Arts and the Charles H. Wright Museum of African American History.[60] Reclaiming abandoned houses along Heidelberg Street where Guyton grew up, just north of the Black Bottom area of Detroit, the Heidelberg Project is a large neighborhood installation employing Guyton's signature painted polka dots as well as dolls, clocks, stuffed animals, and thousands of other discarded objects in sculptures and displays on the vacant houses, empty lots, and trees, creating what I have termed in another context "a contained but alternatively imagined city" produced in collaboration with area kids.[61] The project became a commentary on Detroit abandonment that drew international attention, from appearances on Tom Brokaw's *NBC Nightly News*, the *Oprah Winfrey Show* and *Good Morning America* to the Venice Architecture Biennale, where Guyton represented the United States in 2008.

Twice in the 1990s mayors Coleman Young and Dennis Archer sent in bulldozers to tear down large parts of the project, claiming it produced its own form of urban blight, but undoubtedly motivated more by embarrassment at the attention the project drew to the declining neighborhoods of the city. City officials also reacted against the 1980s activist art project by the group Urban Center for Photography when they turned a grant they had received into a public project called *Demolished by Neglect*, which posted enlarged photos of derelict homes and other structures on outdoor sites. Undiscouraged by the city's demolition of his work, Guyton continued to develop the Heidelberg Project, which became a landmark that attracted about thirty-five thousand nonlocal visitors annually from 140 countries and 49 states.[62] Recent attacks on the Heidelberg Project, however, have had a devastating effect. Arsonists set nine fires in the space of eleven months and burned down five of the remaining seven houses. The last attack was on the beloved Party Animal House, which was covered with stuffed animals nailed to the sides and roof (figure 27). The assault transformed the iconic work into yet another burned out Detroit ruin, blackening a neighboring house and frustrating supporters of the project and arson investigators (figure 28).[63] While Guyton considers the next phase of the project's development, over $54,000 was raised on Indiegogo as well as $18,000 from the Erb Family Foundation and Kresge Foundation to help fund installation of a solar lighting and security plan in the two-block area that is normally in complete darkness.

When bright orange houses began to appear along the city's major freeways, the decrepitude of the Detroit housing stock became even more noticeable. The artists behind the public art project *Object Orange* are largely anonymous (to avoid prosecution) and reveal their first names only, including (at different times) Greg, Jacques, Mike, Andy, and Christian (graduates of Cranbrook Academy of Art). In a series of guerilla actions, the artists painted abandoned

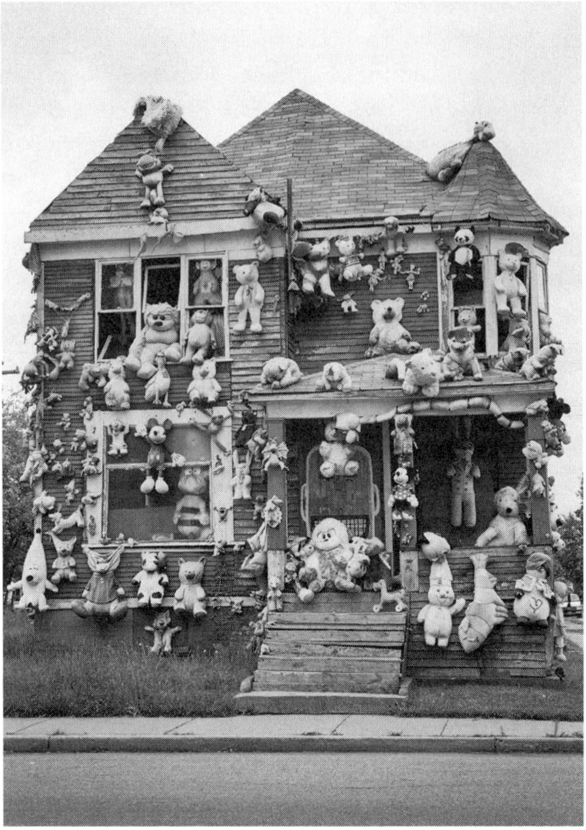

FIG. 27 Party Animal House, Heidelberg Project, Detroit. Photo © 2012 Julie Dermansky.

and structurally unsafe houses the Disney color Tiggerific Orange to accentuate the visibility of the houses. Drawing attention to the dangerously derelict structures and to the problem of abandoned houses blighting the city, the artists painted about sixteen homes starting in 2006. Their primary concern was to make most of them visible to commuters who were rushing home from the city to the northern white suburbs and who might otherwise easily ignore the abandoned houses (figure 29). The group painted only the side of the house most visible to the highway, sparing the neighbors who were already well aware of the decaying houses in their midst. The bright orange houses remind us that the story of abandonment is told not only through shuttered factories and grand architectural landmarks but also through the thousands of ordinary vacant homes, mostly modest wooden structures, and the concomitant desolation of residential neighborhoods. Of the first eleven houses painted,

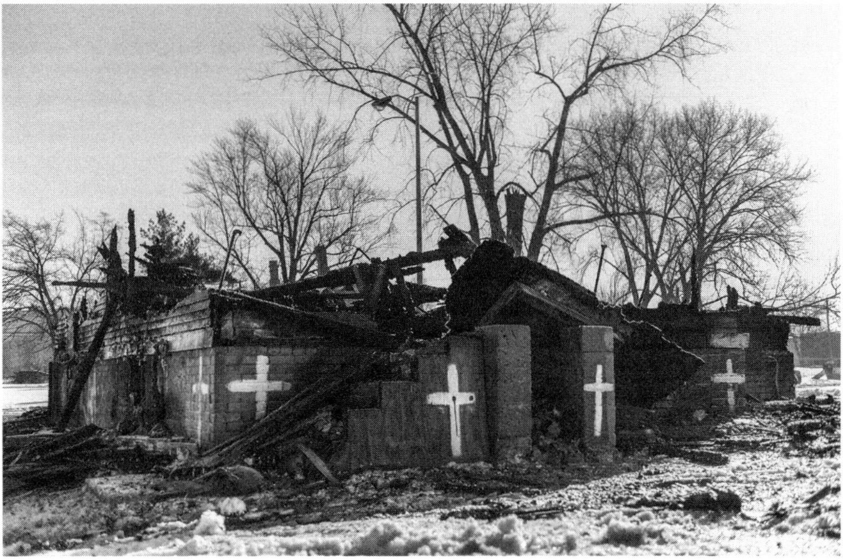

FIG. 28 Party Animal House, Heidelberg Project, Detroit, after the fire on March 7, 2014. Photo: James Fassinger.

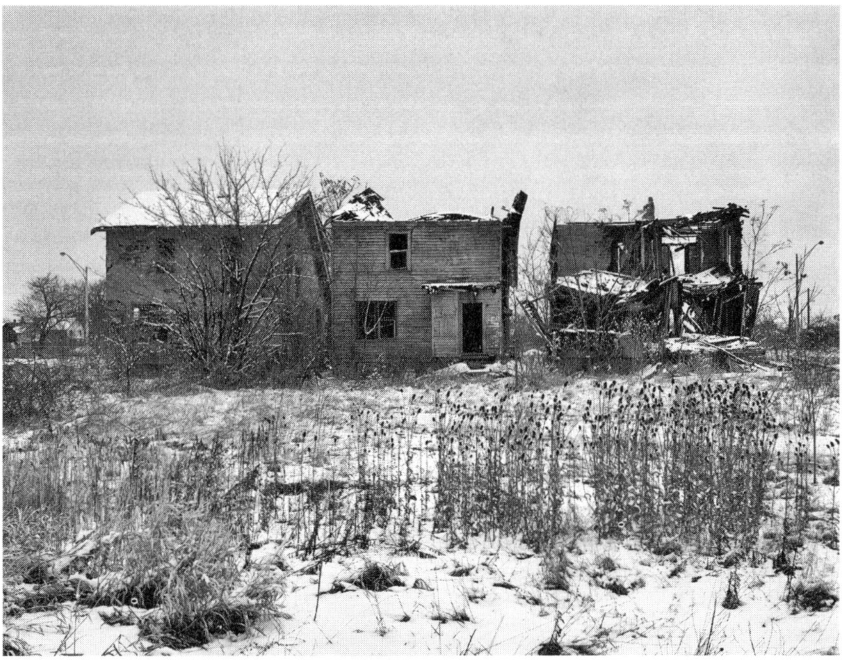

FIG. 29 Andrew Moore, *Houses Painted by Object Orange Artists' Group*, from *Detroit Disassembled*, 2010. © Andrew Moore.

the city almost immediately demolished four, and more have been demolished since. However, the city viewed the project as criminal vandalism and claimed the demolitions were coincidental. Although the demolitions were not initially anticipated by the group, which saw the works as artistic artifacts, they embraced them as a desirable outcome.[64]

Demolishing derelict homes, whose numbers have exponentially grown since *Object Orange* first began, is an expensive undertaking. The Neighborhood Stabilization Program, authorized under the American Reinvestment and Recovery Act of 2008, provides grant money to state and local governments to "acquire and redevelop foreclosed properties that might otherwise become sources of abandonment or blight within their communities." In 2010 former Detroit mayor Dave Bing launched a program to demolish ten thousand homes in three years. About half were torn down at a cost of $72 million. But this is a fraction of the minimum estimate of forty thousand blighted homes in the city that are dangerously derelict.[65] In many cases the cost of home demolition exceeds the property's value. Neighborhoods often respond to blighted homes and the public safety problems they cause with arson; Detroit has more fires than any city in the country, although fire engines are falling apart, gear is outdated or lacking, and firefighters have suffered pay and hiring cuts.[66]

The "Banglatown" projects on the border of Detroit and Hamtramck, a largely Polish-Bangladeshi-Yemeni municipality surrounded by Detroit, have been developed by activists Mitch Cope and Gina Reichert. They originally founded Design 99 in Hamtramck in 2007, a design consulting studio and gallery space that developed into other projects. Working out of their distinctively painted striped house, purchased for $1,900, Cope and Reichert bought or facilitated the sale of ten neighborhood houses to other artists and curators in an effort to help forge an artistic community. In 2008 they developed the Power House as a design lab and experiment in energy self-sufficiency, and in 2009 founded Power House Productions, a nonprofit organization focused on neighborhood stabilization through creative interventions, which has developed a skate park and other neighborhood architectural and clean-up projects as well as artists' residencies.[67] The residencies included the street artists Retna (Marquis Lewis) in collaboration with Richard Colman, Swoon (Callie Curry), Ben Wolf, Saelee Oh, and Monica Canilao, who spent a month in 2009 imaginatively transforming five abandoned houses in Hamtramck under the auspices of *Juxtapoz Magazine* and Power House Productions. Colman and Retna's house, whose interior walls are covered by monochromatic paintings of elegant typographic symbols by Retna and landscape and geometric forms by Colman, is now a recording studio run by artist Jon Brumit.

Indeed, the art scene in Detroit is booming, and the work of Detroit-area artists is supported by a plethora of galleries as well as the Kresge Foundation, founded in Detroit in 1924, which each year offers from twelve to twenty-four unrestricted fellowships of $25,000 each to visual, performing, film, and literary artists. Other community projects include Detroit Soup, which supplies microgrants for creative projects through monthly events in which five dollars buys dinner and the right to vote for your favorite projects (cofounded by Kate Daughdrill and now run by Amy Kaherl), and *Dlectricity*, an annual fall international public arts program since 2012 (founded by Marc Schwartz and the group Art Detroit Now), which invites proposals for projects using light and illuminates the outdoor nighttime landscape of Midtown Detroit's Woodward corridor for two nights in October. Successful nonprofit projects include the Empowerment Plan workshop in Corktown, begun by a College for Creative Studies design graduate, Veronika Scott, when she was twenty-one. Scott employs formerly homeless women to make heat-trapping and waterproof coats that reconfigure into sleeping bags for homeless men and women. Scott's Empowerment Plan, which secured backing from General Motors and Carhartt, has manufactured and distributed more than a thousand coats in Detroit, Ohio, Chicago, and Buffalo since 2010, while Scott herself received an International Design Excellence Award from the Industrial Designers Society of America in 2011.[68]

The city also attracts projects by well-known artists such as Matthew Barney, who performed and filmed *KHU* in Detroit in 2010 as part of his epic opera, *River of Fundament*, employing more than two hundred local musicians, actors, designers, and craftspeople, and produced in collaboration with composer Jonathan Bepler.[69] Inspired by Norman Mailer's novel *Ancient Evenings* and concerned with ancient Egyptian ideas about death and rebirth amid a more contemporary tale of Mailer's quest for immortality, Barney uses Detroit locales for their ability to signify mythic concepts, and highlights the American automobile as a principle character and surrogate for the male ego.[70] In this tale of resurrection, fittingly set in Detroit, Barney "reincarnates" a 1967 Chrysler Imperial as a 1979 Pontiac Firebird Trans Am and then, chillingly, as a 2001 Ford Crown Victoria Police Interceptor.[71]

Mike Kelley's *Mobile Homestead* consists of a sculptural recreation of his childhood home that is now permanently parked at MoCAD (except for a summer 2014 sojourn to the Geffen Contemporary at MOCA in Los Angeles). The life-size replica of the small ranch house where Kelly grew up in the blue-collar Detroit suburb of Westland was initially attached to a tractor-trailer and driven through the streets of Detroit as a "symbolic reversal of the 'white flight' that helped depopulate the city."[72] Kelley's father was a public school janitorial chief in Detroit.

And the ubiquitous guerrilla graffiti artist Banksy created two works at the Packard Plant around the time his film *Exit through the Gift Shop* opened in Detroit in 2010. The Detroit nonprofit 555 Gallery and Studio's removal of one of the works when it faced possible destruction caused intense debate. Gallery artists excavated the fifteen-hundred-pound piece, a seven-by-eight-foot stencil, from the crumbling Packard Plant as bulldozers working nearby got closer, moving the work to the 555 Gallery for public display. Controversy flared again a few years later when the gallery proposed selling the work to support the gallery and artists' studios.[73]

Cheap land and buildings can be bought for a song by artists hoping to pioneer a new way of life based on creative communities, ecological green space, or nonprofit public missions. The move by many artists into Detroit also represents, at least in part, a desire to reject the symbolic order and return to a kind of wild state that is off the grid, a place where big risks can be taken and the cost of failure is low, and where value is determined by standards other than the capitalist market. Success brings the kind of satisfaction that comes with promoting even a small measure of social justice or helping to promote a sense of community solidarity or creative freedom. Although we recognize that such public projects are hardly capable of solving the city's larger problems, seen as exemplary actions, they infuse vitality into their neighborhoods and supportive cohorts. Such public projects also become part of the life of the city and change its narrative, though we must be cautious about romanticizing, as John Patrick Leary observes, "isolated acts of resistance without acknowledging the massive political and social forces aligned against the real transformation, and not just stubborn survival, of the city."[74]

5

Looking for Signs of Resurrection

Detroit is not only the mecca of ruin gazers and urban explorers but also exemplifies both spectacular disaster and fascinating possibilities. The dream of comeback and revival strongly appeals to the newly arrived as well as longtime residents. Savvy corporate advertisers use buoyant narratives of survival and hopes for resurrection to make their merchandise appealing, trading on tradition and the Detroit brand while also suggesting that their products are vaguely edgy and transgressive. Although these upbeat visions of the city may rely more on wishful thinking or hucksterism than on visionary dreams, what is most significant about such corporate advertising is the attempt to signal revival even while constructing Detroit as America's "dark other." Chrysler Corporation's marketing and advertising has made the most notable media efforts to produce a vision that sublimates the city's decline into something thrillingly resilient while simultaneously exotic and elsewhere.

From Industrial Comeback Story to Pastoral Paean

In a series of seductive television commercials from 2011 to 2013, Chrysler attempts to create a redemptive phoenix-from-the-ashes tale that maps Chrysler's own recovery onto the more emotionally feel-good story of Detroit's imagined revival—until this fizzles out. The first of three ads celebrates the city for its industrial heritage as a form of romantic nostalgia, casting the prosperous past forward into the future. The second ad builds on the city's gritty endurance and expands outward from Detroit to the economically struggling nation. As the city headed toward bankruptcy, however, making the theme of resurgence increasingly untenable, a new reality emerges in the third ad, overtaking nostalgia and wishful thinking: the city is entirely abandoned for the agricultural plains. The rise and fall of the comeback narrative, as seen in the arc of these ads over the course of three years, instructively—if unwittingly—evokes the problem of American cities in crisis and the anxiety of decline.

Rolled out during the Super Bowl games when the ads would be watched by millions of people, the two-minute "Born in Fire" 2011 ad pictures Detroit as a teeming urban landscape of steaming factories, 1920s skyscrapers, the monument to Joe Louis sculpture, the Spirit of Detroit sculpture, the doorman at the Guardian Building, area figure skating U.S. ladies champion Alissa Czisny, and the Diego Rivera murals at the Detroit Institute of Arts, among other scenes, as a deep male voiceover asks, "What does this city know about luxury?" The answer is "more than most" because Detroit is "a town that's been to hell and back." Gesturing toward the ruination for which Detroit is known, as well as Chrysler's own bankruptcy in the 2008 economic meltdown, this rhetoric suggests resolute endurance, along with "hard work, conviction, and the know-how that runs generations deep in each and every one of us." If the city has been "to hell and back," the nightmare now seems to be over with the emergence of a new postbankruptcy Chrysler; at the same time, "know-how" transmitted for generations evokes the city's industrial legacy. Eminem's comeback song "Lose Yourself" plays in the background until Eminem himself gets out of a Chrysler 200 sedan and stands in front of the downtown Fox Theater, with a marquee that says "Keep Detroit Beautiful." He enters the theater where members of the Selected of God gospel choir raise their voices in stirring crescendo before Eminem declares, "This is the Motor City. And this is what we do," which cleverly tugs at the pride of every Detroiter. A line of text informs the viewer that the Chrysler 200 has arrived, and then the tag line appears: "Imported from Detroit."

The feel-good ad immediately went viral, inspiring hours of debate on sports-talk radio stations, blogs, and Facebook. Even the *NBC Nightly News* did a segment on it called "Motor City Comeback," explaining that Chrysler sold its newest car by effectively selling Detroit as a city that is still proud and fighting.[1] According to market researchers who track the impact of Super Bowl commercials, it sparked a dramatic increase in online shopping for the company's models. Traffic at the online car research site Edmunds.com shot up 267 percent for the Chrysler brand in the hours after the commercial aired, and 1,619 percent for the Chrysler 200.[2] The message was clear: after the bankruptcies of General Motors (GM) and Chrysler—and the sex and lying scandal that led to Mayor Kwame Kilpatrick's resignation—the city was prepared to overcome its obstacles; more to the point, supporting Chrysler meant

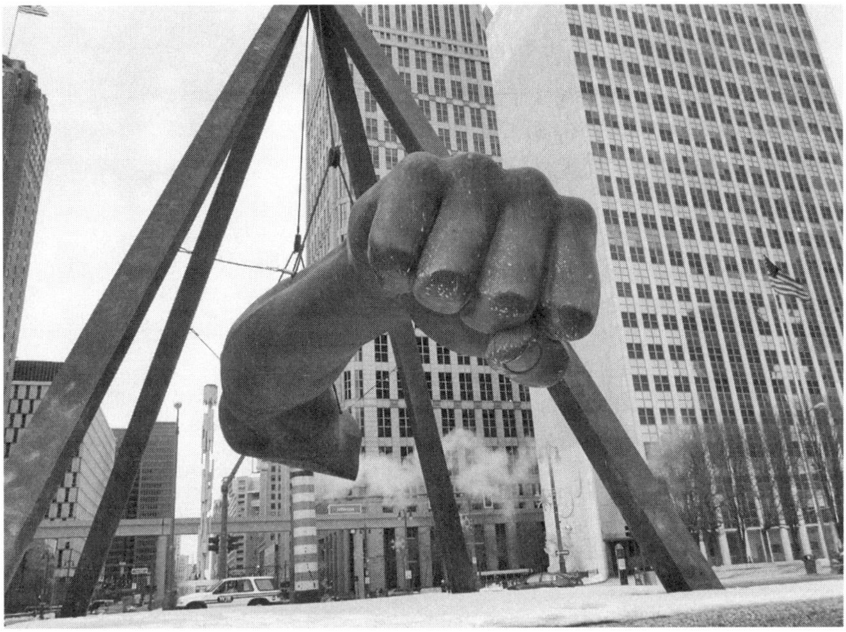

FIG. 30 *Monument to Joe Louis*, 1986, downtown Detroit.

supporting Detroit. The ad makes the two synonymous, and the resurrection of one is merged with the other in a way that evokes a raw emotional impact—everyone loves a comeback story.

The theme of gritty working-class strength and continuity is a heroic tale supported by the images. In an era when white boxers reigned, legendary black boxer Joe Louis held the heavyweight champion title from 1937 to 1949 (ending with a loss to Rocky Marciano). The Detroit Red Wings' hockey arena was named after him, and a giant two-ton sculpture of his forearm and fist, by Robert Graham, donated by Sports Illustrated in 1986, was installed on the corner of Woodward and Jefferson Avenues. It was officially titled *Monument to Joe Louis* but is known as "The Fist."[3] The camera pans around the massive latent power of the horizontally suspended and ungloved black fist as the voiceover says, "The hottest fires make the hardest steel." This suggests strength in adversity even as "The Fist" evokes a horizontal version of the black power salute of an earlier era (figure 30).

The close-ups of Rivera's *Detroit Industry* murals focus on the straining muscles and density of men on the production line at the Ford River Rouge as the voiceover evokes the "the know-how that runs generations deep." Sadly, this is an image that could only be produced by photographing Rivera's mural and could not be made today, where automation has replaced so many men that no such density on the line exists. Ironically, it was not even representative of the production line when Rivera completed the mural in 1933, because Ford had already laid off or reduced the wages and hours of thousands of workers during the Depression. The Rouge was famous in this period for its protest strikes, including the Ford Hunger March in 1932, leading to the shooting deaths of five workers with more than sixty workers injured by Ford's hired goons, the Pinkerton security force led by Harry Bennett. The famed Battle of the Overpass in 1937 marked the showdown between organizers of the fledgling United Auto Workers (UAW) union and the Pinkerton thugs that Ford again used to try to stop them. The poor working conditions and wages in the auto industry that led to the renowned sit-down strike at a GM plant in Flint, Michigan, in 1936–1937 forced recognition of the union by Chrysler and GM and made the UAW a major labor organization. But Henry Ford refused to sign a union contract until 1941, following yet another strike at the Rouge, known as "Master Ford's plantation." It brought ten thousand black members into the UAW.

The focus in the Chrysler ad on tradition and working-class pride suggests a thriving working class that hardly exists in the city; the ad naturally plays down the fact that parts and cars are mostly made in places such as South Carolina, Alabama, and Mississippi, because only Detroit can claim an industrial heritage as a major manufacturing center. Detroit is the place where the automobile production line originated, and the region where the Big Three are still headquartered, although only GM is within the city limits. The thriving factories seen in the beginning of the ad provide little hint of the long history of industrial decline and abandonment.

The emphasis on luxury is particularly jarring as the voiceover suggests that Detroit knows the most about luxury because "That's who we are. That's our story. Now it's probably not the one you've been reading about in the papers, the one being written by folks who've never even been here and don't know what we're capable of. Because when it comes to luxury, it's as much about where it's from as who it's for." Luxury here stands in for modernism itself and Detroit is a metaphor for modernism. Perhaps luxury from a badass beaten-up city (with famous T-shirt slogans such as "Detroit, Where the Weak are Killed and Eaten," or, more recently, "Detroit vs. Everybody") is even more authentic. Invoking a shared story of "who we are" embraces the past triumphs and difficulties of the city and asserts a clear identity that is tied to auto-making. A shared history and identity not only promotes a "community of memory" but also a shared common basis for moving forward into the future.[4] This helps explain why many Detroiters loved this ad, which further states, Detroit is "not New York City, or the Windy City, or Sin City, and certainly no one's Emerald City," distinguishing it from New York, Chicago, Las Vegas, and Seattle. The implications are not only about Detroit's unique identity but also about class, and Detroit—being the Motor City—knows how to get its hands dirty, transforming the ordinary into the aesthetic. Still, what explains the perverse emphasis on luxury?

Finally, there's the tagline, "Imported from Detroit," which suggests that American industry has become superior to foreign automobile imports, or at least as good as anybody in the world. While conveniently ignoring the fact that many foreign cars for the U.S. market are now made in this country, more importantly, the ad constructs Detroit as someplace "else," someplace foreign from which cars can be imported. Playing on Detroit's role in the American cultural imagination as its "dark other," the black city that has become emblematic of America's dystopian "dark side," the tagline capitalizes on the frisson of fear and exoticism this evokes. As a city in the heartland that remains estranged from the host body of the nation, Detroit is nonetheless—or *because* of this—a force to be reckoned with, like the fist of Joe Louis. The city and its largely imaginary black workforce, the ad implies, does the heavy lifting, providing the sweat and blood that is always the sordid underbelly of "luxury" for the affluent.

Thus, Detroit stands in for the auto industry when that industry has effectively abandoned Detroit, and it does this on the basis of a romanticized and vanished past. By constructing a thriving urban center that has overcome its obstacles and is proudly fighting back, the ad neutralizes the role of the auto companies in the city's deindustrialization and decline. Although we are meant to bask in the glow of an unparalleled manufacturing legacy and feel the surge of renewed hope in the industrial might of America that is represented by the idea of Detroit as a scrappy fighter, this hope is founded on economic sacrifices by the workers that ensure only the survival of Chrysler's profitability.

The Chrysler Super Bowl ad of the following year continues the Detroit comeback story but shifts the emphasis to the economic struggles of all Americans, focusing more on faces than on cars and allowing a more elegiac quality to enter the narrative. Starring the flinty eighty-one-year-old Clint Eastwood as America's team coach in "Halftime in America," Eastwood intones, "People are out of work and they're hurting—and they're all wondering what they're gonna do to make a comeback—and we're all scared because this isn't a game." He continues, "The people of Detroit know something about this. They almost lost everything. But we all pulled together." The feel-good boosterism ignores Detroit's continued decline and can only refer, once again, to the bailout of the auto industry and Chrysler's own return from bankruptcy. Although the ad uses some previously shot footage in Detroit, the reality of the city is obscured by the new footage for the two-minute commercial, none of which was filmed in Detroit. The portions with Eastwood are filmed in the Los Angeles Memorial Coliseum and the rest is shot in New Orleans and Northern California.[5]

Images include a protest demonstration in Wisconsin as Eastwood talks about "discord and division" and "times we didn't understand each other," which also seems to be a sly reference to his own film, *Gran Torino*, which was set in Detroit and focuses on the ethnic animosities between a Polish American Korean War veteran and the Hmong family that lives next door. More images of mothers and children and working-class families evoke the Farm Security Administration's Depression-era photographs of Dorothea Lange and Walker Evans, while a sober image of firefighters recalls the fall of the Twin Towers on September 11. Urging us to "come from behind," Eastwood again maps Chrysler's return from bankruptcy onto Detroit when he says, "Detroit's showing us it can be done. What's true about them is true about all of us." He concludes, "This country can't be knocked out with one punch. We get right back up again and when we do the world is going to hear the roar of our engines." Despite the bravado, the intended swell of pride is subdued in this version of the comeback story, which extends the metaphor of knockdown and comeback to the entire nation. It ends with the tagline "Imported from Detroit."

Conservatives such as Karl Rove criticized the ad as an endorsement of the auto bailout of 2008 and 2009. Additional controversy focused on the scene that was taken at a protest in Wisconsin. Originally featuring signs held by members of the Madison teachers union with messages such as, "Care about educators like they care for your child," "Solidarity!" and "Stop the attack on public education," the video frames were digitally edited to remove the pro-union and pro–public education messages while Eastwood's voiceover spoke vaguely about "the fog, division, discord, and blame that made it hard to see what lies ahead." The ad replaced the messages on the signs with bland unspecific phrases such as "Think of our children," and "Say no thanks. It's time [inside a clock]. We don't need another." These changes disguise the identity of the movement to which the protest belonged. Even the description on a statue was removed, which identified Col. Hans Christian Heg, the Wisconsin Civil War hero who rallied a Scandinavian unit to fight for the Union. He became a reference point for the hundreds of thousands of protesters who rallied at the Wisconsin Capitol in February and March of 2011 to defend basic rights against the attacks of Wisconsin governor Scott Walker.[6] As one critic concluded, "Seen through the lens of doctored video footage," the Chrysler ad is more "a pro-corporate, anti-union advertisement than any other kind of political statement."[7]

After Chrysler emerged from bankruptcy in 2009, it became a consolidated subsidiary of Italian multinational automaker Fiat. Olivier François, a French-born executive who runs the Lancia brand for Fiat in Europe, said in a 2011 interview that he "has a lot of ideas about how to make the comeback of Detroit very much a part of the story of Chrysler."[8] Yet it turns out that what has been good for Chrysler has not been as good for Detroit, which continues to decline. Chrysler provides very few jobs for Detroiters, with only about four thousand workers in the city. Government employment provides more than forty thousand jobs; other top employers include the city itself and the Detroit public schools.

In its third ad, with Detroit approaching bankruptcy, Chrysler simply abandoned the Detroit comeback story. Instead, the 2013 Super Bowl ad rolled out a new vision of "America" as an agricultural arcadia in the white Protestant heartland with tractors, pitchforks, bales of hay, and the accompanying slogan, "So God Made a Farmer." Narrated by right-wing radio commentator Paul Harvey, who was popular from the 1950s to the 1990s, "So God Made a Farmer" was taken from a recorded speech Harvey delivered in 1978, during the Carter era, to a Future Farmers of America convention. When Harvey died in 2009, his style was described in a *New York Times* obituary as having "a hypnotic timbre, extended pauses for effect, heart-warming tales of average Americans and folksy observations that evoked the heartland, family values, and the old-fashioned plain talk one heard around the dinner table on Sunday."[9] This summary well describes the recorded text of the farmer speech, which begins, "And on the 8th day, God looked down on his planned paradise and said, 'I need a caretaker.' So God made a farmer," and continues as cheerful scenes of family farm life roll past.

With the disappearance of the city, the ad also drops "Imported from Detroit" and ends with the tagline of "Guts, Glory, Ram." No longer attempting to capitalize on Detroit's former role as a manufacturing center or insisting on the working-class grittiness of the city as a basis for "luxury," the ad instead evokes rugged individualism and offers a paean to the pastoral charms of the Farm Belt. In the interest of selling Dodge Ram trucks at a time when housing construction and truck sales were picking up, the ad reincarnates the postindustrial era as a preindustrial idyll. It returns the viewer, without irony, to the kind of late-nineteenth- to early-twentieth-century existence that was slyly satirized by artist Grant Wood in works such as his 1930 painting *American Gothic*. The Chrysler ad's idealized pastoral images attempt to reify a kind of mythic status that is aimed at an urban/suburban audience, not because they would want an agricultural life but because it plays on the desire for lost plenitude and seems to promise its return—another kind of comeback story. In 2014 Chrysler changed the "Imported from Detroit" marketing line for the Chrysler 200 to the more generic "America's Import."

In similar fashion, part of the post–World War I impulse in the 1920s and 1930s was to seek a nativist tradition that was typically American as an anchor in a world of shattered illusions, especially during the Great Depression, to which the 2008 financial crisis and its continuing aftermath has been repeatedly likened. By returning to the preindustrial, the Dodge Ram Chrysler commercial also tries to find a stable heritage and salvage a "usable past" that connects the bleak present to a more prosperous era. Providing a sense of reassurance and continuity with this more usable past, the ad suggests that midwestern farm life, not the urban metropolis, now stands in for American national culture. The grit and hardiness formerly associated with the workers of the city is shifted to farmers and their families, mapping their hardworking "guts" and "glory" onto "Ram." To be American and to support God and country, the ad implies, means buying a Chrysler truck. Or a Jeep. Chrysler premiered another commercial during the same Super Bowl game that featured Oprah Winfrey narrating scenes of happy domesticity for returning American veterans, identifying Jeep with a nation united ("When you're home, we're more than a family; we are a nation that is whole again," followed by the Jeep logo). The overall message that buying Chrysler products is patriotic is not unlike George W. Bush's suggestion to the country after the 9/11 attacks that the best way to patriotically support the nation was to "go shopping."[10]

The problem is that, for the past several decades, selling cars and trucks by appealing to "luxury" and guilt-tripping patriotism is not as effective as it once may have been. Books such as Bill Vlasic's *Once upon a Car* and Micheline Maynard's *The End of Detroit* tell the stories of the changing fortunes of the car companies and their tin ear when it came to hearing what people wanted in a car and slow-footed response to the superior quality and economy of foreign competition, which quickly became domestic competition as those companies built factories in the United States at the domestic companies own insistence. Toyota and Honda focused on engineering and fuel economy while the Detroit companies focused on style and luxury; the Japanese focused on what the customer wanted while the Detroit companies told the customer what he or she *should* want.[11] As a result, the Big Three have become the Big Five.

Nostalgia for American styling can be seen every summer in Detroit during the annual Dream Cruise, when classic cars such as Cadillacs and Corvettes slowly roll up and down Woodward Avenue from Ferndale to Birmingham in a summer parade of chromed-up, finned-out, block-long cars. Onlookers from the city and from out of town line the avenue in lawn chairs with beers in hand and T-shirt stands behind them in a nostalgic extravaganza. Yet, as Maynard notes, "The fact is that there is no longer a single segment of the car market where Detroit is clearly the leading player, either in profits, quality, or buzz."[12] This includes small, mid-sized, and luxury cars. Today, Birmingham, Alabama, seems to be the capital for a growing number of car companies from Japan, Germany, and Korea. Despite the fact that "Detroit" remains a metonym for the car companies, there is only one auto factory fully within the city limits of Detroit.[13] The shift of factories to areas outside the country altogether, where resources and labor are cheaper and more easily exploited for higher profit margins, has led to the shuttering and abandonment by the Big Three of at least thirty-eight major factories and plants nationally just since 2004.[14]

Another irony in Chrysler's shift from an urban manufacturing to a rural farming identity is the fact that most large farms are not family owned but corporately owned by agribusiness conglomerates. This means they are dependent on migrant labor even as migrant workers are under perpetual attack. In Michigan, reports note "plump red cherries and crisp apples rotting on the ground because there aren't enough workers to pick them" and an asparagus crop left in the field for the same reason.[15] Farmers nationally, from Christmas tree growers in the Appalachians to Wisconsin dairy farmers to fruit and vegetable producers in California, are pleading with lawmakers to ease restrictions so that the forty-five thousand migrant workers needed to pick crops may return. The farming industry insists that its chronic labor shortage is due to the fact that few Americans are willing to deal with the long hours, hot weather, and other hardships of farm labor. "The truth is, not even farm workers are raising their children to be farm workers," said Tom Nassif, a Republican and the president of Western Growers.[16]

The farming industry, among other corporate employers, has come to depend on migrant laborers because they offer subservience and are easily deported and blacklisted if they protest abusive conditions; they are part of a broader phenomenon of subcontracting that shields employers from legal liability for the mistreatment of workers and from labor-organizing efforts. The National Employment Law Project reports that 58 percent of jobs added since the crash of 2008 have been in low-wage sectors, which have high levels of contingent and subcontracted jobs. The *New York Times* reports, "Today, almost all production in global manufacturing involves subcontracting. It is central to the structure of employment in the American construction, warehousing and agricultural industries as well."[17] So much for the slogan "So God made a farmer," as well as the myth that highly exploited and mistreated migrant laborers take jobs from Americans or constitute a menace to the nation; on the contrary, they are crucial to its agricultural success, even as the retro family farm is idealized and mythologized. Of course it would not be nearly as heartwarming to suggest that "God made an agribusiness conglomerate."

Moreover, the business of U.S. agriculture has not prevented or addressed hunger and food insecurity, which is rampant across the nation. Such food insecurity has inspired a different version of the pastoral paean imagined by Detroit's oldest and most famous living radical, Grace Lee Boggs.[18] Boggs leads a group of devoted acolytes who envision Detroit as a collective of communal farms and the world's largest wholly self-sustaining city. Although Detroit has an estimated nine hundred urban farms and community gardens, this remains a far-fetched ideal. Socialism in one city is not a viable option.

Moreover, as David Harvey points out, "While small and localized enterprises can work under the radar and beyond the reach of the laws of competition (acquiring the status of local monopolies, for example), most cannot. So worker-controlled or cooperative enterprises tend at some point to mimic their capitalist competitors, and the more they do so the less distinctive their practices become. Indeed, it can all too easily happen that workers end up in a condition of collective self-exploitation that is every bit as repressive as that which capital imposes."[19]

Nevertheless, the proliferation of urban farms speaks to the ongoing crisis of food insecurity, a critical concern in Detroit and across America, where fifty million people face hunger in a country that has enough food resources to feed them. The adverse health effects of food insecurity are well known, including obesity, diabetes, and heart disease. There are even more dire effects on the cognitive and physical development of children who go hungry for even short periods, compromising health in preventable ways while unnecessarily raising health care costs. The food insecure often live in "food deserts," which are big geographic areas that have no large grocery stores, and 75 percent of food deserts are in cities. The convenience, fast food, and liquor stores that are available to the city poor primarily offer processed foods with little balance in the way of fresh fruits and vegetables, which are far more expensive in any case. This is due to the massive government subsidies to the agribusiness conglomerates that raise crops such as corn, soy, and wheat in order to produce processed foods, while those who raise fresh fruits and vegetables do not enjoy such subsidies. Fresh food is thus out of reach, even when available, for people with food stamp benefits, which average $4.50 per day for recipients in Michigan, or $1.50 per meal.[20] The problem of food insecurity is thus one of poverty, not food shortages; 85 percent of food insecure families have at least one working adult, but they do not earn a living wage, thereby transforming the basic right to food into a daily struggle.

Wayne County, which includes Detroit, ranks fifteenth in the nation for child food insecurity. Los Angeles ranks first, followed by the combined five boroughs of New York City.[21] While the government spends $20 billion to promote processed foods made from corn, soy, and wheat, and has an agricultural policy that supports wealthy corporations and agribusiness, hunger continues to rise in the nation.[22] Urban agriculture groups in Detroit such as the Greening of Detroit, Earthworks Urban Farm, Detroit Food Justice Task Force, and Detroit Black Community Food Security Network have helped increase access to healthy food for impoverished black citizens. In order to resolve the problem of food insecurity in America, however, it must be addressed at a national scale and begin by radically transforming agricultural policy.

Appropriating the Margins: Fashion and Cosmetics

Consumer advertising that employs or sublimates ruin imagery is not limited to companies that originated in Detroit, although ruin imagery often evokes Detroit. Such imagery is deployed by companies that trade on the allure of the safely dangerous and outré, embracing the negative in order to contain the anxiety it produces and transform it into something aesthetically pleasing and desirable. These forms of commercial imagery are produced in the public arenas of photographic display, from magazines to store windows and mall displays, from the Internet to television to the art museum, appealing to overlapping consumer audiences and becoming part of the global network of ruin images.

The cosmetics company Urban Decay, for example, has produced ads that suggest transgressive fantasies drawn from dark urban spaces. Urban Decay signals, by its name, imagery, and ad copy, a rhetorical identity profile that is fierce, rebellious, colorful, glittery, defiant, and trashy. Yet it also suggests an "ethical" identity by virtue of being animal friendly and "vegan." Constructing a "wild creature" in the "urban jungle," yet one that is responsible and socially conscious, Urban Decay transforms urban degeneration into the enticingly forbidden but safe. Offering Gothic urbanity and bold individualism, its cosmetics advertising becomes a way of taming an unsettling reality while simultaneously exploiting it.

The ads initially echoed the language of drug use, but this rhetoric drew online complaints from at least one recovering addict: "So, a few weeks back Urban Decay sent out this awful email through their mailing list that said, 'score some blow and a big fatty'; and 'urban Decay is your pusher'; to advertise their new lip plumper called Blow. I was a little upset to see that sort of thing in my inbox because I've gone through recovery and that is still a sensitive area for me. I thought it really crossed a line."[23] This advertising language, which Urban Decay has since dropped, cavalierly exploits the transgressive thrill of unregulated space and urban drug culture while ignoring the effects of addiction and overdose, a reality that is all too prevalent in the actual centers of urban decay, especially in its abandoned spaces. A 2011 ad offered "Beauty with an Edge," featuring a young woman with a slack mouth and brightly colored eye makeup in greens, blues, pinks, and purples, some of which is running down her cheek. She looks over her shoulder at the viewer with her hands protectively at her throat. The image evokes tears, facial bruising, and a drug hangover, while the drips on the ad copy behind the model suggest the walls of a ruin.[24]

Urban Decay was founded in 1996 and purchased in 2000 by the conglomerate LVMH Moët Hennessy–Louis Vuitton, the world's leading luxury items group. It also became known as Urban Rot and became a "conspiracy brand" in the United States through Sephora, and later was sold through Macy's. It was also sold as City Corrosion through Nordstrom and Bloomingdale's, targeting restless suburbanites and appealing to their instincts for vicarious slumming and fantasized sex and drugs in dark abandoned warehouses.[25] Making a marketable virtue out of frightening anxieties, such advertising fetishizes urban degeneration as a fantasy prerogative that may be freely donned or discarded. Similarly, Swatch Corporation appropriated a ruin image in the form of a clock that was partially melted in a fire at the old Cass Tech High School in Detroit and photographed by Marchand and Meffre as well as Moore. Evoking a sense of collapsed time, Swatch Corporation used it for one of its watch faces, employing the tag line "Melted Minutes." Presumably it is meant to evoke the dreamily surreal melting watches of Salvador Dali, not the fires of abandoned buildings, the sensual and mysterious rather than the apocalyptic. And yet it retains a hint of that, too—a kind of end-of-the-world chic.[26]

In a local example, a high-end clothing store in the northern Detroit suburb of Birmingham capitalized on the thrillingly trashy allure of the dangerous city in its winter 2012 window display, reassuring its anxious customers of their secure status while distancing and othering Detroit. Expensive dresses and shoes were carefully arranged in an installation containing yellow police tape and an 8 Mile street sign, evoking the infamous border between Detroit and the suburbs, with jumbled pages torn from Julia Taubman's *Detroit: 138 Square Miles* littered across the display floor. The staged "crime scene" became another way of titillating the well-heeled while taming a frightening reality for the affluent white residents of Detroit's wealthy suburbs. Like the transgressive aesthetic of "heroin chic" popular in fashion in the 1980s, or the exhibition *Punk: Chaos to Couture* at the Metropolitan Museum of Art in 2013, the edgy and provocative social margins are appropriated by the center, their terror defused and rendered sexy and safely consumable. The Urban Decay ads, Swatch's melting watch face, and a crime scene window display in a high-end clothing store all vicariously engage with the anxieties of decline by evoking and exoticizing the allure of dark urban nightscapes through the modern ruin aesthetic of the deindustrial sublime.

Cool Survivalism: City Films, Music, and Theatre Bizarre

A growing number of city films and documentaries about Detroit offer detailed views of the metropolis, its storied histories and cultural complexities.[27] Unlike photography, such films are better able to produce narratives that attempt to account for the processes of ruination. Because they approach their subjects with compassion and sorrow, an elegiac quality often pervades documentaries about the rise and fall of the city, conveying a sense of mourn-

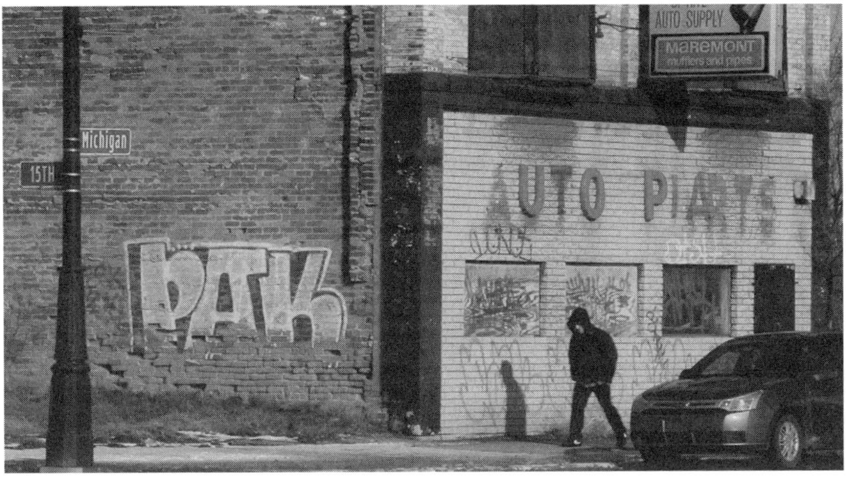

FIG. 31 *Detropia*, directed by Heidi Ewing and Rachel Grady, 2012, film still.

ful resignation and commemoration even while searching the city for signs of resurrection and conveying the determined pride of city residents who tenaciously endure. Films such as *Detropia*; *Detroit: Requiem for a City?*; and *Deforce* offer historical insights, though they usually end, perhaps inevitably, with indeterminate conclusions.

The documentary *Detropia* by Heidi Ewing and Rachel Grady earned an editing award at the 2012 Sundance Film Festival and has played the national circuit, making it one of the more popular recent films about Detroit (figure 31). A quiet meditation on Detroit's decline, the film touches on issues of class, deindustrialization, the cutbacks of city services, right-sizing, the continuing inability of Detroit car companies to adapt to foreign competition, and artists moving downtown, though it does not explore any of these issues in depth. Instead, *Detropia* weaves together the observations of a variety of interview subjects, from a young black female blogger to a union local president to a black bar owner, but lacks an authoritative voiceover, sometimes compensating for this by providing on-screen texts with statistics. The camera often dwells on the haunting decay of the city. The most wrenching part of the narrative occurs early in the film at a meeting of Local 22 of the UAW, which is held in response to the demand of the American Axle company that workers submit to large pay cuts under threat of a plant shutdown. The stunned workers refuse, as much in opposition to the humiliation and denigration of the value of their work as to the economic blackmail. A screen text informs us that the plant was closed shortly afterward.

Exorbitant salaries at the top of such corporations exacerbate the disgrace of this form of economic blackmail. An AFL-CIO data report on 350 companies shows that "the CEO to worker pay ratio was 331:1 and the CEO to minimum wage worker pay ratio was 774:1," with CEOs earning, on average, $11.7 million in total compensation.[28] "Even as companies argue that they can't afford to raise wages," notes a reporter, "the nation's largest companies are earning higher profits per employee than they did five years ago. In 2013, the S&P 500 Index companies earned $41,249 in profits per employee, a 38% increase."[29] These profits per employee are greater than the average employee's take-home pay of $35,239.[30] Profits take precedence not just over employees' wages but also over consumer safety. Both Toyota and Ford have been fined for "hiding safety defects," while GM recalled a whopping thirty-nine million cars in 2014 after willfully concealing design flaws that caused at least thirteen deaths and numerous severe injuries in crashes.

Another telling moment in *Detropia* is offered by Tommy Stevens, the owner of the Raven Lounge, the last black-owned blues bar in the Detroit area, which is barely hanging on after nearby factories have been shuttered. Stevens attends the annual Detroit Auto Show where he is impressed by a new Chinese electric car, called "Build Your Dream," that sells for $20,000. Speaking with sales reps for GM's Volt, an electric car with a price tag of $40,000, he questions the huge difference in price and is told that the Volt has many more "luxury options" and is "better made." Stevens reminds them that this is what Detroit automakers said when Japanese cars first entered the American market and that it seems to him that American automakers still have their "heads in the sand" when it comes to overseas competitors. Toward the end of the film he muses that the continuing destruction of the middle class may lead to revolution.

For the most part, the film's poetic, collage-like quality induces a kind of melancholia and severs emotional connection as we jump from one thread to another, from a town hall meeting where residents emotionally convey the devastating effects of cuts in bus service that prevent them from getting to work, to young dudes on their front porch joking about the effects of right-sizing and imagining a fight over tomatoes in a city garden. For those who are unaware of the desperate conditions of the poor in Detroit, however, the film provides an odd awakening, prompting David Denby, a critic for *New Yorker*, for example, to call it "the most moving documentary I've seen in years." Charmed by the African American Detroit Opera tenor Noah Stewart's sonorous singing of Puccini in the cavernous Michigan Central Station, Denby declares that "the filmmakers' aestheticism turns into an explicit promise of renewal."[31] This is more wishful thinking than evidence-based, despite the colorful gestures and determined loyalty to the city of the subjects we follow. Thus another reviewer observes, "To a one, those subjects are an admirable lot, standing strong and proud—and in stark contrast to the city crumbling around them. But they are not experts—they are anecdotes."[32] While the tone of poetic melancholy may render the film, as a third reviewer observes, "all but a eulogy for Detroit,"

Detropia mediates the fear of urban decline through the tenacious endurance of its selected spokespersons and its beautifully shot scenes of the city.[33]

At a showing at the Main Theater in Royal Oak on September 14, 2013, Ewing and Grady, who were present for discussion following the film, responded to audience frustration about the lack of proposed political solutions by asserting that the film was only meant to be "a meditation," and noting that the deliberately indeterminate title *Detropia* was meant to incorporate the possibilities of both dystopia and utopia. More dystopic than otherwise, the film nonetheless points to a paradoxical structure of feeling which suggests that even in a dystopian setting, the utopian impulse flickers to life. Yet the signs of resurrection, mainly represented as artistic initiatives in the city, are tentative and necessarily limited in nature; the enduring form of existence most of the film's subjects display is a combination of frustration, tenuous hope, and cool survivalism.

Other films are more self-consciously political and historical. Daniel Falconer's documentary *Deforce: A History of Tyranny in the Heart of America* (2010) reviews Detroit's modern history, often using archival material, and shows how it grew as a city and became the "Arsenal of Democracy" during World War II, the industrial machine that produced the Allies' military hardware. It discusses the racist housing policies and redlining that enforced segregated housing, cop terror, and the 1967 riots; the failed racist "war on drugs" that incarcerates such a high percentage of young black men; and the high rate of early deaths among them.[34] It also focuses on corruption in the city government and racist state and federal policies. *Deforce*, though far less subdued than *Detropia*, concludes with urgent but vague calls for community solidarity.

A third example is Julien Temple's *Requiem for Detroit?* Although the question mark leaves room for the possibility of a future resurrection, one can already hear the funeral dirge the film title suggests.[35] In his *Guardian* essay, "Detroit: The Last Days," which accompanied the release of his film, Temple displays a certain thrill at witnessing the decay of the city:

> Approaching the derelict shell of downtown Detroit, we see full-grown trees sprouting from the tops of deserted skyscrapers. In their shadows, the glazed eyes of the street zombies slide into view, stumbling in front of the car. Our excitement at driving into what feels like a man-made hurricane Katrina is matched only by sheer disbelief that what was once the fourth-largest city in the US could actually be in the process of disappearing from the face of the earth. The statistics are staggering—40 square miles of the 139-square-mile inner city have already been reclaimed by nature.[36]

This excited amazement and view of residents as stumbling "street zombies" is redolent of a kind of schadenfreude and sense of the city as alien and other, even as it conveys post-apocalyptic anxieties. Such rhetoric contributes to the local resentment of voyeuristic outsiders who seem insensitive to the effects of decline on the lives of real people. As critic John Patrick Leary ruefully observes, "the exuberant connoisseurship of dereliction; the unembarrassed rejoicing at the 'excitement' of it all" leaves a sour taste.[37]

This sense of excitement also pervades the film, which juxtaposes archival footage of better times with burned-out cars, crumbling buildings, fire, and devastation, providing a rapid-fire but shocking ruin tour of the city as Temple narrates a voiceover, in addition to talking heads such as Lowell Boileau, Grace Lee Boggs, Tyree Guyton, auto executive Paul Thal, and others. Temple glibly illustrates the "end of the line" for auto manufacturing in Detroit with footage of a test car smashing into a wall. He employs Martha and the Vandellas' upbeat Motown song "Dancing in the Streets" for scenes of the 1967 riot, as if it were a party. Characterizing the city as a "slow-motion Katrina," "war zone," and landscape similar to "the last days of the Maya," Temple presents Detroit as a cautionary tale for the industrialized world but overdraws the lesson by suggesting that we have "traveled a thousand years into the future." The film attempts a redemptive moment by concluding with the assertion that "even in the worst environment, life takes hold." This observation is illustrated by greenery among the ruins as Temple lamely suggests that the city will be revitalized through urban farms and gardens. The narrative arc of *Requiem for Detroit?* constructs a trajectory that may be understood, ironically, as similar to that of the Chrysler ads: a return to a vanished preindustrial past as a vision for the future, a hope based on the resurrection of nature and its implied promise of plenitude.

Dan Georgakis, a longtime Detroit leftist, film reviewer, and author of more than twenty books, including, most famously, *Detroit: I Do Mind Dying: A Study in Urban Revolution* (with Marvin Surkin and Manning Marable), aptly articulates the larger problem with this crop of films as a failure of political perspective: "The makers of *Detropia*, *Deforce*, and *Requiem for Detroit?* ultimately seem to be as bewildered and dazed by what they have observed as the Detroiters with whom they interact."[38] Perhaps the films' primary contribution, and others like them, is the warning they represent, the exposure of the empty myth of class mobility that informs hundreds of other cities across America. While it may be tempting to see Detroit as existing in its own parallel universe of time and space, in July 2013 RealtyTrac reported that the five states with the highest home foreclosure rates, for example, did not even include the state of Michigan. It was outranked by Florida, Maryland, Ohio, Connecticut, and New Mexico. Evoking the deindustrial sublime, the pleasure these films offer is the domestication of terror through the safety and distance of representation. Yet even as they contain the anxiety that ruination produces and make it belong to someone else, such films demonstrate the devastating effects of deindustrialization and the evaporation of jobs and opportunities for the impoverished and unemployed everywhere.

Fictional representations of the city also play upon the sense of a regressive downward spiral. *Low Winter Sun* (2013), for example, the subdued title of an AMC police drama set in Detroit, grapples with the complexities of the struggle between good and evil. Unlike AMC's *Breaking Bad*, which is set in sunny Albuquerque and tempers its violence with a quirky humor, *Low Winter Sun* is muted, restrained, and relentlessly dark. It focuses on two Detroit homicide cops who murder one of their own and struggle to cover it up, as well as drug lords, informants, prostitutes, and small-time hoods in the business of drugs, sex, and murder in Greektown and surrounding Detroit neighborhoods. The city itself becomes a character in the downbeat show, which had a large temporary production facility on East Grand Boulevard next to the Packard Plant. The activities of scrappers, the high death rate of young black men, the loss of union jobs, and the closing of plants are themes threaded into the story lines of the first three episodes, along with the deindustrialized landscape, trash-strewn alleys, and broken-down houses.

And yet, as with most Detroit stories, a counternarrative of gritty resilience and survival at all costs is reflected in the endurance of the characters within their depressed environment. *Low Winter Sun* was adapted for AMC by Chris Mundy, who notes, "The whole show is about second chances and what the characters are willing to do to get a second chance. The people who are here will not give up on Detroit, and as part of that, they have sort of doubled down on the pride of being from here."[39] But the Detroit of *Low Winter Sun* is too demoralized and alienated a place to make watching it feel good. The struggle to survive and keep despair at bay becomes the overriding theme as its leading characters seem to hang on by their fingernails, persisting through sheer stubbornness, habit, luck, and, occasionally, flashes of hope for a new beginning. The season ended, not surprisingly, with a major drop in viewers and bad reviews. As one reviewer dourly notes, "In case we were wondering about the dire state of the Motor City, at one point a stray dog trots by with a rat in its mouth."[40] A Michigan resident perhaps best captures the conflicted nature and cool survivalism of the Detroit story with his blog comment, "Great acting and I watched every episode but this show is tough to watch and one of the bigger bummers on TV. But I like it."[41]

In music, the hot, soulful sounds of Motown, the American record company founded in Detroit by Berry Gordy in 1959, generated vast pride in the city. The "Motown Sound," which often used a call-and-response singing style that originated in gospel music, shaped the sound of a generation and helped achieve the racial integration of popular music. Motown had more than a hundred top ten hits by groups and singers such as The Miracles, with Smoky Robinson; The Marvelettes; Mary Wells; Gladys Knight & the Pips; Diana

Ross & the Supremes; The Jackson 5; The Four Tops; Stevie Wonder; and Marvin Gaye. The Hitsville, U.S.A. Motown building on West Grand Boulevard, which served as Motown's headquarters from 1959 until 1968, became the Motown Historical Museum in 1985.[42]

The quintessential example of cool survivalism, however, is techno music, an early 1980s Detroit invention that embodies in musical form a way of existing in a landscape of decline. Techno was a product of its dystopian environment in the deindustrialized landscape following a period of recession and layoffs in the auto industry in the late 1970s. The first wave of techno producers and DJs, including Juan Atkins, Derrick May, and Kevin Saunderson, were the sons of unionized black auto workers and observed how robotics and automation replaced humans on the line, producing in them an ambivalent relationship with technology.[43] Ridley Scott's film *Blade Runner* (1981), which problematized the issue of telling the difference between robots and humans, was also important to the retrofuturistc nature of techno and a favorite film of its producers and DJs.

Techno was characterized by its robotic repetitiveness, 4/4 beat, lack of lyrics, and use of alarm bells, sirens, and sonar. Its production used retrofitted, antiquated, and accidental tools and equipment appropriate to a dystopian environment. Both in its production and its continuous sound, as critic Richard Pope asserts, techno projected an ethos of cool survivalism in a hopeless, dystopian environment, one not easily appropriated by mainstream culture because it was not properly a "subculture," having no uniform, no lyrics, no focus on seeing and being seen. Indeed, the renowned techno parties in the Packard Plant in the early to mid-1990s, where second-wave techno DJs played their music to growing crowds, took place in near-total darkness, defying visual representation.[44] Pope argues that techno survivalism goes further than punk in accepting the end of history: "Where punk rails against the end of history, techno blips, bleeps and grooves."[45]

Nonvocal techno-rock with a 4/4 beat has become the music of a contemporary phenomenon known as Detroit Jit, a largely African American male dance form conducted as successive duels and dance battles. Based on intense body movement, high energy, and rapid footwork yet highly individual, the dance form traces its roots through Motown and the Detroit dance group Jitterbugs that started in the 1970s and won national fame. Alistair Macaulay, *New York Times* dance critic, describes Jit as a form of "throbbing speed and vitality and pride."[46]

One of the most remarkable annual events produced in Detroit is Theatre Bizarre, described as "part carney side show, part burlesque theater, and part performance art" and "a bloody imaginative fantasy party" with some Grand Guignol and Weimar cabaret thrown in.[47] It originated as a carnivalesque Halloween masquerade in a decaying residential neighborhood near the old

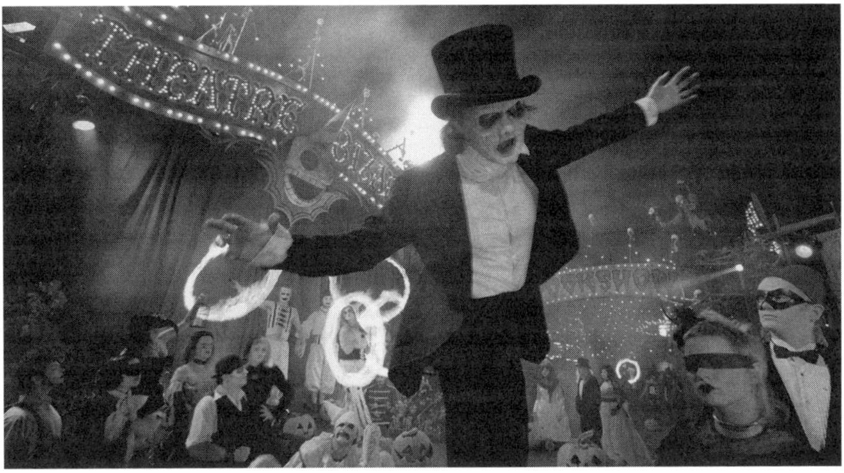

FIG. 32 Theater Bizarre, with John Dunivant in front of Main Stage, West State Fair Road, Detroit, 2009. Photo: Brett Carson/Courtesy John Dunivant.

Michigan State Fairgrounds in the northern part of Detroit. Begun by commercial illustrator and multimedia artist John Dunivant with Ken Poirer in 1999, Theatre Bizarre for one night turned a half-block area of houses, alleys, and vacant lots surrounded by burned-out houses into a replica of an abandoned amusement park and wicked wonderland for a couple thousand people. It was produced by dozens of volunteers who came from all over the country in the weeks leading up to the event to construct the stages and attractions, including a Ferris wheel and haunted house featuring more than 150 performers. In 2010 the City of Detroit shut down the project, citing various zoning and code violations, but Theatre Bizarre moved briefly to the Fillmore Theater before finding a permanent home at Detroit's Masonic Temple—the largest Masonic Temple in the world—drawing over four thousand partygoers from around the globe in 2012 and 2013 to "the greatest masquerade on earth" (figure 32). With mandatory costumes and masks and featuring live musical performances, fire-eaters, burlesque performers, freaks, and side shows in a festival atmosphere of debauched anonymity, Theatre Bizarre richly embodies the funky decadence, communal hedonism, and hallucinatory fantasies that feed the vitality of Detroit. This, too, becomes a way of surviving in a depressed environment.

6

Surviving in the Postapocalyptic Landscape

The recovery of Detroit, and, by extension, that of all deindustrialized and declining cities, is a hope set against the fear of a downward spiral of progress that often manifests as apocalyptic catastrophe. Yet even apocalyptic collapse is not necessarily regarded as the end of everything but as another possible beginning. Indeed, the notion of new beginnings is integral to the structure of most apocalyptic narratives throughout the centuries. In post–World War II sci-fi thrillers, and more recent zombie and disaster films and television shows, such new starts are central to postapocalyptic scenarios that depend upon imagining survivors and their adventures, no matter how hostile or devastated the environment in which they find themselves may be. Such films help to domesticate the anxiety of decline while the pictured or implied evils that result in these postapocalyptic fantasies are always firmly rooted in the problems of the present.

Nuclear Fear and Sci-Fi Thrillers

In "The Imagination of Disaster," Susan Sontag's 1965 essay about postwar sci-fi thrillers, she observed that "the freakish, the ugly, and the predatory all converge—and provide a fantasy target for righteous bellicosity to discharge itself, and for the aesthetic enjoyment of suffering and disaster."[1] Sontag identifies here the key elements of disaster films: the horrifying and frightening, the legitimation of unrestrained violence, and the ability to enjoy it all at an aesthetic remove. She regarded sci-fi films as normalizing and neutralizing that which is psychologically unbearable, thereby "inuring" us to it, which might be another way of saying that disaster films are a way of containing and controlling our cultural anxieties, although the terrors of disaster can never be entirely normalized, nor are we ever completely desensitized to the fears that haunt our era. Indeed, the greater the fears, the more rapidly the imagery meant to domesticate those fears multiplies; crucially, the imagery is always anchored in the real. One of the pleasures of these films, as Sontag points out, is the imagined ability to survive a planetary catastrophe, to fantasize starting all over again in a ravaged environment with a small group of people.

The anxieties regarding global catastrophe have shifted in the last fifty years. In the 1950s and 1960s, nuclear fear followed the incineration of Hiroshima and Nagasaki and spawned a sci-fi cast of alien invaders, mutants, and monsters. Today, zombie thrillers and postapocalyptic narratives have largely replaced them with the living dead, and address contemporary anxieties about viral pandemics, migrant populations, global warming, ecological destruction, and struggles for limited resources as well as the explosive growth of social inequality. The convergence of the freakish and the predatory with righteous violence and aesthetic enjoyment endures. A key difference, however, between contemporary zombie films and postwar sci-fi thrillers is that scientists and the military, who usually collaborated to save the day at the end of sci-fi movies, are malevolent, impotent, or nonexistent in most contemporary zombie movies. In half a century, public confidence in the beneficent promise of science, technology, and the global cooperation of the military and the state has drastically eroded.

The primary continuity between sci-fi thrillers provoked by nuclear fear and recent zombie and disaster films is the collective imagination of catastrophe and the apocalyptic threat of total social breakdown. There is an important difference, however. Engaging the anxiety of global decline, the postapocalyptic landscapes found in zombie and disaster films are dominated by the iconic landscapes of the abandoned and decaying city, for which Detroit serves as a global metaphor. But first let us briefly examine the imagery and effects of nuclear fear, which have never left public discourse and continue to infuse the contemporary imagination of ruin imagery.

Anxiety about humanist progress, national catastrophe, and urban ruination has served as modernism's dark underbelly for at least two centuries. It burst into full flower in the United States first with Orson Welles's 1938 "War of the Worlds" radio broadcast about Martians landing, which caused a nationwide panic, and then, in a more sustained way, when the U.S. government deliberately conjured a vision of national nuclear destruction following World War II as a prelude to ramping up the security apparatus of the state. From the late 1940s and 1950s onward, the Cold War state went to great lengths to invent an American landscape of future nuclear ruin. Test programs called for actively imagined national nuclear warfare and forced schoolchildren to hunker down under their desks and families to huddle in bomb shelters. These tactics were combined with large-scale response exercises such as the evacuation of cities, all as part of the psychological reprogramming of the American public by the government to justify new security and surveillance measures.[2]

By the mid-1950s the ostensible threat level reached absurd heights of alarmism. As anthropologist Joseph Masco observes: "It became a civic obligation to collectively imagine, and at times theatrically enact through 'civil defense,' the physical destruction of the nation-state."[3] The fomenting of national fear that characterizes the post-9/11 "war on terror" rhetoric and the enactment of draconian security measures in response to this fear was prefigured by the Cold War logics of nuclear fear and the security state built in response to it. The visions of nuclear war and nuclear ruins promoted by the state more than fifty years ago, writes Masco, "installed an idea of an American community under total and unending threat, creating the terms for a new kind of nation-building which demanded an unprecedented level of militarism in everyday life as a minimum basis for 'security.'"[4]

In response to the events of 9/11, George W. Bush (and his lieutenants, Condoleezza Rice and Colin Powell) mobilized the nation by deploying the reliable Cold War rhetoric of nuclear fear, even though this was not an actual threat. On October 7, 2002, when Bush addressed the nation to justify a preemptive war against Iraq, although it was unconnected to the attacks of 9/11, he invoked a nuclear threat by conjuring a mushroom cloud, the unmistakable visual icon of nuclear destruction: "Facing clear evidence of peril, we cannot wait for the final proof, the smoking gun that could come in the form of a mushroom cloud."[5] Despite the different nature of the attack on the World Trade Center, that site was dubbed "Ground Zero," just like the detonation site in Hiroshima, thus figuring the collapse of the Twin Towers in terms of the nuclear destruction of a city and mapping the former onto the latter.

The mentality of the security state continues apace under the Obama administration with the unprecedented scope of the National Security Agency's (NSA) domestic surveillance and the massive invasion of privacy, as revealed by whistle-blower Edward Snowden. Fear is increasingly instrumentalized by the state for control of the population through ever stronger security measures, including spying and wiretapping, in which the government seizes enormous quantities of phone records and electronic data while cracking down on press freedom and trampling on constitutional rights—even as it claims the opposite in Orwellian newspeak. Both the *Guardian* and the *Washington Post* published accounts in June 2013 about the ability of NSA technicians in the United States to comb through vast troves of audio, video, photos, e-mails, and documents from industries such as Microsoft, Google, YouTube, Facebook, Yahoo, Skype, and Apple, using data-mining tools such as Boundless Informant to assemble individual profiles—and they have been secretly doing so for years.

Despite the government's mobilization of nuclear fear after 9/11 by invoking the mushroom cloud, this iconic image of nuclear war is highly deceptive and conveys little sense of the actual destructive effects of atomic bombs on human populations. As Kyo Maclear argues, the mushroom cloud became a powerful and memorable Cold War symbol both because it was "a technocratic vision" that could be seen as "the culmination of scientific progress" and because it elided all human presence and the destructive effects of the bomb. Producing an image of what might be called the "technological sublime," precisely by keeping its effects at an abstract distance, the mushroom cloud became the *only* image to represent the dropping of the A-bomb, obscuring the human cost and scale of wreckage. The U.S. government actively censored other images of the war, which were concealed from the public until 1980, when pictures of the irradiated body were first made public.[6] As late as 1994 a controversy arose at the Smithsonian Institute over a proposed exhibition of the refurbished B-29 bomber *Enola Gay* that was to discuss the use of the atomic bomb and display artifacts that demonstrated its destructive power. The original concept for the exhibition was abandoned after a veterans' group successfully lobbied for the removal of all items and references to the effects of the bombs.[7]

By occluding any view of trauma and its destructive effects, such distancing and image repression makes witnessing impossible and has racist overtones to boot.[8] Like the abstract photos taken from the eye of "smart bombs" during the U.S. bombing of Iraq in the 1991 Gulf War, which made tens of thousands of Iraqi deaths invisible, and the absence of the impoverished black population in most Detroit ruin imagery, erasing the human is a strategy meant to quell dissent, cultivate complacency, and garner support for dominant political policy.

Nevertheless, it is difficult to censor fear and trepidation, which finds its own formats for expression.[9] Sci-fi thrillers about biological mutation and battles with aliens became enormously popular in the post–World War II period, functioning as ways of coming to terms with nuclear trauma, the terror of radiation, and the fear of mass incineration. Between 1948 and 1962 Hollywood released more than five hundred science-fiction features.[10] As vehicles for the experience of the technological sublime, they attempted to tame the horror of planetary crises and make them enjoyable. The most classic film of the genre is *Godzilla*, which was made not in Hollywood but in Japan by director Inoshiro Honda in 1954, a film that has been remade several times recently. It tells the story of a giant Jurassic monster roused from the murky depths of Bikini Atoll by nuclear testing, and culminates with Godzilla rampaging indiscriminately through Tokyo, wreaking death and destruction while pleasurably terrifying audiences everywhere.[11]

Bare Life and the Zombie Apocalypse

In the past several decades, but especially since the attacks on the World Trade Center and Pentagon in 2001, the proliferation of zombie and disaster films, books, television shows, and video games attest to new fears about national and global calamities, which proliferate as inequality and globalization accelerates. *The Hunger Games* trilogy of films starring Jennifer Lawrence, for example, based on the science-fiction best sellers by Suzanne Collins, focuses on themes of poverty, starvation, oppression, and gladiatorial-style fights for survival in a postapocalyptic world. *The Hunger Games* films follow in the tradition of other notable postapocalyptic films such as the *Terminator* series (1984, 1991, 2004) and the *Matrix* series (1999, 2003), in which the world is destroyed in nuclear holocausts, and the future is left to self-replicating systems of artificial intelligence and intelligent machines that either obliterate or enslave the human race, and the *Left Behind* series of best-selling books and films that focus on the Christian dispensationalist end times.[12] Postapocalyptic television shows include the BBC series *Survivors*, about a small band of people who survive a deadly unknown strain of influenza that kills most of the world's population; *Jericho*, about the survival of a town after the nuclear destruction of twenty-three other American cities; *The Lottery*, about a world in which humans can no longer reproduce; *The Leftovers*, in which a part of the population has inexplicably disappeared; *Under the Dome*, in which a town is isolated under a mysterious dome; *The Last Ship* and *The Strain*, both about destructive viruses; *Falling Skies*, about an alien invasion that devastated the planet; *Revolution*, about a permanent global blackout; *The Colony*, a reality show about ten people thrown together in a warehouse after a simulated epidemic has destroyed civilization; and *The 100*, set ninety-seven years after civilization has been destroyed by nuclear war, when one hundred juvenile survivors are sent back in a spaceship to repopulate Earth.

Cinema and television are particularly well-suited for plumbing our collective cultural anxieties and dreams of disaster, cultivating the ruin imaginary as we contemplate the obliteration of the world in the safety of darkened theaters or our own living rooms. Just as the explosion of cinematic fantasies of global disaster in the form of postwar sci-fi thrillers was a response to the real effects of nuclear incineration, the recent surge in zombie and disaster films and television responds to contemporaneous threats of catastrophe in an era when the state is widely perceived as either corrupt or unable to protect and sustain its populations against any number of possible threats. The imagined economic and social collapse in these narratives consists of two key elements: wrecked

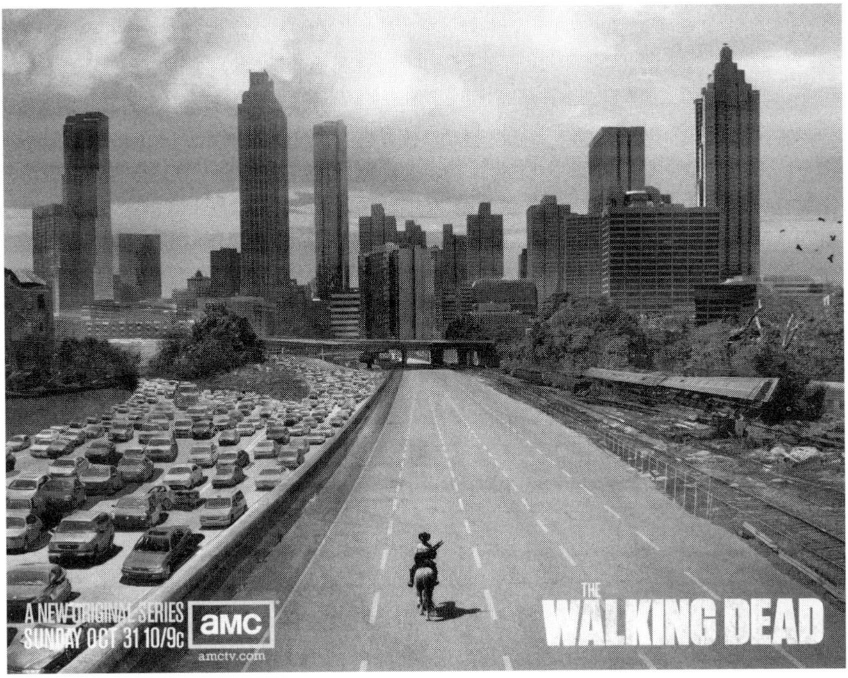

FIG. 33 *The Walking Dead*, AMC television series, 2008–present, poster.

urban environments and survivors who are reduced to the conditions of bare necessity. At the same time, the zombie has become the central alien figure in our culture.

Danny Boyle's film *28 Days Later* (2002) sparked the renaissance of the zombie genre following 9/11. The film opens with a man who wakes up from a coma in a London hospital to find that a raging viral pandemic has devastated all of England within a month. It suggests fears of AIDS, cholera, anthrax, avian and swine flus, and other biohazards. Central London is destroyed and deserted, evoking a whole population of such images, for which the imagery of downtown Detroit serves as the paradigmatic example. Indeed, the image of abandoned skyscrapers in the city center arguably has emerged as the quintessential urban disaster image, the central signifier of the end of progress and the ruin of modernity.

Similarly, the AMC television series *The Walking Dead*, which began in 2010—based on Robert Kirkman's 132-issue (and counting) comic book series *The Walking Dead*, which began in 2003—portrays a man who wakes up in a hospital to discover that an unexplained zombie apocalypse has occurred. He makes his way to Atlanta—also the home base for the Centers for Disease Control and Prevention—only to discover that the city has been deserted and overtaken by zombies (figure 33). Kirkman focuses on the moral and ethical quandaries of the postapocalyptic world as well as the characters' strategies for survival, which become struggles to maintain a sense of humanity in the wrecked and dangerous environment. Wildly popular, *The Walking Dead* became the most-watched program on television, with 12.9 million viewers for the 2013 season three finale, which was topped by 16.1 million viewers for the 2013 season four premiere.

Marc Forster's *World War Z* (2013), inspired by the eponymous 2006 apocalyptic novel and bestseller by Max Brooks, begins with a family caught in a traffic jam during a terrifying zombie onslaught in Philadelphia that leads to panic and anarchy as the city is overrun. Later the film takes us to Jerusalem, where the Israelis have allowed the uninfected, including Palestinians, into the city, but joyful singing attracts the zombies outside the walls. They madly scramble atop each other until they form a giant anthill high enough to get over the wall and invade the city, pointedly demonstrating the ineffectiveness of walls in keeping out the other. Commenting on wall-building and the conflict between nation-state sovereignty and the processes of globalization, political theorist Wendy Brown asserts, "Rather than resurgent expressions of nation-state sovereignty, the new walls are icons of its erosion. While they may appear as hyperbolic tokens of such sovereignty, like all hyperbole, they reveal a tremulousness, vulnerability, dubiousness, or instability at the core of what they aim to express—qualities that are themselves antithetical to sovereignty and thus elements of its undoing."[13] The scene in Jerusalem is viewed from above as if from a television news helicopter, producing an image format that is easily mapped onto other scenes of recent mass political protests in countries across North Africa as well as countries such as Turkey, Greece, and Brazil. These dystopian film narratives therefore must be understood as critical responses to the contemporary anxiety of social unrest and economic decline coupled with a loss of confidence in progress and the state. By the time the zombie threat finally ends in *World War Z*, the scope of devastation and city ruination is massive, just as it is in countries such as Iraq and Syria today.

In addition to viral threats and the exigencies of basic survival, zombie films connect to a variety of political issues. George Romero's *Land of the Dead* (2005), set in Romero's hometown of Pittsburgh, for example, portrays the financial elite hoarding all remaining resources in the aftermath of a zombie apocalypse while trying to insulate themselves against both the zombies that have overtaken the devastated city and the living survivors that reside in a slum beneath the gleaming high-rise enclave of the wealthy. The enclave is called Fiddler's Green, bringing to mind Nero fiddling while Rome burned. Fiddler's Green is protected by barricaded bridges, electric fences, and armed guards with standing orders to shoot any intruder on sight. The zombies, however, eventually become tool users, picking up weapons, walking underwater to cross a river, and finally storming the citadel of power through determination

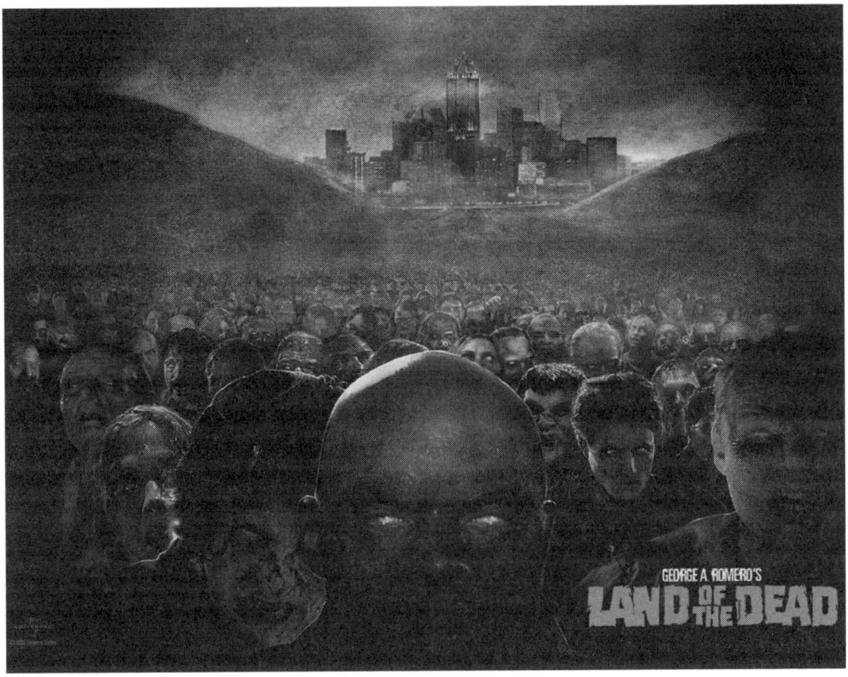

FIG. 34 *Land of the Dead*, directed by George Romero, 2005, poster.

and sheer force of numbers. Evoking the anxiety of immigrants crossing the Mexican border into the United States at a time when the government was proposing to build a border fence and deploy National Guard troops, Fiddler's Green becomes a metaphor for the United States itself, a paranoid xenophobe's dream of extreme security and a simultaneous critique of American immigration policy.[14]

Like other zombie films, *Land of the Dead* reiterates and reframes images of city ruination; it also connects postapocalyptic decay with the hoarding of wealth by the ruling minority and the forcible impoverishment of the majority. The signature image of *Land of the Dead* is the derelict landscape inhabited by the poor and the zombies set before the shining tower of the wealthy (figure 34). Like the poster for *The Walking Dead*, it evokes an image by Camilo José Vergara of Detroit's own desolate city landscape, with its vacant lots in the shadow of the Renaissance Center and the pre-Depression skyscrapers in its once-thriving downtown (figure 35). As the imagery of city ruination is reproduced in postapocalyptic narratives, its power is intensified by new patterns of connection to social issues such as class privilege, extreme inequality, immigration, and the security state.

Detroit ruination also evokes the inequalities of the developing world. In a typical example, veteran CBS correspondent Bob Simon, following a visit to

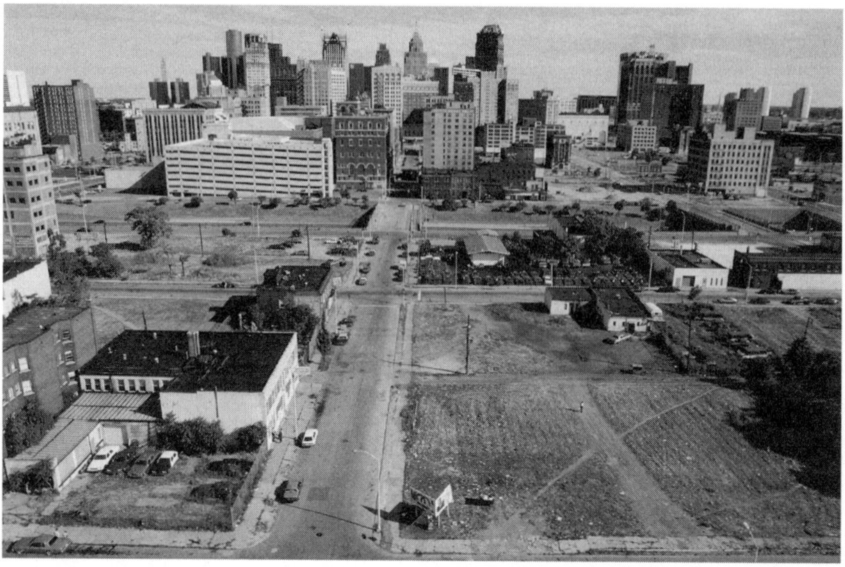

FIG. 35 Camilo José Vergara, *Downtown Detroit, 1991, View from Sibley Street down Park Avenue*, from *The New American Ghetto*, 1995. © Camilo José Vergara.

Detroit, compared it to Mogadishu, the impoverished and strife-torn capital of Somalia, a so-called failed state.[15] Recalling filmmaker Julien Temple's excited encounter with "street zombies" in an abandoned part of downtown Detroit when shooting *Requiem for Detroit?*, both responses underline Detroit's ongoing marginalization and isolation, a city both within and without the nation that resonates as easily with postapocalyptic film landscapes as it does with cities in poor developing countries ravaged by civil war. Both responses construct Detroit as a reigning metaphor for decline.

As the contradictions of capitalism have become steadily exacerbated over the last several decades, so has the figure of the zombie evolved in response to deepening anxieties. Zombies first appeared in modern form in George Romero's now classic 1968 film *Night of the Living Dead*, which started the flesh-eating form of the genre. Prior to this, zombies did not consume others. First appearing in Haitian folklore at the beginning of the twentieth century (although Central and West African sources have been postulated), zombies were thought to be the reanimated corpses of former slaves that were brought back from the dead to be enslaved again; they worked in the fields and were controlled by their masters, having no will of their own. In modern South Africa, anthropologists Jean Comaroff and John Comaroff show that fear of zombies of this nature has been produced by the extremes of joblessness juxtaposed with the great prosperity of the wealthy whose wealth seems to have no obvious source because it is based on market speculation and abstract financial instruments. This abstract source of wealth leads to the suspicion that the affluent employ magical means, embodied by the unseen labor of zombies, to produce their wealth.[16]

Romero popularized zombies as lumbering, awkward figures that sway from side to side as they walk and want to consume you. Since 1968, however, zombies have gathered strength and speed. As reimagined in *28 Days Later*, they run at high velocity and are violently aggressive. Moreover, the time to transition, once bitten, from living to undead has been greatly reduced. Whereas before, death occurred first and it took many hours for a corpse to reanimate as a zombie, in *28 Days Later* it takes only twenty seconds, with no intervening death state; in *World War Z*, it takes only twelve seconds. The zombie thus embodies the sudden transformation from a sustainable condition of life to a near instant loss of autonomy.

Romero's *Land of the Dead* also suggests, for the first time, the possibility of coexistence between the zombies and the living poor based on the essential sameness of the disfranchised survivors and the zombies. The zombies are loosely organized and led by Big Daddy, a black zombie who communicates with his fellow zombies through grunts and gestures. The zombies appear to be exhausted sources of value-producing labor, still recognizable by the clothing of their former day jobs, like Big Daddy himself, a former gas station attendant. During a run into the city for supplies, the protagonist, Riley, and his sometime rival, Cholo, offer a revealing exchange as they observe Big Daddy uselessly attempting to pump gas. "They're pretending to be alive," says Cholo. Riley replies, "Isn't that what we're doing? Pretending to be alive?" Romero begins to humanize the zombies, making them more sympathetic and complex characters with their own personalities and motivations. Kyle Bishop, a film scholar, observes that Romero is thus "encouraging audience identification with the very monsters he had formerly taught them to fear."[17] At some moments Romero uses close-ups to forge audience identification with Big Daddy when he howls to express his rage and grief; at other times Riley is visibly disgusted by the gratuitous slaughter of zombies or their abuse for entertainment purposes, recalling the abusive treatment of Arab and Muslim prisoners at Abu Ghraib prison by American troops in Iraq, a scandal that became public in 2004, only a year before the film's release.[18]

Kaufman, the head of the tenants' board of Fiddler's Green, could stand in for Nero, or any sovereign, while both the zombies and impoverished survivors become metaphors for the world's expendable populations.[19] Romero himself identified Kaufman as Donald Rumsfeld and the board as the Bush administration. Kaufman evokes Rumsfeld with his repeated assertions that he "won't negotiate with terrorists," meaning the ragged survivors struggling for concessions from the wealthy Kaufman.[20] After his downfall, the zombies are rendered equivalent to the survivors as Riley and Big Daddy exchange looks and Riley decides to leave the zombies alone and move on with his own group, establishing a mutual detente in a depressed and ruined world.

As Bishop argues, Romero gradually humanizes zombies in the films following *Night of the Living Dead*, including *Dawn of the Dead* (1978) and *Day of the Dead* (1985), culminating in *Land of the Dead*, because his overarching thesis is that humans and zombies are essentially the same.[21] Romero's films therefore must be understood as antiracist, anticapitalist parables that deliver social and cultural critiques. *Night of the Living Dead* addresses issues of patriarchy and the nuclear family; *Dawn of the Dead*, set in a mall, satirizes rampant consumerism; *Day of the Dead*, set in an underground bunker, takes on militarism and the abuses of technology; and *Land of the Dead* attacks the racist and oppressive security state that legitimizes itself as an enemy to terrorism.

Like Romero, Robert Kirkman creates a paradoxical equivalence between zombies and survivors in *The Walking Dead*. For a long period in both the comic books and the TV series, the protagonist, Rick Grimes, a former sheriff's deputy, along with the survivor group he leads, ironically secure their freedom by settling into a prison complex, the ultimate "gated community," while zombies roam freely in the surrounding cities and countryside. When Grimes learns early on from a scientist (who commits suicide) at the Centers for Disease Control that everyone is already infected and will turn into zombies when they die, whether or not they are bitten, he exclaims, "We *are* the walking dead!"[22] Even in satirical zombie films, or "zomedies," such as Edgar Wright's 2004 *Shaun of the Dead* (an homage to Romero's *Dawn of the Dead*), stumbling zombies become indistinguishable from living drunks, and Shaun even keeps his friend Ed, who has turned into a zombie, chained up in his garden shed so they can continue to play video games together after the British army has killed the remaining zombies.

The zombie and disaster genres, which operate in the future anterior, represent futures in which the contemporary era has been ruined for reasons that are always anchored in the viewer's present[23]—scarcity of resources, class, race, and ethnic hatred, unemployment, dispossession, viruses, and a wrecked environment. In this way postapocalyptic films deliberately slow down or halt any idea of progress and operate at the level of ideology critique.

Nationalism versus Globalization

The apocalyptic imagination has a long history as one of the oldest narrative forms, one that is well developed in the doctrines of Judaism, Christianity, and Islam. In the twentieth century, however, apocalyptic narratives became increasingly secular as well as increasingly dystopian. Although culturally pervasive, the apocalyptic imagination has shifted over the course of the last century from faith in human survival and utopian promise to a pessimistic view of humanity and its prospects that instead sees humanity's future as one of violence, disintegration, and collapse. Mervyn Bendle, a scholar of religion, suggests that this shift occurred as a result of global events, especially the horrors of World War I, and worsened after the genocides of World War II, becoming more prominent in the 1990s as the millennium approached. That event set off exaggerated concerns about the alleged "Year 2000" (Y2K) computer problem and prompted the FBI to establish a domestic terrorism task force that led to the debacle of the FBI siege on the Branch Davidian compound near Waco, Texas, killing seventy-four cult members in 1993, and helping to radicalize extreme right-wing groups in the nation. One of their members, Timothy McVeigh, blew up a federal government building in Oklahoma City two years later. The 2001 attacks on the World Trade Center and Pentagon only accelerated this darkening apocalyptic imagination.[24]

Yet there have been many horrific wars, plagues, and catastrophic environmental events across the centuries that did not trigger such a lasting change in perspective. This fact suggests that more is at stake in the accelerated shift from utopian to dystopian apocalyptic fantasies than the wars and traumatic events of the last century, although these certainly contributed to the loss of faith in the Enlightenment ideals of progress and rationality. We must also look to the more fundamental reorganization of the global capitalist system that has gradually subverted and destabilized the very foundations of modern society. It seems no coincidence that the popularity of vampires and Gothic horror coincided with the advent of the Industrial Revolution in the late eighteenth and early nineteenth centuries, which induced a fear of technological monstrosity—even Karl Marx used the language of vampires to describe the bloodsucking effects of capitalism. Similarly, the mainstream popularity of zombies today coincides with the globalization of capitalism and deindustrial decline in the traditional manufacturing centers with its attendant impoverishment of millions of people. Industrialization and deindustrialization bookend the modern period; the vampire and the zombie are the figures of excess that embody the fears and anxieties induced by these seismic economic and social transformations. Although both the vampire and the zombie are undead, the aristocratic vampire is the figure that enslaves while the zombie has come to represent the modern equivalent of the enslaved: the socially expendable laborer, the migrant, the refugee, the asylum seeker, the impoverished, the unemployed, the productively "useless"—that is, the figure without autonomy who is consigned to a biopolitical existence.

Indeed, the zombie may be understood as the natural victim of the vampire. This notion is explicitly realized in Jim Jarmusch's *Only Lovers Left Alive* (2014). The film's sophisticated, centuries-old vampire lovers, Adam and Eve, who obtain their sanguinary nourishment from medical professionals, live in separate cities until Eve arrives from Tangier to rescue Adam, a reclusive rock musician, from profound depression. Adam lives in Detroit, occupying a rundown Victorian house in a deserted neighborhood.[25] His complaint is that the "zombies" have ruined the world, and by zombies he means ordinary humans. Adam is particularly depressed by the dismissive treatment of great scientists in their day, such as Galileo, Einstein, Tesla, the continuing controversy over Darwin, and, by extension, the continuing rejection of scientific rationality. Adam and Eve take nocturnal drives (in a vintage Jaguar) down empty streets to gaze at the darkly evocative abandoned houses, open spaces, and derelict factories of the city. They visit the Michigan Theater while Adam explains that it once was the site of Ford's invention of the original prototype for the automobile and then a grand movie theater before becoming a desolate parking garage; they dispose of a body, sucked dry by Eve's bratty younger sister, into an acid pool at the Packard Plant, understood as the best place to dump corpses in Detroit, just as the Thames River once was when Adam and Eve lived in London in another century. "Everyone has left," says Adam gloomily, while Eve insists that because it has water, Detroit will come back when the South gets too hot, predicating the city's speculative revival on the destructive effects of global warming. Detroit becomes a metaphor for everything grand the world once was as well as the ruination for which it is now headed. Adam and Eve retreat to Tangier only to find that their old vampire friend, a contact source for blood, is dying due to blood contamination, another "zombie" atrocity. As desperation and addiction withdrawal set in, they return to their old bloodsucking ways, preparing to prey upon a pair of young lovers, two "zombies" that are helpless before their approach. We might read this as the destructive imperative of capital despite the best intentions of individuals.

The Industrial Revolution (and the rise of the vampire) coincided with the establishment of the modern nation-state. Today, nationalism conflicts with globalization (and the rise of the zombie), which depends on free trade on a global scale and the unconstrained circulation of people, capital, and goods. This perceived need for unrestrained global circulation suggests that nation-states are becoming obsolete, constituting an unresolved contradiction between globalization and nationalism. As the free flow of people, capital, and goods occurs, the state nonetheless tries to keep out migrants, or locks them into detention camps and centers. "'Illegality,'" notes sociologist Willem Schinkel, "a label attached to a state of *being* instead of a state of *acting*, becomes the basis of incarceration and forced repatriation."[26] Migrants are effectively turned into zombies by a state that has become deindustrialized and thus incarcerates potential workers seeking employment. "Yet," writes

Schinkel, "the fact remains that 'being illegal' is not a *legal* category, and incarcerated irregular immigrants are not convicted of a crime."[27] The state thus casts the migrant into a liminal category, which is neither criminal nor legal but merely a state of bare life, exposing the problem of citizenship in a globalized world and creating pressure for universal citizenship. This idea is resisted precisely because it compromises the traditional notion of the nation-state and the control of national subjects that citizenship is meant to secure, even as the foundations for citizenship continue to erode.[28] The wandering zombie, who remains animate and hungry, therefore threatens to overwhelm the "legitimate" citizens of the nation-state, highlighting the central contradiction of contemporary capitalism: the clash between nationalism and globalization. Alarmingly, although citizenship has been considered a right that cannot be taken away, citizenship is also being stripped from citizens because of their actions even if it leaves them stateless.[29]

Zombies are thus associated with rapidly changing conditions of work under capitalism, generated by the rise of neoliberalism on a global scale that has greatly intensified market competition and created vast migrant populations. These peripatetic immigrants in search of employment are automatically coded as "nonwhite" and thereby racialized and demonized. Zombies are a potent metaphor for the new "nonstandard" laborers, the migrants who travel in "hordes," "stream across borders," who threaten to "flood" and overwhelm the nation. Indeed, the same language is used for both zombies and migrants.[30] Zombies are those who have lost control over their own labor power, who are stateless and rightless. Noting that the number of displaced peoples and refugees in the last few decades has increased exponentially while the 9/11 attacks further increased anxieties over border protection, cultural critic Jon Stratton asserts, "Zombies provide a monster for our time because they express our anxieties over the relationship between bare life and the modern state."[31]

Alfonso Cuarón's film *Children of Men* (2006), set in 2027, illuminates the problem of migrants. Although ostensibly concerned with global infertility, the film constructs Britain as overrun with racialized asylum-seekers who are placed in cages on the streets and into a massive detention camp. The film critically pictures the inhumane treatment of and hostility toward large displaced populations. The Roma today are another example of a despised and rightless population who are regarded as an invasive species and not legitimate citizens. Persecuted for centuries, they have been attacked across Europe, where they make up the largest and one of the most oppressed minorities, estimated at a population of ten million to twelve million. Excluded from employment and housing, they are made to live in abysmal and unsanitary conditions while being targeted as scapegoats for the worsening economic crisis and rising unemployment. In Greece, they have been falsely accused of stealing children; in France, where they are forced to live in squalid encampments on the outskirts of Paris, the French interior minister Manuel Valls declared that the Roma were incapable of "integrating" into a civilized society and called for their forcible removal. As the Trotskyist newspaper *Workers Vanguard* observes, "The truth is that decaying capitalism is incapable of 'integrating' the Roma and all the more so in periods of crisis. The French state, including its PCF [French Communist Party] mayors, chases them from one shantytown to another and then uses the pretext that they are not official residents to refuse to enroll the children in school."[32]

Neill Blomkamp's film *Elysium* (2013), set in 2154, imagines the entire Earth as a squalid encampment for a rightless and rigidly policed population. The wealthy live on a different planet, a luxurious man-made space station called Elysium, with access to private medical machines and instant cures, while everyone else lives on an overpopulated and ruined Earth inundated by poverty and crime. Those on Earth are forcibly kept from emigrating to Elysium. When asked whether the film revealed his view of the future, Blomkamp responded, "No, no, no. This isn't science fiction. This is today. This is now."[33] In *The Already Dead*, Eric Cazdyn suggests that as the ideologies of democracy and equality continue to weaken, the existing harsh realities will become even more transparent and a global two-tier system of preemptive medicine will grow even stronger in which only those who can afford to pay for life-saving care will receive it.[34] The United States today already has the highest first-day infant mortality death rate among all industrialized countries, with more than double the incidence for black women than white women.[35]

The fear evoked by zombies of being overwhelmed and consumed by alien others thus suggests the nature of contemporary zombies, who turned cannibalistic as post–World War II deindustrialization accelerated and the globalization of capital created vast unemployed, disfranchised, and migrant populations. These migrants, often disconnected from their families, place, and cultural life and community, are feared, despised, and distrusted by resident populations, who feel increasingly threatened by a similar fate.

The Zombie as Racialized Other

The slaughter of film zombies, justified as defense of the species, gives rise to killing sprees of unbridled violence that may be seen as a metaphor for colonial violence, activating a state of exception, in Giorgio Agamben's terms, that allows for the elimination of whole categories of people. Cultural critic Gerry Canavan suggests that the racialized nature of the zombie and the sense of justified violence that zombies unleash are perhaps most clearly seen in the real-world analogies of the black victims of Hurricane Katrina in 2005 and the destructive earthquake in Haiti in 2010.[36]

When isolated doctors and nurses at Memorial Medical Center in New Orleans came to believe that "crazy black people who think they've been oppressed for all these years by white people" would storm the hospital looking for drugs, or raping people, they began refusing treatment to select patients to conserve resources and deliberately euthanized as many as twenty-four people.[37] Similarly, at the Danziger Bridge in New Orleans, two black people were killed and four wounded when they were shot by five police officers who then invented a cover story to explain opening fire with assault rifles on an unarmed family looking for food and water. A New Orleans Federal Court jury convicted the five officers of myriad counts in 2011, including the deprivation of civil rights (however, citing prosecutorial misconduct on the part of federal lawyers who made anonymous comments online, a New Orleans judge threw out the convictions in 2013 and granted a new trial). In both cases the black victims effectively became zombies, conjuring "racial panic" and the conviction that they needed to be actively eliminated, thereby instantiating historical and ongoing racist and colonial violence.[38]

Likewise, Haitians were immediately consigned to a state of exception by white authorities following the earthquake, which is to say, Haitian life, even under such dire circumstances, was seen as threatening, untrustworthy, and even undeserving of life. As a result, the U.S. military, which took control of the international aid effort, established as its first priority its own security, bringing in thousands of troops to secure the island while diverting international aid flights and before allowing any food drops from the air. As Ben Ehrenreich reported on Slate.com, the U.S. military

> built a wall around itself, commandeering the Port-au-Prince airport and constructing a mini-Green Zone. While thousands of tons of desperately needed food, water, and medical supplies piled up behind the airport fences—and thousands of corpses piled up outside them—Defense Secretary Robert Gates ruled out the possibility of using American aircraft to airdrop supplies: "An airdrop is simply going to lead to riots," he said. The military's first priority was to build a "structure for distribution" and "to provide security." (Four days and many deaths later, the United States began airdropping aid.)[39]

Canavan observes that this is what we do when zombies strike, even though "outside the walls there are only other people just like us."[40] The zombie is always the racialized other, the outcast, the walled-off, the displaced, the one who is excluded, left to die or killed outright.

In Madison, Wisconsin, during the demonstrations against Gov. Scott Walker's bill limiting bargaining rights for most of the state's unions, one of the ways protesters chose to show their opposition was to dress as zombies. This masquerade suggests both their perceived sense of delegitimization as workers and the threat to their autonomy that deunionization represented. The zombie as a figure of protest demonstrates that the icons of the ruin imaginary can be mobilized to produce political critique and protest. As the racialized other in a state of exception and a figure of exhausted value-producing labor, the zombie is emblematic of what we fear becoming.

From the perspective of the state, disempowered migrants differ only in degree from citizens who are chronically unemployed or underemployed. The ruling elites view the poor with contempt, seeing them as relentlessly consuming resources rather than producing wealth and contributing to the state, a view that defines the ethos of neoliberal capitalism. Mitt Romney clearly articulated this perspective during the 2012 U.S. presidential election when he was secretly recorded at a fundraising dinner making the following speech:

> There are 47 percent of the people who will vote for the president [Obama] no matter what. All right, there are 47 percent who are with him, who are dependent upon government, who believe that they are victims, who believe that government has a responsibility to care for them, who believe that they are entitled to health care, to food, to housing, to you name it. That's an entitlement. And the government should give it to them. And they will vote for this president no matter what. And I mean, the president starts off with 48, 49, 48—he starts off with a huge number. These are people who pay no income tax. Forty-seven percent of Americans pay no income tax. So our message of low taxes doesn't connect. And he'll be out there talking about tax cuts for the rich. I mean that's what they sell every four years. And so my job is not to worry about those people—I'll never convince them that they should take personal responsibility and care for their lives.[41]

There is no ambiguity here: food, housing, health care are all regarded as "entitlements" for which Romney and the corporate capitalists he represents see themselves as bearing no responsibility. Rather than looking to the government to support the population, corporate capitalists believe that *they* should be supported by the nation's citizens. In particular, they believe they should not have to pay taxes because they have taken "personal responsibility" for their lives and should be able to keep the profits they have earned for themselves. What is left out of view is the direct relationship between the impoverishment of the majority and the wealth of the minority, not to mention the basic democratic principles of a society organized for the maximum benefit of all its members. Instead the scions of capital today regard the "unproductive" as an "alien-nation" who are "entitled" to exactly nothing, while the impoverished and downwardly mobile sink further into despair and dark visions of the future. In the neoliberal state, where rights are dependent on one's economic worth and contribution to the welfare of the state, the more menial, humiliating, and alienating the form of labor, the higher the rate of zombification and loss of autonomy.

Z World Detroit and Doomsday Preppers

Perhaps it was only a matter of time before zombies attempted to lay claim to Detroit, haunted as it is by the specter of apocalyptic decline. In 2012 Detroit-area native Mark Siwak proposed the creation of Z World Detroit, a zombie theme park that would colonize two hundred acres of abandoned city land and derelict buildings. Throughout the night, zombies would chase paying customers, who, if caught, would also become the walking dead and help chase others. Offered as a way of revitalizing the city through entertainment and by creating jobs, Siwak attempted to raise the necessary funds to open Z World Detroit on the website Indiegogo. Atlanta, the initial setting for *The Walking Dead*, already has a zombie theme park on a smaller scale. Participants at Atlanta Zombie Apocalypse are given a paintball gun and enter a dark motel where they are chased by zombies, run up and down stairs, in and out of buildings and through woods, equivalent to about three city blocks. The Zombie Apocalypse website entices potential participants with promises to scare them witless: "You will be terrified, you will run for your life, you will feel like you are living in the zombie apocalypse as you play a role to survive. Will you make it? People have had heart attacks! Soiled their pants! Took the chicken exit after the first room! What will you do when the zombies come for you?"[42] The terror, safely circumscribed, is the appeal.

Siwak's proposal for Z World Detroit did not receive sufficient funding to be realized, and city leaders opposed the idea in any case. Perhaps they feared that turning two hundred acres into a permanent zombie theme park, even if successful as an entrepreneurial venture, would openly identify Detroit as an expendable symbol of a decaying capitalist metropolis, a zombie city that could no longer be revived in the ways that city leaders, business owners, and venture capitalists would like to imagine. Nonetheless, "zombie walks," in which participants dress as zombies, often with elaborate makeup, have become hugely popular, including World Zombie Day Walk against Hunger in Detroit and its suburbs of Royal Oak and Ferndale, which has taken place annually since 2007 (figure 36).[43] Zombie "fun runs," races, and chases are popular across North America. In July 2013, 750 zombies chased 7,500 runners over a three-mile obstacle course on a Christmas tree farm in Medford, New Jersey, during a Run for Your Lives zombie-themed race. It began as a one-time event in 2011 in a Baltimore suburb and attracted 12,000 people from around the world. Run for Your Lives hosted twenty-two events in 2013 in the United States and Canada, while the rival Zombie Run hosted sixteen events.[44] Just as the ongoing crisis of poverty extends well beyond the United States to encompass

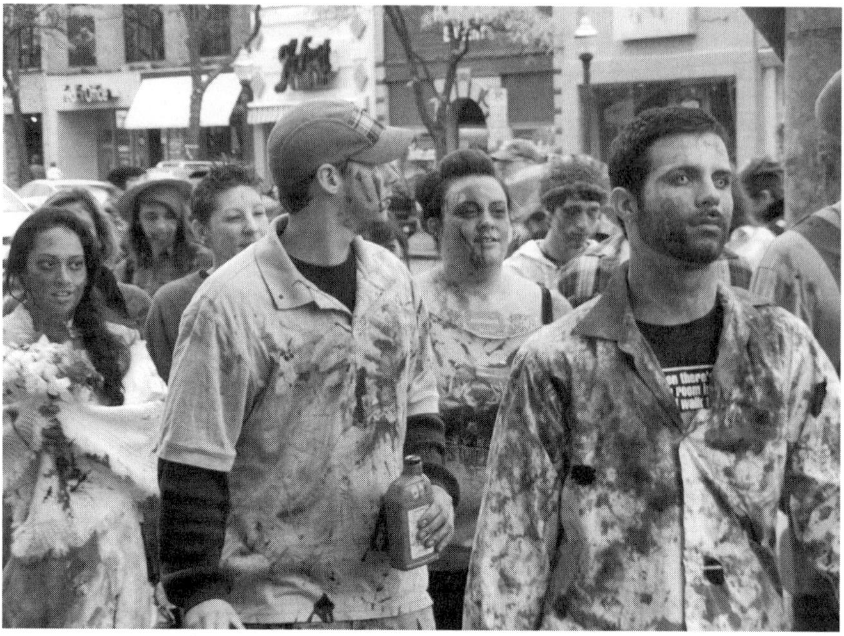

FIG. 36 Zombie Walk Detroit, 2012. Courtesy DeathByZombie.com.

the globe, zombie walks, races, and chases now take place throughout the world in cities such as Rio de Janeiro, Singapore, Brisbane, Nottingham, Dublin, and Santiago.

Two seasons of a History channel series, *Life after People* (2009–10), speculated about what would happen to the environment after human extinction. No longer indulging the fantasy of a small band of survivors who manage against all odds, the series explores the question, "What would happen if every human being on Earth were to suddenly vanish?" The two-hour premiere in 2008, including footage of Detroit's Packard Plant, was the most-watched program ever on the History channel.[45] Tapping into zombie mania and survivalist fantasies, the Centers for Disease Control produced *Zombie Preparedness 101*, a comic book on how to prepare for zombie attack, which coincides with preparedness for natural disasters. Zombie videogames bring in $2.5 billion in annual sales. *Resident Evil*, for example, originally released for Sony PlayStation in 1996, sold 25 million units by 2004 and inspired the eponymous film, the fiftieth-highest-grossing film globally, which was followed by two sequels. The *Resident Evil* media franchise, which also includes comic books, novels, and action figures, is based on scenarios of survival horror produced by recurrent outbreaks of zombies and other monsters caused by the release of an artificially created virus as a biological weapon. In literature, Seth

Grahame-Smith's bestseller *Pride and Prejudice and Zombies* introduces zombies into Jane Austen's 1813 novel.[46]

Fears of losing economic autonomy and independence perhaps most affect the young at the beginning of their productive lives, making them the biggest fans of the zombie genre, which mitigates the anxieties of bare life while aestheticizing the apocalyptic. But people of all ages are apprehensive about the end times, partly in response to events such as 9/11 and Hurricane Katrina. All over the nation, disaster "preppers" prepare for the collapse of civilization with "bug-out bags" containing basic survival gear such as compasses, iodine pills, and digital road maps as well as items such as dehydrated lentils, magnesium fire starters, and rat traps (for catching and eating). The massive flooding and destruction of Hurricane Sandy on the eastern coast of the United States in 2012 attracted new recruits to what has become known as the Prepper movement.[47] Preppers are unexpectedly diverse, including, according to the *New York Times*, "doctors, doormen, charter school executives, subway conductors, advertising writers, and happily married couples from the Bronx," and the movement is rapidly growing.[48] The National Geographic Channel premiered the reality series *Doomsday Preppers* in 2012, which features people across the country extensively preparing for the end times, building hideouts and arks, storing provisions, creating perimeter security systems, and explaining their thinking as they go. At the end of each program, the preppers' efforts are rated by the program's experts, and their doomsday postulations are contextualized with statistics (that often undermine their apocalyptic assumptions). *Doomsday Preppers* is the most-watched series and highest-rated show in the history of the National Geographic Channel, garnering an audience that is 60 percent male with an average age of forty-four.[49]

As with other apocalyptic narratives, preppers tend to regard scientists and government leaders as corrupt or unreliable and ineffective, instead supporting the ideology of heavily armed survivalism promoted by figures such as Wayne LaPierre, the National Rifle Association executive vice president. LaPierre is the man who chillingly proposed putting armed guards in elementary schools as a way to protect children from mass shooters after the Newtown, Connecticut, school massacre; he also urges the accumulation of arms by civilians to facilitate a quick transition to a survivalist mentality in the event of social breakdown.[50]

Contemporary apocalyptic anxiety may be understood as being connected to the violence at the core of capitalism itself. The fact that the modern nation cannot exist without violence stands in direct conflict with the basic narrative of the state as seeking peaceable coexistence with others, a comforting fiction that obscures the nature of the state as perpetually militarized and focused on security and surveillance in order to protect the wealthy ruling elite. The global ruin imaginary may be understood as a response to global zombification, and as a pessimistic product of what British theorist Mark Fisher calls "capitalist realism." Echoing Fredric Jameson, Fisher defines capitalist realism as "the widespread sense that not only is capitalism the only viable political and economic system, but also that it is now impossible even to *imagine* a coherent alternative to it."[51]

And yet, by depicting our technologically advanced civilization in states of ruination and decay, postapocalyptic narratives render our own society as other and encourage us to ask whether the empire of capital represents lasting progress or a road to decline—just as Detroit once represented the industrial powerhouse of the nation and now stands for an abstract postapocalyptic elsewhere. Zombie and disaster films exemplify and instantiate the fear of a dystopian futurity. Yet even as they seek to mitigate that fear by rendering the terror pleasurable, they also offer a radical critique of the status quo and the violence at its core, exploring the conditions of decline amid the debris of late capitalism.

As real-world conditions continue to deteriorate, so have the emergent behaviors of zombies in their postapocalyptic worlds evolved in response. Through their multiplying numbers, accelerating speed, and development of personality, zombies paradoxically are becoming more powerful, suggesting the possibility of rebellion. This combative potential harkens back to the Haitian origins of zombies and the late-nineteenth-century Haitian Revolution in which slaves successfully revolted against their French colonial masters and established a republic. Their battle cry was said to be, "We have no mother, no child; what is death?"[52] Zombies become metaphors for the disfranchised masses that have nothing to lose and a world to gain. The destruction of the habitable environment and the dire conditions of bare life that characterize global ruin and its representation may be mobilized to serve emergent protest movements and anticapitalist struggles that would ultimately create a planned economy based on social need, not profit.

Conclusion

Your Town Tomorrow

The zombie metaphor not only suggests the dispossessed victims of capitalism but also evokes the idea of the zombie city that has been consumed and abandoned as a shell of its former self. As the largest deteriorating former urban manufacturing center, Detroit is the paradigmatic zombie city while the state of "zombism" becomes the condition that awaits us all when the state withdraws its protection from those it no longer considers contributing citizens. In the neoliberal version of the state, where rights are dependent on what people can offer to the state's economic well-being, rather than vice-versa, the lost protection of the state means vastly inadequate living conditions and the most menial and unprotected forms of labor in cities that are divested of many of their social services and left to their own devices. Detroit continues to fail—notwithstanding the resilience and determination of the local population, the neighborhood cleanup efforts, the demolition of blighted houses, the thriving arts and culture, the creative interventions and urban farms, or the downtown renewal efforts—because there are as yet no massive employment programs, civic rebuilding programs, mass transportation programs, and concrete plans for regionalizing the economy. Often selected as the backdrop for dystopian Hollywood movies and crime films, Detroit is always-already regarded as a racialized and zombified city that is foreign to the host body of the nation, an "alien-nation" within. This suggestion of a zombie city due to its "otherness" implicitly blames the failure of the city on itself, scapegoating the victims of decades of class and race oppression.

Yet Detroit occupies a contradictory position in the ruin imaginary. Although it is the quintessential ruined city because of the scope and scale of its industrial, civic, and residential abandonment as well as the high rates of unemployment and poverty, these are in evidence in many other declining towns and cities as well. Detroit, however, is also marginalized and isolated as a failing *black* city in a country where African Americans are less than 13 percent of the total population. According to the 2010 Census, blacks comprised 12.3 percent of the total population, or forty million people, down from 14.8 percent in 2000. The two popular versions of Detroit suggest either that the city symbolizes the historical inevitability of industrial decline in the traditional manufacturing centers, or that it represents a singular example of a poor racialized city with only itself to blame for its bankrupt conditions. These two accounts work well together in exempting the auto companies from responsibility for industrial disinvestment and deunionization, the state for its corporate support at the expense of the city population, and the policies of racial discrimination at the city, state, and federal levels that all helped foster the abandonment and decline of Detroit and continue to victimize the poor and black population. At the same time, the popular explanations of inevitability and local financial recklessness serve as disciplinary warnings about future fiscal austerities for towns and cities across the nation.

In Michigan, "emergency management" has become a norm in many cities with large black populations, including Allen Park, Flint, Hamtramck, and Lincoln Park, while Benton Harbor, Ecorse, and Pontiac are in receivership and transitioning to a nine-member financial advisory board that has the power to vacate collective bargaining agreements once contracts have expired. Pontiac, which was placed under an emergency manager (EM) in 2009, experienced extensive privatization of services before emergency management ended in 2013, while EMs ran Highland Park from 2001 to 2009 and its status is again under review. Inkster, Royal Oak Township, and River Rouge operate under a consent agreement, which stops short of an EM but places city control under a financial advisory board.[1] In addition, Detroit Public Schools, Muskegon Heights School District, and Highland Park School District are all under emergency management, while Benton Harbor schools are under review. With Kevyn Orr's appointment as EM in Detroit, about half of the state's black population, which makes up 14 percent of the state's total population, is under emergency financial control and deprived of democratically elected leadership.[2] In a gesture of protest, the liberal think tank Michigan Forward and the Detroit branch of the NAACP sent a letter to Gov. Rick Snyder asserting that the emergency manager law represents "a clear example of voter disenfranchisement."[3]

Notwithstanding the specificity of its racial demographics and history, Detroit has become only the most extreme example of what is happening in the nation's declining cities, which are suffering the effects of capitalist disinvestment and are slowly "erasing" themselves. A Brookings Institution study found that from 2000 to 2010, the number of vacant houses in the country increased by 44 percent, adding 4.5 million abandoned homes to the national count, while a report from the University of California at Berkeley found that over the past fifteen years, 130 cities, mostly with smaller populations, have dissolved themselves entirely. As cities decline, instead of planning based on growth and expansion, planning is based on "ungrowth," a negative calculation premised on disinvestment patterns that help determine what should be saved and what should be torn down or allowed to return to forest and meadow.[4] Large-scale urban demolition is under way in cities such as Baltimore, Philadelphia, Cleveland, Cincinnati, St. Louis, and Buffalo. Many city governments are searching for ways to ameliorate the devastating effects of poverty and unemployment while others, including large cities such as Chicago and Los Angeles, are watching Detroit's bankruptcy proceedings to see if they, too, can cut pensions for retired public workers. As former Detroit mayor Coleman Young wrote in his 1994 autobiography, "In the evolutionary urban order, Detroit today has always been your town tomorrow."[5]

In response to worsening conditions, the federal government is "militarizing" social science to develop "operational tools" that target peaceful activists and protest movements. Nafeez Ahmed, an international security journalist and academic, shows that the U.S. Department of Defense is preparing for mass civil breakdown by funding a variety of university research programs with millions of dollars through the "Minerva Research Initiative." It was established in 2008, the year of the global financial meltdown. One such program at the University of Washington is meant to determine how to "uncover the conditions under which political movements aimed at large-scale political and economic change originate," a project that covers fifty-eight countries.[6] Other projects "gauge the risk of civil unrest due to climate change" (University of Maryland) or produce "counter-radical Muslim discourse" (Arizona State University). The militarization of the social sciences in order to counteract grassroots movements is grounded in the view that popular unrest is far more dangerous than the conditions that give rise to that unrest. As Ahmed writes, "In their unswerving mission to defend an increasingly unpopular global system serving the interests of a tiny minority, security agencies have no qualms about painting the rest of us as potential terrorists."[7] This comes on top of the militarization of the police in towns across America since September 2001, as vividly seen in the St. Louis suburb of Ferguson in August 2014. Following the police killing of Michael Brown, an unarmed eighteen-year-old black teenager, police responded to unarmed protesters with armored vehicles, assault rifles, tear gas, and rubber bullets. This show of military-style force only further inflamed local and national outrage, making news around the world, before escalating to the arrival of the actual military in the form of the National Guard in the majority-black city.

When the Los Angeles 2020 Commission presented a report that catalogued the failings and decline of Los Angeles—widespread poverty, job stagnation, huge debt, paralyzing traffic—some civic leaders grew incensed, not because they disputed the facts but because articulating them publicly represented a blow to the city's image. Russell Goldsmith, president of City National Bank in Los Angeles, called the description of the city "an unfortunate characterization" that painted "an unduly negative picture." In response, one of the report's authors observed, "If the report is seriously sobering, maybe it's because the facts are seriously sobering."[8]

Denial of the systemic causes of poverty and inequality is rampant. Charles Blow reports that in a recent NBC News / *Wall Street Journal* Poll, the primary cause for the continuing poverty crisis was understood as "too much welfare that prevents initiative," blaming welfare for creating poverty rather than for attempting to alleviate its worst effects.[9] In line with this perspective, Congress passed a farm bill that cut down the food stamp program at a time when more Americans than ever depend upon it. A report by the United States Conference of Mayors in December 2013 found that all but four of twenty-five cities surveyed reported increases in requests for emergency food aid since 2011, and that they expected those requests to increase further. The report also found increases in homelessness and expected homelessness to increase further. The idea that capitalist economies can expand forever is not only deeply mistaken but also ignores the fact that a sharp decline in living standards and an end to economic growth has already occurred in the United States and other advanced economies. As liberal economist Stephen King observes, "We are reaching the end times for Western affluence. . . . Policy makers simply pray for a strong recovery. They opt for the illusion because the reality is too bleak to bear. But as the current fiscal crisis demonstrates, facing the pain will not be easy. And the waking up from our collective illusions has barely begun."[10] Blaming the victim is nonetheless a favorite tactic of the ruling elites that regard poverty, hunger, homelessness, and joblessness for millions of people as problems resulting from personal irresponsibility to be solved individually. The poor are reviled and distrusted in the same way as undocumented immigrants. They may as well be zombies.

The hegemony of globalized capitalism and the failures of Stalinist states should not paralyze or blind us to the continuing need for an egalitarian alternative based on need and not profit. Relying on the most extensive income and wealth datasets ever compiled, economist Thomas Piketty, in his study of inequality, demonstrates that wealth concentration is inherent to capitalism; not only do the rich get much richer while the poor get much poorer but we are rapidly moving toward a society of "patrimonial capitalism" on a global scale, especially in the United States—that is, a society run by an oligarchy based on inherited wealth. In other words, capitalism's long history supports widening inequality, which has dire consequences for democracy and social justice. Piketty's book has become a best seller because it hits a raw nerve, codifying and documenting with a raft of statistics what many already know and fear: that the American dream of greater equality and widening opportunity without the burden of oppressive class distinctions is largely a myth.

Yet Piketty rejects a solution that appropriates private property and does away with the capitalist market, instead suggesting that capitalism and continuing wealth inequality might be reformed through a progressive global tax on wealth requiring a high level of global cooperation. He admits this would be a utopian solution. It would certainly be rejected by the elite that controls the vast majority of the world's wealth and wields global political power. As history shows, this is not a class that can be morally persuaded. In his critique of Piketty's book, David Harvey observes that while Piketty shows statistically that "capital has tended throughout its history to produce ever-greater levels of inequality," this was also Marx's conclusion at the end of volume 1 of *Capital.* But Piketty is no Marxist and has declared himself "very much in favour of private property and private capitalism."[11] His analysis, moreover, is unable to account for historically specific trends and events and cannot explain, for example, the crash of 2008 or "help us understand why growth is currently so sluggish in the U.S. as opposed to China and why Europe is locked down in a politics of austerity and an economy of stagnation."[12] Harvey also points out a central difficulty with Piketty's argument, which is that it rests on a mistaken definition of capital as wealth: "Capital is a process not a thing. It is a process of circulation in which money is used to make more money often, but not exclusively, through the exploitation of labor power."[13] Harvey also asserts the need for an "alternative economic engine." Following Marx, he writes, "Capitalism will never fall on its own. It will have to be pushed. The accumulation of capital will never cease. It will have to be stopped. The capitalist class will never willingly surrender its power. It will have to be dispossessed."[14]

By evoking the very fears they mean to pacify, ruin images make visible our continuing fall into widening inequality and decline. Whether lamenting Detroit's descent into a deindustrialized wasteland, engaging in romanticized reveries on the struggles between nature and culture, suggesting alternative utopian futures, or imagining survival in postapocalyptic landscapes that return to a preindustrial past, the densifying network of ruin images offers visions of a global capitalism that is unable to sustain the overwhelming majority of the world's population. The social and cultural power of this image network intensifies as connections to social and political issues multiply, whether focusing on the effects of war, climate change, environmental catastrophe, viruses, and biohazards, or on deindustrialization, joblessness, homelessness, access to health care, food insecurity, and all the other devastating effects of capitalist globalization and worsening inequality. Ruin imagery thus helps open up the space for anticapitalist struggle that would begin with basic demands for adequate housing and city services and ultimately reorganize economic and social relations to serve the needs of everyone, protect the environment, and make rational use of the earth's resources.

Once we apprehend our own society heading toward catastrophe, it is impossible to make an optimistic claim for lasting progress and rationality. The contradictions embodied by ruin imagery therefore raise different possibilities. We may indulge in the appeal of ruins as a form of decadent consciousness, which aestheticizes our own decline, and enjoy the liberating sensual materiality of ruins, the haunting ambiguity of time, the sense of mythic mystery, the access to unregulated space, and the seductive beauty of decay. Yet even as ruin imagery domesticates the terror of decline and makes it pleasurable, it is difficult to ignore the downward spiral toward greater deprivation, dispossession, and suffering it represents. The landscapes of ruin across the nation and around the world compel us to recognize that the story of Detroit is not only an exemplary story but also the evolving story of all declining cities and the entire ecosystem. As Harvey writes, "Capital cannot help but privatize, commodify, monetize and commercialize all those aspects of nature that it possibly can. Only in this way can it increasingly absorb nature into itself to become a form of capital—an accumulation strategy—all the way down into our DNA."[15] While Detroit's history is inflected by extensive patterns of racial discrimination, the destructive effects of industrial disinvestment and globalization in the perpetual drive for profit have impoverished people everywhere. The imagery of ruination challenges us to imagine a society that would eliminate the bankruptcy of cities and the impoverishment of their inhabitants, and to ask how ruin imagery might be harnessed to an emancipatory struggle that would eliminate the constant drive for accumulation, privatization, commodification, and monetization—for to look at Detroit's beautiful terrible ruins and talk about its decline is to talk about everything that is wrong with global capitalism today.

Notes

Introduction: Modernity in Ruins

1 Adam Gopnik, "Stones and Bones: Visiting the 9/11 Memorial Museum," *New Yorker*, July 7, 2014.

2 Sarah Boxer, *New York Times*, May 23, 2002, quoted in Weena Perry, " 'Too Young and Vibrant for Ruins': Ground Zero Photography and the Problem of Contemporary Ruin," *Afterimage* 36, no. 3 (November–December 2008): 8.

3 Ibid. See also Joel Meyerowitz, *Aftermath: World Trade Center Archive* (New York: Phaidon Press, 2006); Steve McCurry's image gallery "September 11, 2001" is on his website at http://stevemccurry.com/galleries/september-11-2001; also *Here Is New York: A Democracy of Photographs*, exh. cat., Alice Rose George, Gilles Peress, Michael Shulan, eds. (New York: Scalo, 2002), and many other 9/11 photography books.

4 Terry M. Neal, "Hiding Bodies Won't Hide the Truth," *Washington Post*, September 8, 2005.

5 Tania Ralli, "Who's a Looter? In Storm's Aftermath, Pictures Kick up a Different Kind of Tempest," *New York Times*, September 5, 2005.

6 See Samuel R. Sommers, Evan P. Apfelbaum, Kristin N. Dukes, Negin Toosi, and Elsie J. Wang, "Race and Media Coverage of Hurricane Katrina: Analysis, Implications, and Future Research Questions," *Analyses of Social Issues and Public Policy* 6, no. 1 (2006): 1–17, doi:10.1111/j.1530-2415.2006.00103.x.

7 For a trenchant critique of the magazine essay, see Joshua Akers and John Patrick Leary, "Detroit on $1 Million a Day," *Guernica*, July 28, 2014.

8 Jerry Herron, *After Culture: Detroit and the Humiliation of History* (Detroit: Wayne State University Press, 1993), 9.

9 Todd Samuel Presner, "Hegel's Philosophy of World History via Sebald's Imaginary of Ruins: A Contrapuntal Critique of the 'New Space' of Modernity," in *Ruins of Modernity*, ed. Julia Hell and Andreas Schönle (Durham, NC: Duke University Press, 2010), 194; also see Andreas Huyssen, "Authentic Ruins: Products of Modernity," in *Ruins of Modernity*, 17–28.

10 Thomas Piketty, *Capital in the Twenty-First Century* (Cambridge, MA: Belknap Press, 2014), 28.

11 John Russo and Sherry Lee Linkon, "The Social Costs of Deindustrialization," Center for Working-Class Studies, Youngstown State University, at http://cwcs.ysu.edu/resources/CWCS-publications/social-costs-of-deindustrialization.
12 Ibid.
13 Ibid.
14 See Dave Jamieson, "Pittsburgh's Largest Employer Draws Hundreds of Protestors over 'Poverty' Wages," *HuffPost Business*, March 3, 2014; and Ann Belser, "Statistics Show Pittsburgh Region's Workers Make Less against Inflation," *Pittsburgh Post-Gazette*, July 6, 2014.
15 Between 2000 and 2012, the real (inflation-adjusted) wages of young high school graduates declined 12.7 percent, and the real wages of young college graduates declined 8.5 percent. Heidi Shierholz, Natalie Sabadish, and Nicholas Finio, "The Class of 2013: Young Graduates Still Face Dim Job Prospects," *Economic Policy Institute*, April 10, 2013.
16 Cliff DuRand, "The American Dream Is Dead; Long Live the New Dream," *Truthout*, May 10, 2013.
17 Charles M. Blow, " 'A Town without Pity,' " *New York Times*, August 10, 2013.
18 Ann Laura Stoler, introduction to *Imperial Debris: On Ruins and Ruination*, ed. Ann Laura Stoler (Durham, NC: Duke University Press, 2012), 11.
19 Douglas Brinkley, Foreword to *American Ruins*, by Arthur Drooker (New York: Merrell, 2009), 8.
20 Jill Bennett, *Practical Aesthetics: Events, Affects and Art after 9/11* (London: I. B. Tauris, 2012).
21 Ibid., 2–3, 4–5.

Chapter 1. Ruin Terrors and Pleasures

1 Georg Simmel, "The Ruin//1911," in *Ruins*, Documents of Contemporary Art, ed. Brian Dillon (London: Whitechapel Gallery; Cambridge, MA: MIT Press, 2011), 23–24. For a tour through celebrated ruins, see Christopher Woodward, *In Ruins: A Journey through History, Art, and Literature* (New York: Vintage Books, 2001).
2 Dylan Trigg, *The Aesthetics of Decay: Nothingness, Nostalgia and the Absence of Reason* (New York: Peter Lang Publishing, 2006), 146.
3 Gilda Williams, "It Was What It Was: Modern Ruins//2010," in *Ruins*, Documents of Contemporary Art, ed. Brian Dillon (London: Whitechapel Gallery; Cambridge, MA: MIT Press, 2011), 96.
4 See Shane McGowan, "The Sublime Working of History: Travel, Ruins, and the Romantic Origins of the Post-Apocalyptic Aesthetic" (paper presented at Humanities Center symposium The Apocalyptic Landscape, Wayne State University, Detroit, November 16, 2012).
5 Ibid.
6 Ibid.
7 Julia Hell, "Imperial Ruin Gazers, or Why Did Scipio Weep?" in *Ruins of Modernity*, ed. Julia Hell and Andreas Schönle (Durham, NC: Duke University Press, 2010), 175–176.
8 Ibid., 171.
9 Ibid., 180–181.
10 Ibid., 182.
11 In literature, early texts that pictured decline within the West include Anna

Barbauld's poem "Eighteen Hundred and Eleven" and Mary Shelley's *The Last Man*. See McGowan, "Sublime Working of History."

12 Rose Macaulay, "A Note on New Ruins//1953," from *Pleasure of Ruins*, in *Ruins*, Documents of Contemporary Art, ed. Brian Dillon (London: Whitechapel Gallery; Cambridge, MA: MIT Press, 2011), 27.

13 Ibid., 27–28.

14 Quoted in Alexander Regier, "Foundational Ruins: The Lisbon Earthquake and the Sublime," in *Ruins of Modernity*, ed. Julia Hell and Andreas Schönle (Durham, NC: Duke University Press, 2010), 367.

15 Ibid., 366.

16 Russell Berman, "Democratic Destruction: Ruins and Emancipation in the American Tradition," in *Ruins of Modernity*, ed. Julia Hell and Andreas Schönle (Durham, NC: Duke University Press, 2010), 106.

17 Benjamin's essay is "Erdleben von Lissabon," in *Gesammelte Schriften*, cited in Regier, "Foundational Ruins," 370–371.

18 Quoted in Regier, "Foundational Ruins," 371.

19 Ibid.

20 Edmund Burke, *A Philosophical Enquiry into the Origin of Our Ideas of the Sublime and Beautiful*, ed. Adam Phillips (New York: Oxford University Press, 1990), 36.

21 Luke White, "Damian Hirst's Shark: Nature, Capitalism, and the Sublime," in *The Art of the Sublime*, ed. Nigel Llewellyn and Christine Riding, January 2013, http://www.tate.org.uk/art/research-publications/the-sublime/luke-white-damien-hirsts-shark-nature-capitalism-and-the-sublime-r1136828.

22 Richard B. Woodward, "Disaster Photography: When Is Documentary Exploitation?" *Art News*, February 6, 2013. I thank James Griffioen for this reference.

23 Thomas Morton, "Something, Something, Something, Detroit: Lazy Journalists Love Pictures of Abandoned Stuff," *Vice Magazine*, August 1, 2009.

24 I myself used the phrase in the title of a lecture at the Harvard Graduate School of Design in 2013, before thinking better of it.

25 Woodward, "Disaster Photography."

26 Ibid.

27 Ibid.

28 Ibid.

29 James Griffioen, e-mail to author, July 11, 2014.

30 Michael Chanan, "*Detroit: Ruin of a City*—A Reception Diary," *Journal of Media Practice* 6, no. 3 (2005): 136–137.

31 Michelle Andonian, conversation with author, Grand Rapids, MI, June 12, 2012.

32 Quoted in Alec Quig, "Interview with Photographer Andrew Moore (Uncut)," *Alec Quig's Blog*, November 14, 2011, at http://alecquig.wordpress.com/2011/11/. I thank Katie Lynch-Tapia for this reference.

33 Linda Williams, *Hard Core: Power, Pleasure, and the "Frenzy of the Visible"* rev. ed. (Berkeley: University of California Press, 1999, x.

34 George Steinmetz, "Drive-By Shooting: Vision and Division in the Documentation of Detroit," *Michigan Quarterly Review* 45, no. 3 (2006): 491–492.

35 Charlie LeDuff, *Detroit: An American Autopsy* (New York: Penguin Press, 2013), 138; also see Charlie LeDuff, "Life Goes on around Body Found Frozen in Vacant Detroit Warehouse," *Detroit News*, January 29, 2009. How the story was broken by LeDuff also became contentious. See Curt Guyette, "Anatomy of a Story," *Metro Times*, February 25, 2009.

36 Steinmetz, "Drive-By Shooting," 492.
37 LeDuff, *Detroit: An American Autopsy*, 129.
38 Steinmetz, "Drive-By Shooting," 503.

Chapter 2. Fear and Longing in Detroit

1 Evan McMurry, "George Will on ABC: 'Cultural Collapse,' 'Unwed Mothers,' 'Voting for Incompetents' Bankrupted Detroit," *Mediaite*, July 28, 2013.
2 James Politi, "Contentious NAFTA Pact Continues to Generate a Sparky Debate," *Financial Times*, December 2, 2013.
3 David Harvey, *The Enigma of Capital and the Crisis of Capitalism* (Oxford: Oxford University Press, 2011); and Naomi Klein, *The Shock Doctrine: The Rise of Disaster Capitalism* (New York: Picador, 2007).
4 Harvey, *Enigma of Capital*, 219.
5 Mark Binelli, "Detroit's Davos," *Detroit Free Press*, May 30, 2013; and Diane Bukowski, "Detroit EM Orr's Report Envisions a Nightmare Future," *Voice of Detroit*, May 16, 2013.
6 Matt Helms, Nancy Kaffer, and Stephen Henderson, "Detroit Files for Bankruptcy, Setting Off Battles with Creditors, Pensions, Unions," *Detroit Free Press*, July 19, 2013; for a comprehensively detailed overview of events, see Curt Guyette, "Anatomy of a Takeover," *Metro Times*, April 2–8, 2014, 24–36.
7 Maude Barlow, "Water Cut-offs in Detroit Are a Violation of Human Rights," *Eco Watch*, May 28, 2014.
8 Steve Neavling, "Water Gushes in Thousands of Vacant Buildings as Detroit Shuts off Occupied Homes," *Motor City Muckraker*, July 21, 2014.
9 Barlow, "Water Cut-offs in Detroit."
10 See Teddy Wilson, "'Water Is a Human Right': Advocates Call for End to Detroit Water Shutoffs," *RH Reality Check*, July 17, 2014; and Amel Ahmed, "UN Panel: Detroit Water Cutoffs Violate Human Rights," *Aljazeera America*, June 25, 2014. The UN assessment came days after a coalition of welfare rights groups, including the Detroit People's Water Board, Food and Water Watch, and the Canada-based Blue Planet Project pleaded in an open letter for UN intervention.
11 John Swaine, "Detroit Residents Fight Back over Water Shutoff: 'It's a Life or Death Situation,'" *Guardian*, July 21, 2014.
12 See Jeff DeBruyn, "Hyper-Gentrification, Community Engagement, and Detroit Future City," *Opening of Detroit*, May 27, 2014.
13 John Russo and Sherry Lee Linkon, "The Social Costs of Deindustrialization," Center for Working-Class Studies, Youngstown State University, http://cwcs.ysu.edu/resources/cwcs-publications/social-costs-of-deindustrialization.
14 Quoted in John Nichols, "Against Austerity in Detroit: 'Water Is a Human Right,'" *Nation*, July 11, 2014.
15 Mike Duggan, who moved to Detroit from the white suburb of Livonia just prior to the mayoral election of 2013, managed to accrue 46 percent of the primary vote as a write-in candidate in the black city against Wayne County Sheriff Benny Napoleon, and received 55 percent of the vote in the general election. Interestingly, Duggan was a classmate of both Snyder and Orr at University of Michigan Law School and, as CEO of the Detroit Medical Center, he led the hospital into privatization. His largest bloc of support and campaign financing came from real estate mogul Dan Gilbert and employees at Quicken Loans. See Victoria Collier and Ben-Zion

Ptashnik, "Protesters Gain Detroit Water Shut-Off Moratorium, Demand Investigation of Suspected Rampant Corruption," *Truthout*, August 17, 2014.

16 Amy Goodman, "Detroit Faces 'Humanitarian Crisis' as City Shuts Off Water Access for Thousands of Residents," *Democracy Now!*, October 10, 2014.

17 David Sirota, "Don't Buy the Right-Wing Myth about Detroit," *Salon*, July 23, 2013.

18 Georgia Daskalakis, Charles Waldheim, and Jason Young, introduction to *Stalking Detroit*, ed. Georgia Daskalakis, Charles Waldheim, and Jason Young (Barcelona: Actar, 2001), n.p.

19 Russo and Linkon, "Social Costs of Deindustrialization."

20 Ryan Felton, "Is There Detroit after Bankruptcy?" *In These Times*, August 12, 2013. Detroit residents also were concerned about the privatization of Belle Isle, a 982-acre island park in the Detroit River designed in part by Frederick Law Olmsted in the late 1800s, with a conservatory designed by Albert Kahn in 1904. The State of Michigan signed a thirty-year lease, however, allowing it to take over the maintenance and operation of Detroit's Belle Isle and turn it into a state park.

21 Ibid.

22 These included "high-pressure salesmanship to target elderly and vulnerable homeowners, as well as misleading borrowers about their loans, and falsifying property appraisals and other information to push through bad deals." Quoted in Alain Sherter, "Mortgage Mess: Why Quicken Loans May Not Be as Squeaky Clean as It Claims," *Money Watch*, February 8, 2011. The quote is from Michael Hudson, a staff writer for the Center for Public Integrity, who further notes, "A group of ex-employees, meanwhile, have gone to federal court to accuse Quicken of abusing workers and customers alike. In court papers, former salespeople claim Quicken executives managed by bullying and intimidation, pressuring them to falsify borrowers' incomes on loan applications and to push overpriced deals on desperate or unwary homeowners." Sherter notes that Quicken Loans may have cleaned up its act since the suits were filed. In 2012 an appeals court sided with Quicken Loans and upheld a 2011 court verdict in their favor against more than four hundred employees who claimed the company owed them overtime.

23 John O'Brien, "Quicken Loans Ordered to Pay $3.5M in Mortgage Case, Appeals," *West Virginia Record*, August 7, 2013.

24 Ben Austen, "The Post Post-Apocalyptic Detroit," *New York Times Magazine*, July 11, 2014. Also see Matthew Dolan, "Billionaire's Detroit Buying Spree Starts to Spread," *Wall Street Journal*, December 17, 2013; for a breakdown of buildings, occupancy, master leases, and parking lots and structures, see David Muller, "The Latest Facts and Figures on Dan Gilbert and Co.'s Massive Downtown Detroit Real Estate Empire," *MLive*, July 16, 2013.

25 David Harvey, *Rebel Cities: From the Right to the City to the Urban Revolution* (London: Verso, 2012), 99.

26 Ibid.

27 Timothy Williams, "Cities Mobilize to Help Those Threatened by Gentrification," *New York Times*, March 3, 2014.

28 Martha Rosler, "Culture Class: Art, Creativity, Urbanism: Part III," *E-Flux* (2011). Her essays are now published as *Martha Rosler: The Culture Class* (E-Flux Journal) (Berlin: Sternberg Press, 2013).

29 John Patrick Leary, "All the Young Technocrats," *Huffpost Detroit*, April 16, 2013. "Solutionism" was coined by Evgeny Morozov in *To Save Everything, Click Here*.

30 Rosler, "Culture Class."

31 Ibid.
32 John Caramanica, "The Next Branding of Detroit," *New York Times*, August 22, 2013.
33 Ibid.
34 Also see Rebecca Solnit, "Detroit Arcadia: Exploring the Post-American Landscape," *Harpers* (July 2007).
35 Paul Clemens, "Breakdown: A Journalist and Detroit Native Searches for Clues to the City's Fate," review of *Detroit: An American Autopsy* by Charlie LeDuff, *New York Times*, February 24, 2013. Also see Clemens's own books about Detroit, *Made in Detroit* (New York: Doubleday, 2005); and *Punching Out: One Year in a Closing Auto Plant* (New York: Doubleday, 2011).
36 Felton, "Is There Detroit after Bankruptcy?"
37 Diane Ravitch, "School Privatization Is a Hoax, Reformers Aim to Destroy Public Schools," *Salon*, September 15, 2013; excerpted from Diane Ravitch, *The Reign of Error: The Hoax of the Privatization Movement and the Danger to America's Public Schools* (New York: Knopf, 2013). Also see Andrew Delbanco's review, "The Two Faces of American Education," *New York Review of Books*, October 10, 2013, 4–9.
38 Jerry White, "Snyder Administration Plot to Privatize Michigan Schools Exposed," *World Socialist Web Site*, April 24, 2013.
39 Robert Kleine, "How the State of Michigan Helped Bankrupt Detroit—and Is Keeping It Down," *Detroit Free Press*, August 4, 2013.
40 "Michigan Leads Nation in Massive Corporate Tax Breaks (The Untold Story of Detroit's Decline)," *Real News*, August 2, 2013.
41 Harvey, *Enigma of Capital*, 108.
42 Ibid., 263–264.
43 George Packer, "Don't Look Down: The New Depression Journalism," *New Yorker*, April 29, 2013, 72.
44 Ron Nixon, "House Republicans Pass Deep Cuts in Food Stamps," *New York Times*, September 19, 2013. This bill has been watered down by the Senate to a proposed $4 billion reduction, which would still come on top of significant cuts to the food stamp program that went into effect on November 1, 2013, as a result of the expiration of the 2009 stimulus law. See Editorial, "Budget Grief for the Poor and Jobless," *New York Times*, November 2, 2013.
45 Letter from Michael Reisch, professor of social justice, *New York Times*, September 28, 2013.
46 Bill Vlasic, *Once upon a Car: The Fall and Resurrection of America's Big Three Automakers—GM, Ford, and Chrysler* (New York: William Morrow, 2011), 207.
47 Dan Hoffman, "Erasing Detroit," in *Stalking Detroit*, ed. Georgia Daskalakis, Charles Waldheim, and Jason Young (Barcelona: Actar, 2001), 101.
48 "The Fiscal Condition of the City of Detroit," Citizens Research Council of Michigan, Report 361, Summary, April 2010, http://crcmich.org/PUBLICAT/2010s/2010/rpt361.html.
49 Sandra MacNeill, "Beware: Zombie Foreclosures Haunting Homeowners," *CBS Detroit*, February 24, 2013; and Barbara Liston, "Zombie Foreclosures: 300,000 'Undead' Properties Stalk Ex-owners," *Christian Science Monitor*, March 28, 2013.
50 Monica Davey, "$1.85 Billion Renewal Plan for Bankrupt Detroit," *New York Times*, May 28, 2014.
51 The term "negative ruins" is George Steinmetz's. See "Colonial Melancholy and Fordist Nostalgia: The Ruinscapes of Namibia and Detroit," in *Ruins of Modernity*,

ed. Julia Hell and Andreas Schönle (Durham, NC: Duke University Press, 2010), 315.

52 Eric Cazdyn, *The Already Dead: The New Time of Politics, Culture, and Illness* (Durham, NC: Duke University Press, 2012), 5.

53 "Detroit Pension Robbery," *Workers Vanguard*, June 13, 2014, http://www.icl-fi.org/english/wv/1048/detroit.html.

54 "Economic News Release: Union Members Summary," *Bureau of Labor Statistics*, January 24, 2014, http://www.bls.gov/news.release/pdf/union2.pdf.

55 Greg Grandin, "Empire's Ruins: Detroit to the Amazon," in *Imperial Ruins: On Ruins and Ruination*, ed. Ann Laura Stoler (Durham, NC: Duke University Press, 2013), 119.

56 Greg Grandin, *Fordlandia: The Rise and Fall of Henry Ford's Forgotten Jungle City* (New York: Metropolitan Books, 2009), 16.

57 Ibid., 359.

58 Grandin, "Empire's Ruins," 123–124.

59 George Steinmetz, "Guest Editorial," *Environment and Planning D: Society and Space* 27 (2009): 761.

60 Grandin, "Empire's Ruins," 124–125.

61 Kevin Boyle, "The Ruins of Detroit: Exploring the Urban Crisis in the Motor City," *Michigan Historical Review* 27, no. 1 (2001): 111.

62 Thomas J. Sugrue, *The Origins of the Urban Crisis: Race and Inequality in Postwar Detroit*, rev. ed. (Princeton, NJ: Princeton University Press, 2005), 86.

63 Ibid., 144–149.

64 Boyle, "Ruins of Detroit," 118.

65 Robert Fishman, "On Big Beaver Road: Detroit and the Diversity of American Metropolitan Landscapes," *Places: Forum of Design for the Public Realm* 19, no. 1 (2007): 42. According to the 2010 census, Detroit was 8 percent white and 7 percent Hispanic. See "2010 Census Data for City of Detroit Neighborhoods," *SEMCOG Quick Facts*, http://library.semcog.org/InmagicGenie/DocumentFolder/2010CensusDataDetroitQuickFacts.pdf, April 5, 2011. For detailed demographic, economic, and housing trends, see *Data Driven Detroit*, at datadrivendetroit.org.

66 Fishman, "On Big Beaver Road," 43.

67 See "Detroit Transit History," at detroittransithistory.info; and "General Motors Streetcar Conspiracy," at wikipedia.org.

68 Harvey, *Rebel Cities*, 117.

69 Sugrue, *Origins of the Urban Crisis*, 47.

70 The Twelfth Street area was a Jewish neighborhood in the 1930s, but Jews moved out as blacks moved in after World War II. The bulldozing of Black Bottom ultimately made way for Lafayette Park, a residential project designed by Mies van der Rohe and built six years later. Some Black Bottom residents relocated to the large public housing projects of Brewster-Douglass Housing and Jeffries Homes. For a description of living in Black Bottom and being forced to move to the Twelfth Street area, see the chapter "Urban Passages" in Coleman Young and Lonnie Wheeler, *Hard Stuff: The Autobiography of Mayor Coleman Young* (New York: Viking, 1994). On Lafayette Park, see Francesca Scotti, ed., *Lafayette Park, Detroit: The Form of the Settlement* (Como, Italy: Libraccio, 2006); and Danielle Aubert, Lana Cavar, and Natashi Chandani, eds., *Thanks for the View, Mr. Mies: Lafayette Park, Detroit* (New York: Metropolis Books, 2012).

71 Sidney Fine, *Violence in the Model City: The Cavanaugh Administration, Race*

Relations, and the Detroit Riot of 1967 (East Lansing: Michigan State University Press, 2007), 4.

72 Sugrue, *Origins of the Urban Crisis*, 259.

73 Dominic J. Capeci Jr. and Martha Wilkerson, *Layered Violence: The Detroit Rioters of 1943* (Jackson: University Press of Mississippi, 1991), 145.

74 Fishman, "On Big Beaver Road," 45.

75 Ibid., 46. For the primer on what promotes or defeats the vitality of a city, see Jane Jacobs, *The Death and Life of Great American Cities* (New York: Vintage Books, 1992).

76 Boyle, "Ruins of Detroit," 126.

77 Walter Russell Mead, "Rogue Democrats Loot Detroit as Nation Sleeps," *American Interest*, May 5, 2012, http://www.the-american-interest.com/wrm/2012/05/05/rogue-democrats-loot-detroit-as-nation-sleeps/.

78 Nolan Finley, "Face It, DIA Artwork Will Be 'Monetized,'" *Detroit News*, September 29, 2013.

79 Quoted in Mark Stryker and John Gallagher, "DIA's Art Collection Could Face Sell-Off to Satisfy Detroit's Creditors," *Detroit Free Press*, May 24, 2013.

80 Quoted in Randy Kennedy and Monica Davey, "Detroit's Creditors Eye Its Art Collection," *New York Times*, July 20, 2013.

81 Quoted in ibid.

82 Hrag Vartanian, "New Yorker Art Critic Justifies Looting of Detroit Museum," *Hyperallergenic*, July 24, 2013; Peter Schjeldahl, "Should Detroit Sell Its Art?" *New Yorker*, July 24, 2013; and Schjeldahl, "What Should Detroit Do with Its Art? The Sequel," *New Yorker*, July 26, 2013.

83 Terry Teachout, "Protecting Detroit's Artwork Is a Job for Detroit," *Wall Street Journal*, August 1, 2013.

84 The deal depends on raising $466 million from private foundations and the DIA and $195 million from the state, as well as the approval of retirees and the bankruptcy judge. Although most of the retirees feel they should never have faced cuts to their pensions in the first place, they voted in favor of the plan.

85 Steven Yaccino and Monica Davey, "As Detroit Pensioners Rejoice, Bankruptcy Experts Are Wary," *Detroit Free Press*, April 17, 2014; Yaccino and Davey, "Optimism as Detroit Makes Pacts on Finances," *Detroit Free Press*, April 29, 2014; Mary Williams Walsh, "Detroit Bankruptcy Deadline May Be Missed, Imperiling State Funds," *New York Times*, May 16, 2014; and David Firestone, "The Koch Brothers Kick Detroit While It's Down," *New York Times*, May 21, 2014, http://takingnote.blogs.nytimes.com/2014/05/21/the-koch-brothers-hit-detroit-while-its-down/.

86 Slavoj Žižek, *Violence: Six Sideways Reflections* (New York: Picador, 2008).

87 Quoted in Randy Kennedy, "Fate of City's Art Hangs in the Balance," *New York Times*, December 4, 2013.

88 Schuette quoted in Randy Kennedy and Monica Davey, "Detroit's Creditors Eye its Art Collection," *New York Times*, July 19, 2013; and Snyder quoted in Chad Livengood and Daniel Howes, "Snyder Asserts City Assets, Including DIA Art, at Risk If Detroit Goes Bankrupt," *Detroit News*, May 30, 2013.

89 For links to PDFs of both the summary and full report by Christie's, see Mark Stryker, "What's DIA Artwork Worth? New Christie's Report Has the Numbers," *Detroit Free Press*, December 19, 2013.

90 Randy Kennedy, "Christie's Reveals Detroit Art Appraisal," *New York Times*, December 5, 2013.

91 Michael Hodges, "Report for Detroit Creditor Nearly Doubles Value of DIA Collection at 8.5B," *Detroit News*, July 27, 2014.

92 Roberta Smith, "Selling Art and Selling Out: The Perils Involved in Detroit's Appraisal of Its Museum's Collection," *New York Times*, September 11, 2013.

93 Kennedy, "Fate of the City's Art."

94 The term is David Joselit's.

95 Quoted in Smith, "Selling Art and Selling Out."

96 Another offer to "monetize" the artworks, which would have sabotaged the grand bargain and was supported by major creditors, was made by Art Capitol Group, a Manhattan-based company that issues loans against fine art. Art Capitol proposed using the DIA collection as collateral for a $4 billion loan to the city. The plan was rejected and the city reached settlements with the two largest bond insurers, pending the court's approval. Syncora would get a twenty-year extension on its deal to operate the Detroit-Windsor Tunnel, a thirty-year lease on a city parking garage, and millions in bonds and options to purchase city property; it is estimated that Syncora would ultimately collect up to $50 million. Financial Guaranty Insurance Co. would get the rights to build a hotel, retail, and condominium complex on the five-acre site of the Joe Louis Arena; the rights to a parking garage on the site; and two types of notes from the city with a total value of about $146 million.

97 Zach Schonfeld, "Protests Sparked in Detroit over the Dumping of Black History Books," *Atlantic Wire*, July 9, 2013.

98 Vickie Thomas, "Exclusive: Inside Highland Park's Black History Collection," *CBS Detroit*, July 10, 2013; and Stateside Staff, "Outrage after Highland Park High School's Library Material Gets Dumped in the Trash," *Michigan Radio*, July 9, 2013.

99 Thomas Sugrue, "Workers' Paradise Lost," *New York Times*, December 14, 2012.

100 It should be noted that many legislators themselves have not completed a college education. About one in four of the nearly 7,400 elected representatives across the country do not possess a four-year college degree, according to a report based primarily on self-reported biographical information by officials. In Michigan, 27 percent of state elected officials lack college degrees. Scott Smallwood and Alex Richards, "How Educated Are State Legislators?" *Chronicle of Higher Education*, June 12, 2011.

101 Following Gerald Ford's 1975 speech denying federal assistance to spare New York from bankruptcy, the *Daily News* published a famous headline that read, "Ford to City: Drop Dead." Although not an actual quote, it captured the essence of the speech and may have cost him the presidency the following year, even though Ford later signed legislation to provide federal loans to the city. See also Thomas J. Sugrue, "Notown," *Democracy: A Journal of Ideas* 28 (Spring 2013).

102 Mike Alberti, "Detroit Consigned to an Unnecessarily Bleak Future?" *Remapping Detroit*, December 21, 2011, 3.

103 Felton, "Is There Detroit after Bankruptcy?"

104 Alberti, "Detroit Consigned."

105 Joseph E. Stiglitz, "The Wrong Lesson from Detroit's Bankruptcy," *New York Times*, August 11, 2013.

106 Kevin Rizzo, "Crime in America: Top 10 Most Dangerous Cities over 200, 000," *Law Street*, November 25, 2013.

107 Alberti, "Detroit Consigned," 5.

108 Mike Alberti, "Squandered Opportunities Leave Detroit Isolated," *Remapping Detroit*, January 11, 2012, 1.

109 Ibid., 6.
110 Quoted in ibid., 7.
111 Ibid., 9–10.
112 Mike Alberti, "Detroit's Woes Can Be Eased, but Region's Officials Avert Their Eyes," *Remapping Detroit*, January 25, 2012, 1.
113 Ibid., 8.
114 Harvey, *Rebel Cities*, xviii.

Chapter 3. Urban Exploration: Beauty in Decay

1 *Anthony Bourdain Parts Unknown: Detroit*, Season 2, Episode 8, which aired on November 10, 2013.
2 Steven High and David W. Lewis, *Corporate Wasteland: The Landscape and Memory of Deindustrialization* (Ithaca, NY: Cornell University Press, 2007), 48.
3 Ninjalicious, "No Disclaimer," *Infiltration*, at http://www.infiltration.org/ethics-nodisclaimer.html. Chapman, a liver-transplant recipient, died of cancer at the age of thirty-one in August 2005. Current access to the website and the twenty-five issues of *Infiltration* are only available for a fee of $65, although "No Disclaimer" is still available for free.
4 RomanyWG, "Collectors: Our Passion to Preserve," in *Beauty in Decay: Urbex* (Berkeley: Gingko Press and Carpet Bombing Culture, 2010), n.p. Credits cite "compiled: RomanyWG" and "words: Patrick Potter." RomanyWG is Jeremy Gibbs; in 2012 he compiled *Beauty in Decay II.*
5 Ibid.
6 See my chapter "Historical Reenactment: Romantic Amnesia or Counter-Memory?" in *War Culture and the Contest of Images* (New Brunswick, NJ: Rutgers University Press, 2012).
7 RomanyWG, "History," in *Beauty in Decay*, n.p.
8 Ibid.
9 RomanyWG, "Contemplation" and "Challenge," in *Beauty in Decay*, n.p.
10 High and Lewis, *Corporate Wasteland*, 42–44.
11 RomanyWG, "What's the Story with Urban Exploration?" in *Beauty in Decay*, n.p.
12 RomanyWG, "Outside of Time," in *Beauty in Decay*, n.p. The nineteenth-century American romantic writer Henry David Thoreau asserted in *Walden* (1808–1810), "The mass of men lead lives of quiet desperation."
13 Quoted in High and Lewis, *Corporate Wasteland*, 50–51.
14 Ibid.
15 Ibid., 58.
16 Brian Dillon, "Introduction: A Short History of Decay," in *Ruins*, Documents of Contemporary Art, ed. Brian Dillon (London: Whitechapel Gallery; Cambridge, MA: MIT Press, 2011), 12–13.
17 RomanyWG, "Outside of Time," in *Beauty in Decay*, n.p.
18 Robert Smithson, "A Tour of the Monuments of Passaic, New Jersey//1967," quoted in *Ruins*, Documents of Contemporary Art, ed. Brian Dillon (London: Whitechapel Gallery; Cambridge, MA: MIT Press, 2011), 49.
19 George Steinmetz, "Colonial Melancholy and Fordist Nostalgia: The Ruinscapes of Namibia and Detroit," in *Ruins of Modernity*, ed. Julia Hell and Andreas Schönle (Durham, NC: Duke University Press, 2010), 315.

20 See Dylan Trigg, *The Aesthetics of Decay: Nothingness, Nostalgia and the Absence of Reason* (New York: Peter Lang, 2006).
21 RomanyWG, "Archive Fever: Urban Exploration and the Digital Artform," in *Beauty in Decay*, n.p.
22 For more on Kristine Diven, see her photo series *Cathedrals of Decay: Self Portraits from Within*, at http://cathedralsofdecay.tumblr.com/; on Miru Kim, see "TED Talks: Nude Photography in Urban Ruins," at http://videosift.com/video/Miru-Kim-Making-art-of-urban-ruins.
23 I thank Nicole Kristich for calling my attention to these video games.
24 Andrea Huyssen, "Authentic Ruins: Product of Modernity," in *Ruins of Modernity*, ed. Julia Hell and Andreas Schönle (Durham, NC: Duke University Press, 2010), 24–25.
25 Ibid., 26.
26 Tim Edensor, *Industrial Ruins: Space, Aesthetics and Materiality* (New York: Berg, 2005), 168–169.
27 For a critique of heritage sites, see, for example, Kevin Walsh, *The Representation of the Past: Museums and Heritage in the Post-Modern World* (New York: Routledge, 1992).
28 Lebbeus Woods, *War and Architecture*, quoted in Edensor, *Industrial Ruins*, 165.
29 Edensor, *Industrial Ruins*, 15–16.
30 Ibid., 7.
31 High and Lewis, *Corporate Wasteland*, 60.
32 Edensor, *Industrial Ruins*, 28.
33 Ibid., 50.
34 Edensor, *Industrial Ruins*, 165.
35 Edensor, *Industrial Ruins*, 171–172.
36 Trigg, *Aesthetics of Decay*, 9–10.
37 Ibid., 183.
38 Ibid., 184–185.
39 Ibid., 116.
40 Ibid., 148.
41 Ibid., 221.
42 Ibid., 233.
43 "It seems to be easier for us today to imagine the thoroughgoing deterioration of the earth and of nature than the breakdown of late capitalism; perhaps that is due to some weakness in our imaginations," Fredric Jameson, *The Seeds of Time*, cited in Eric Cazdyn, *The Already Dead: The New Time of Politics, Culture, and Illness* (Durham, NC: Duke University Press, 2012), 209n46.

Chapter 4. Detroit Ruin Images: Where Are the People?

1 Nate Millington, "Post-Industrial Imaginaries: Nature, Representation and Ruin in Detroit, Michigan," *International Journal of Urban and Regional Research* 37, no. 1 (2013): 287.
2 Ibid., 290.
3 Monica Davey, Bill Vlasic, and Mary Williams Walsh, "Detroit Ruling Lifts a Shield on Pensions," *New York Times*, December 4, 2013.
4 Detroit-born and Chicago-based photographer Dave Jordano's "Re-Photography

Survey" also revisits many Detroit sites years later. See his current ongoing series "Detroit—Unbroken Down," on his website at davejordano.com.

5 Camilo José Vergara, "Downtown Detroit: 'American Acropolis' or Vacant Land—What To Do with the World's Third Largest Concentration of Pre-Depression Skyscrapers?" *Metropolis* 33 (April 1995): 33–38. Also see Vergara's *The New American Ghetto* (New Brunswick, NJ: Rutgers University Press, 1995); his *American Ruins* (New York: Monacelli Press, 1999); his 2012–2013 exhibition at the National Building Museum in Washington, D.C., *Detroit Is No Dry Bones*; and the online exhibition *Tracking Time* at camilojosevergara.com.

6 Vergara, "Downtown Detroit," 35. Art critic Richard Woodward suggests, "Had the authorities heeded his suggestion [for a skyscraper park] instead of scorning it, they might have created a tourist attraction to rival New York's High Line." See Richard Woodward, "Disaster Photography: When Is Documentary Exploitation?" *Art News*, February 6, 2013.

7 Yves Marchand and Romain Meffre, *The Ruins of Detroit* (Göttingen: Steidl Publishers, 2010).

8 Yves Marchand, e-mail to author, August 15, 2014.

9 See Daniel Okrent, "Notown," *Time*, October 2009: 26–34.

10 Marchand and Meffre, *Ruins of Detroit*, 182.

11 Erik Eckholm, "No Longer Ignored, Evidence Solves Rape Cases Years Later," *New York Times*, August 3, 2014. Among other cities, more than 12,000 kits were incompletely tested or untested in Memphis; nearly 4,000 in Cleveland. In addition to financial constraints, uncaring and haphazard responses to charges of sexual assault and slow recognition that rape kits could help identify serial rapists are other reasons for the lax handling. Kym L. Worthy, the Wayne County prosecutor, has pursued full testing of the Detroit rape kits and the first 1,600 analyzed have identified 455 suspects in twenty-three states, including 87 involved in multiple assaults.

12 Dan Austin and Sean Doerr, "Michigan Central Station," in *Lost Detroit: Stories behind the Motor City's Majestic Ruins* (Charleston, SC: History Press, 2010), 101–118.

13 Susan Berfield, "Matty Moroun, Detroit's Border Baron," *Bloomberg Businessweek*, May 3, 2012; and Paul Egan, "Moroun Bids $1.2M for Vacant Southwestern High School in Detroit," *Detroit Free Press*, February 28, 2014.

14 Austin and Doerr, "Michigan Central Station," 116.

15 Dylan Trigg, *The Aesthetics of Decay: Nothingness, Nostalgia and the Absence of Reason* (New York: Peter Lang, 2006), 5.

16 See Anthony Vidler, "Architecture Dismembered//1992," in *Ruins*, Documents of Contemporary Art, ed. Brian Dillon (London: Whitechapel Gallery; Cambridge, MA: MIT Press, 2011), 55.

17 Bill McGraw, *Detroit Free Press*, November 2009, quoted in Austin and Doerr, "Michigan Central Station," 116.

18 Thomas J. Sugrue, *The Origins of the Urban Crisis: Race and Inequality in Postwar Detroit*, rev. ed. (Princeton, NJ: Princeton University Press, 2005), 146.

19 Steven Kurutz, "Life in the Ruins," *New York Times*, February 7, 2013.

20 See, for example, "TPlex Wedding Photography ... Detroit," *ArsMagna*, http://www.arsmagnastudio.com/2013/06/tplex-wedding-photography-detroit/.

21 J. C. Reindl, "Packard Plant's New Owner Networking at Auto Show as Redevelopment Project Needs $350 M," *Detroit Free Press*, January 12, 2014. Short videos on the Packard Plant abound on YouTube; also see Jennifer Dixon, "The Packard Plant:

Why It Has to Go," special section of the *Detroit Free Press*, December 2, 2012; and Chris Christoff, "Packard Plant Buyer Predicts Rebirth for Symbol of Detroit Decay," *Detroit Free Press*, December 17, 2013.

22 Marchand and Meffre, *Ruins of Detroit*, 142.

23 Ibid., 192.

24 Austin and Doerr, "Lee Plaza," in *Lost Detroit*, 80–83.

25 I thank Katherine Toole for drawing my attention to this. The closing of Lee Plaza was followed by the architectural theft of the magnificent terra-cotta lion heads adorning its exterior (which turned up in Chicago) and more than $2 million in damage to the building.

26 Andrew Moore, "Detroit Undone," *National Geographic* 218, no. 5 (2010): 9.

27 See James Elkins, "Against the Sublime," https://www.academia.edu/163451/Against_the_Sublime. It was posted, with an introduction, on jameselkins.com and was originally published in *Beyond the Finite: The Sublime in Art and Science*, edited by Roald Hoffmann and Iain Boyd Whyte (New York: Oxford University Press, 2011), 20–42.

28 Andrew Moore, Lecture in conjunction with the exhibition *Cities in Transition*, Grand Rapids Art Museum, Grand Rapids, Michigan, June 12, 2012.

29 See Julia Reyes Taubman, *Detroit: 138 Square Miles* (Detroit: Museum of Contemporary Art Detroit, 2011); also see Taubman's discussion of the book at detroitpocketsofcool.com/videos/julie-taubman; and Nick Paumgarten, "Detroit Valentine," *New Yorker*, December 12, 2011. Taubman explains at the back of the book that since Detroit is 138.8 miles, she was advised that 138 miles sounded better than 139.

30 Jerry Herron, "The Forgetting Machine: Notes toward a History of Detroit," *Design Observer Group*, January 9, 2012, https://placesjournal.org/article/the-forgetting-machine-notes-toward-a-history-of-detroit/.

31 Jerry Herron, "Living with Detroit," in *Detroit: 138 Square Miles* (Detroit: Museum of Contemporary Art Detroit/D.A.P. 2011), 14.

32 Ibid.

33 See Jill Bennett's discussion of compassion in *Practical Aesthetics: Events, Affects and Art after 9/11* (London: I. B. Tauris, 2012), 182–184. The term "distant suffering" is Luc Boltanski's.

34 Ted Loos, "Picturing Motor City: Julia Reyes Taubman Trains Her Lens on Detroit," *Vogue*, November 15, 2011; and Pedro Vélez, "*Detroit: 138 Square Miles:* Ruin Porn Galore for Both Rich and Poor," January 19, 2012, http://www.artnet.com/magazineus/books/velez/detroit-138-square-miles-1-19-12.asp.

35 Comment quoted in Loos, "Picturing Motor City"; book signature cited in Paumgarten, "Detroit Valentine."

36 The other three Grand Rapids exhibitions were *What Happened Here? GRAM, Ecliptic, and Rosa Parks Circle*; *Detroit: Then/Now/Next*; and *Perspectives on the City: Four Centuries of Drawings, Prints and Photographs.*

37 Detroit-based painters who represent the urban and industrial landscape include artists such as Stephen Magsig, Nancy Mitchnick, and Clinton Snider.

38 Alec Quig, "Interview with Photographer Andrew Moore (Uncut)," *Alec Quig's Blog*, November 14, 2011, http://alecquig.wordpress.com/2011/11/.

39 In the summer of 2014, the DIA opened *Detroit: Bruce Weber*, an exhibition underwritten by Condé Nast and based on two photo shoots by Weber for *W* magazine and Shinola. The show was meant to celebrate Detroit's vitality and residents. See Mark Stryker's thoughtful critique, "Bruce Weber Photo Doesn't Tell Whole Story

of DIA Exhibit Subject's Life," *Detroit Free Press*, August 3, 2014; the Detroit Artists Market opened *313* in honor of Detroit's 313th birthday (313 is also the Detroit telephone area code) in 2014, including works by Carlos Diaz, Bruce Giffin, Scott Hocking, Oscar Hoff, Ali Elisabeth Lapetina, Vanessa Miller, Bill Rauhauser, Bill Schwab, and Tom Stoye.

40 Herron, "Forgetting Machine."

41 Warren Whatley and Gavin Wright, "Getting Started in the Auto Industry: Black Workers at the Ford Motor Company, 1918–1947," *The Cliometric Society*, Allied Social Science Associations Meetings, December 28, 1990, http://cliometrics.org/conferences/ASSA/Dec_90/Whatley-Wright_Abstract/.

42 Greg Grandin, *Fordlandia: The Rise and Fall of Henry Ford's Forgotten Jungle City* (New York: Metropolitan Books, 2009), 272n.

43 Scott Martelle, *Detroit: A Biography* (Chicago: Chicago Review Press, 2012), 108–109.

44 See Martelle's chapter, "The Black Legion," in *Detroit*, 127–132.

45 Barry James, "Detroit: The Rise and Fall of a Labor/Black Stronghold," *Workers Vanguard*, April 18, 2014, 9; also see Dominic J. Capeci Jr., and Martha Wilkerson, *Layered Violence: The Detroit Rioters of 1943* (Jackson: University Press of Mississippi, 1991).

46 The Book Beat, "Detroit: 138 Square Miles: Elegance, Rust & Soul," May 12, 2011, http://www.thebookbeat.com/backroom/2011/12/05/detroit-138-square-miles-elegance-rust-soul/.

47 Julia Hell, "Imperial Ruin Gazers, or Why Did Scipio Weep?" *Ruins of Modernity*, ed. Julia Hell and Andreas Schönle (Durham, NC: Duke University Press, 2010), 174.

48 As an extreme example, Chinese artist Ai Weiwei's projects on the tragic effects of the 2008 Sichuan earthquake, protesting shoddy governmental school construction that contributed to the deaths of thousands of Chinese schoolchildren, precipitated his imprisonment by the Chinese government for eighty-one days in 2011 on the pretext of tax evasion charges. See the eighteen-minute video "Ai Weiwei—Wenchuan Rebar.mov"; and Melissa Block, "In 'According to What?' Ai Weiwei Makes Mourning Subversive," *NPR.org*, January 23, 2013.

49 Daniel Fuller, "An Arctic Lecture: Detroit Deconstruction," *Art in America*, March 25, 2010. The house was located at 3920 McClellan Street.

50 Ben Rooney, "Rust and Sun Belt Cities Lead '07 Foreclosures," *CNN Money*, February 13, 2008; and Les Christie, "Foreclosures Fall to Lowest Level since 2007," *CNN Money*, January 12, 2012. Foreclosures fell dramatically in 2011 only because of processing delays.

51 Diane Sweet, "3.5 Million Homeless and 18.5 Million Vacant Homes in the US," *Occupy America*, December 30, 2011.

52 Matthew Radune, e-mail to author, March 3, 2013.

53 Ibid. For an interview with Holm and Radune and slide shows, see Sarah Rich, "Ice House Detroit," *Dwell Magazine*, February 10, 2010. Holm has since moved back to Detroit and opened the restaurant Antietam.

54 Santiago Colas, "Why Don't We Stop Here?" in *Stalking Detroit*, ed. Georgia Daskalakis, Charles Waldheim, and Jason Young (Barcelona: Actar, 2001), 147.

55 Mark Jacobs, "Officials Turn Blind Eye to Detroit's Growing Homeless Crisis," *Deadline Detroit*, June 3, 2013; and Michigan Educational Association, "Michigan Facing Growing Number of Homeless Children," October 4, 2013, http://mea.org/michigan-facing-growing-number-homeless-children.

56 Mitch Cope, e-mail to author, July 21, 2014; also see Vince Carducci's review "'Zen and the Art of Garbage Hunting and the Protectors of the Refuse': Mitch Cope at Popps Packing," *Motown Review of Art*, March 26, 2014, http://motownreviewofart.blogspot.com/2014/03/zen-and-art-of-garbage-hunting-and.html.

57 Sandra Osip, e-mail to author, January 30, 2014. Also see sandraosip.com.

58 Hocking also writes, "The form of an egg has traditionally represented the unborn potential yet to be hatched; the new beginning; the gestating idea; the primordial matter; creation. While cairns have been used as markers of tombs, caves, or pathways; places of significance; astronomical and navigational tools; and points of mystical or religious importance." See "The Egg and the MCTS 2007–present," at http://scotthocking.com/egg.html.

59 Michael H. Hodges, "Birth, Death, Regeneration Mix in New Scott Hocking Exhibit," *Detroit News*, December 24, 2012, http://scotthocking.com/bibliography/2012_12_24_Birth_Death_Regeneration_Mix_Hodges_Detroit_News.pdf.

60 Anna Clark, "Detroit Is Burning: Mysterious Arson Fires Plague Renowned Public Art Project," *NBC News*, December 18, 2013.

61 See Dora Apel, *Imagery of Lynching: Black Men, White Women, and the Mob* (New Brunswick, NJ: Rutgers University Press, 2004), 207.

62 See "The Heidelberg Project: Impacting the Local Community," Center for Creative Community Development, Williamstown, MA, http://web.williams.edu/Economics/ArtsEcon/library/pdfs/HPSocNetwork.pdf.

63 See www.heidelberg.org; also James Fassinger, "Who Is Burning Down Detroit's World-Famous Street Art?" *Daily Beast*, March 14, 2014; and Keith Matheny and Tammy Stables Battaglia, "What Now for Heidelberg, as It Battles Fires and Tax Problems?" *Detroit Free Press*, December 29, 2013. In addition to the Party Animal House (also known as the Doll House), the other burned houses include the Obstruction of Justice House, the House of Soul, the War House, and the Clock House.

64 Telephone interview with Greg, January 11, 2014; Linda Yablonsky, "Artists in Residence," *New York Times Style Magazine*, September 22, 2010; also see Julie Pincus and Nichole Christian, *Canvas Detroit* (Detroit: Wayne State University Press, 2014); and the group's original statement at http://www.thedetroiter.com/nov05/disneydemolition.html; and a video presented by GOOD Magazine, at woostercollective.com/post/detroits-object-orange. They were originally known as the DDD or Detroit. Demolition. Disneyland.

65 Joann Muller, "Bill Pulte: From Home Builder to Detroit's Unlikely Blight Buster," *Forbes*, October 9, 2013; and Todd Spangler, "Michigan Gets OK to Use $100M to Demolish Vacant Homes, Fight Blight," *Detroit Free Press*, June 6, 2013.

66 Tom Putnam and Brenna Sanchez, "*BURN* Brings Detroit's Battle to the Big Screen," *HuffPost Home*, November 16, 2012; and Charlie LeDuff, "Fire," in *Detroit: An American Autopsy* (New York: Penguin Press, 2013).

67 See www.powerhouseproductions.org.

68 Pincus and Christian, *Canvas Detroit*, 243; also see empowermentplan.org. The Empowerment Plan is housed in Pony Ride, a repurposed factory building that is now a community of shops, businesses, and nonprofits established in 2011 by Phil Cooley, owner of Slow's Bar-B-Q, who bought the thirty-thousand-square-foot space at the foreclosure rate of $100,000 to renovate and offer low rents to businesses.

69 Mark Stryker, "Artist-Filmmaker Matthew Barney Sees 'So Many Possibilities' in Detroit," *Detroit Free Press*, May 31, 2014. The film is also set in New York and Los

Angeles. As we go to press, African American artist Nick Cave is scheduled to be in Detroit in 2015 for ten months of events before and during his solo exhibition at Cranbrook Art Museum. His largest planned performance series to date, these events will include impromptu flash-mob Soundsuit Invasions throughout the city; Dance Labs at MoCAD; a new performance filmed in the Michigan Theater; *Heard Detroit*, planned for students from the Detroit School of Arts; costuming workshops with children; and, in culmination, *Figure This: Detroit*, a massive performance downtown for an audience of thousands.

70 Rebecca R. Hart, "Matthew Barney, Alchemist," in *Canvas Detroit* (Detroit: Detroit University Press, 2014).

71 See the *River of Fundament* film libretto; the five-hour-and-twenty-minute film was shown at the Detroit Film Theater of the Detroit Institute of Arts on June 1, 2014.

72 Mike Rubin, "A Battered City, through Local Lenses: Filmmakers from Detroit Take Their Own Looks at the City," *New York Times*, April 29, 2012.

73 See Mark Stryker, "Gallery's Plan to Sell Packard Plant's Banksy Mural Sparks Uproar," *Detroit Free Press*, March 14, 2014.

74 John Patrick Leary, "Detroitism," *Guernica*, January 2011.

Chapter 5. Looking for Signs of Resurrection

1 Available at nbcnews.com/id/21134540/vp/41465523#41465523.

2 Brent Snavely and B. J. Hammerstein, "Chrysler Super Bowl Ad: How It All Came Together," *Detroit Free Press*, February 8, 2011; also see Neal Boudette, "Eminem Super Bowl Ad Sparks Lasting Buzz for Chrysler," *Wall Street Journal*, February 8, 2011.

3 Richard Bak, *Detroitland: A Collection of Movers, Shakers, Lost Souls, and History Makers from Detroit's Past* (Detroit: Wayne State University Press, 2011), 263. The Fist made news when Jerry Vile, artist provocateur and organizer of the Detroit annual Dirty Show, one of the nation's largest exhibitions of erotic art, placed a large replica of a Crisco can under the sculpture with a sign that said, "Helping to EASE THE PAIN of Detroit's Bankruptcy." The city removed it the same day. See Bill McGraw, "Update: City Trashes Crisco Can Artist Installed at Fist to 'Ease Bankruptcy Pain,'" *Deadline Detroit*, July 29, 2013.

4 John Russo and Sherry Lee Linkon, "The Social Costs of Deindustrialization," Center for Working-Class Studies, Youngstown State University, http://cwcs.ysu.edu/resources/CWCS-publications/social-costs-of-deindustrialization (first appeared in *Manufacturing a Better Future for America*, ed. Richard McCormack, The Alliance for American Manufacturing, 2009).

5 AP, "'Halftime in Detroit' Ad Creates Political Debate," February 6, 2012, http://www.foxnews.com/us/2012/02/06/halftime-in-america-ad-creates-political-debate/.

6 John Nichols, "Chrysler Super Bowl Ad Edits out Wisconsin Union Signs," *Nation*, February 6, 2012.

7 Michael Shaw, "Reading the Pictures: The Clint Eastwood 'Halftime in America' Controversy, and the Doctored Wisconsin Footage," *HuffPost Media*, February 7, 2012.

8 David Kiley, "Opinion: Chrysler's Eminem Super Bowl Commercial Advertises Detroit with Wrong Car," *Autoblog*, February 7, 2011.

9 Garance Franke-Ruta, "Paul Harvey's 1978 'So God Made a Farmer' Speech," *Atlantic*, February 3, 2013.

10 Bush said, "As we work with Congress in the coming year to chart a new course in Iraq and strengthen our military to meet the challenges of the 21st century, we must also work together to achieve important goals for the American people here at home. This work begins with keeping our economy growing. . . . And I encourage you all to go shopping more." Amanda Terkel, "With Recession Looming, Bush Tells America to 'Go Shopping More,'" *ThinkProgress*, December 20, 2006.

11 Micheline Maynard, *The End of Detroit: How the Big Three Lost Their Grip on the American Car Market* (New York: Doubleday, 2003); and Bill Vlasic, *Once upon a Car: The Fall and Resurrection of America's Big Three Automakers—GM, Ford, and Chrysler* (New York: William Morrow, 2011).

12 Maynard, *End of Detroit*, 19.

13 This is Chrysler's Jefferson North Plant, which makes Jeep Grand Cherokees, and has more than 4,600 workers. Chrysler's Conner Avenue Assembly Plant, which makes the Dodge Viper and is subject to shutdowns, has only about 150 employees. General Motors also operates a car plant that is partly in Detroit and partly in the neighboring city of Hamtramck. See Bill Vlasic, "Last Car Plant Brings Detroit Hope and Cash," *New York Times*, July 15, 2013; and Brett Beyer, "Where the Viper Gets Its Vroom," *New York Times*, January 13, 2013.

14 Vlasic, *Once upon a Car*, 365–366.

15 AP, "As Lawmakers Debate Immigration Reform, Farmers Lament They're 'Running out of Time,'" *Latino Fox News*, July 8, 2013, http://latino.foxnews.com/latino/politics/2013/07/08/as-lawmakers-debate-immigration-reform-farmers-lament-theyre-running-out-time/.

16 Ibid.

17 Jennifer Gordon, "Subcontractor Servitude," *New York Times*, September 2, 2013. The level of exploitation and abuse of immigrant workers has reached such depths that more than 150 Jamaican "guest workers" who clean luxury hotels and condos in Florida went on strike, a rare event, after being coerced, mistreated, and defrauded. Gordon estimates that seven hundred thousand to a million guest workers and their families enter the country each year, mostly to work in low-wage, menial jobs, but also as nurses, teachers, and computer programmers.

18 Boggs wrote and directed a film about herself entitled *American Revolutionary: The Evolution of Grace Lee Boggs*, released in 2013.

19 David Harvey, *Rebel Cities: From the Right to the City to the Urban Revolution* (New York: Verso, 2012), 122.

20 Sophie Milam, "SNAP (Food Stamps): Facts, Myths and Realities," *Feeding America*, 2013.

21 Kathleen Miles, "U.S. Child Hunger Rates by County: 2013 Report Reveals Most Food-Insecure Places for Children," *HuffPost Los Angeles*, June 19, 2013.

22 See the film *A Place at the Table* (2013), directed by Kristi Jacobson and Lori Silverbush (who also directed *Food, Inc.*, 2008).

23 Makeup Talk at makeuptalk.com/t/25264/urban-decay.

24 The ad can be seen online at Urban Decay Collage/Publish with Glogster. Urban Decay denied use of the image.

25 In 2011, Urban Decay was sold to Castanea Partners, a personal collateral organization based in California.

26 For a comparison of the image and watch face, see Helen Bienvenu, "Detroit 'Ruin Porn' Goes Commercial—In a Swatch," *HuffPost Detroit*, December 20, 2011. The watch was designed by Jeremy Scott for Swatch Corporation.

27 An incomplete list of documentaries includes Harvey Ovshinsky's *Land Grab: The Taking of Poletown* (1980); Ovshinsky's *The Voodoo Man of Heidelberg Street* (1990); the HBO documentary *Come Unto Me: The Faces of Tyree Guyton* (1999); the Vision TV documentary *Urban Shrines* (2005); the French documentary *Detroit: The Cycles of the Mental Machine* (2007); Stewart Bird, Rene Lichtman, and Peter Gessner's *Finally Got the News* (1970), about the activities of the League of Revolutionary Black Workers; Michael Moore's *Roger and Me* (1989); *Detroit: Remember When, vols. I & II* (1996); Aviva Kempner's *The Life and Times of Hank Greenberg* (1998); George Steinmetz and Michael Chanan's *Detroit: Ruin of a City* (2005); Gary Bredow's *High Tech Soul* (2006), about Detroit techno music; Mascha and Manfred Poppenk's *Grown in Detroit* (2009), about a farming program at the Catherine Ferguson Academy; Aaron Wolf's *Blueprint America: Beyond the Motor City* (2009), on public transportation reform; Alan Bradley's *Rollin': The Fall of the Auto Industry and the Rise of the Drug Economy in Detroit* (2009); Al Profit's *Detroit Mob Confidential* (2009); Johnny Knoxville's *Detroit Lives* (2010); Oren Goldenberg's *Our School* (2010), a critical study of the Detroit public school system; Mark MacInnis's *Urban Roots* (2010); *Living with Murder* (2011), made by the *Detroit Free Press*; Tony D'Annunzio's *Louder than Love: The Grande Ballroom Story* (2011); *Detroit in Overdrive* (2011), a three-part miniseries by the Discovery Channel; Florent Tillon's *Detroit Ville Sauvage* (Detroit Wild City, 2011); Renee Tajima and Christine Choy's *Who Killed Vincent Chin?* (1989); Tony Lam's *Vincent Who?* (2009); Philip Lauri's *After the Factory* (2012); Erik Proulx's *Lemonade: Detroit* (2012); Malik Bendjelloul's *Searching for Sugarman* (2012); Oren Goldenberg's *Brewster Douglass: You're My Brother* (2012); Amir Bar-Lev's *Re:Generation Music Project* (2012); American Music Research Foundation's *Detroit Blues & Beyond* (2012); *Motor City Pride* (2012), a short about Detroit's gay community; Sasha Reuther's *Brothers on the Line* (2012); and *Burn: One Year On the Front Lines of the Battle to Save Detroit* (2013), directed by Brenna Sanchez and Tom Putnam, about Detroit's firefighters, which won the Audience Award at the 2012 Tribeca Film Festival.

Fictional films set in Detroit include Paul Schrader's *Blue Collar* (1978); Paul Verhoeven's *Robocop* (1987); Curtis Hanson's *8 Mile* (2002), starring Detroit rapper Eminem; Bill Condon's *Dreamgirls* (2006); Clint Eastwood's *Gran Torino* (2008); and Rola Nashef's *Detroit Unleaded* (2012). Cop stories include Craig Baxley's *Action Jackson* (1988); Arthur Marks's *Detroit 9000* (1973), set in the racially volatile Detroit of the 1970s; and the television series *Detroit 1-8-7* (2010–2011), a police procedural.

28 Meteor Blades, "Report: CEOs Earn 331Times as Much as Average Workers, 774 Times as Much as Minimum Wage Earners," *Daily Kos*, April 16, 2014.

29 Ibid.

30 Ibid.

31 David Denby, "Good Fights: 'Detropia' and 'The Eye of the Storm,'" *New Yorker*, September 10, 2012.

32 Mike Scott, "'Detropia' Review: Documentary Boasts Artistry but Lacks Intellectual Punch," *Times-Picayune*, November 29, 2012.

33 Tom Keogh, "'Detropia': A Nightmarish Look at Once-Great Detroit," *Seattle Times*, October 18, 2012.
34 Although people of color make up 30 percent of the U.S. population, they account for 60 percent of the prison population, so one in three black men can expect to go to prison in their lifetime. In addition, black and Hispanic students face harsher punishments in school, are arrested far more often, are more likely to be sent to adult prisons and receive longer sentences, are disproportionately affected by felony voter laws, and have lower wage trajectories than their white peers. See Sophia Kerby, "The Top 10 Most Startling Facts about People of Color and Criminal Justice in the United States," *Center for American Progress*, March 13, 2012.
35 The film is available for free viewing at documentarystorm.com/requiem-for-detroit/.
36 Julien Temple, "Detroit: The Last Days," *Guardian*, March 10, 2010.
37 John Patrick Leary, "Detroitism," *Guernica*, January 2011.
38 Dan Georgakis, "Detroit: An Urban Zombie: Motown Images in Three New Documentaries," *Cineaste* 37, no. 4 (2012): 21.
39 Quoted in David Carr, "Broken Men, Broken Place: 'Low Winter Sun' Gives Detroit a Leading Role," *New York Times*, August 4, 2013.
40 Maureen Ryan, "'Doctor Who' Stars Go for Broke in 'Broadchurch'; 'Low Winter Sun' Gives off No Heat," *Huffpost TV*, August 6, 2013.
41 Bryan Egmont Key in response to Eric Lacy, "AMC 'Low Winter Sun' Producer Addresses Future of Detroit-themed Cop Drama," *MLive*, October 24, 2013.
42 Diana Ross, Mary Wilson, and Florence Ballard, founding members of the Supremes, as well as comedian and actress Lily Tomlin, all lived in the historic fourteen-acre Brewster-Douglass Housing Projects, built for the "working poor" (and named after Frederick Douglass) in Brush Park near the Chrysler Freeway. The last of the projects' uninhabited buildings, however, was demolished in 2014.
43 Richard Pope, "Hooked on Affect: Detroit Techno and Dystopian Digital Culture," *Dancecult: Journal of Electronic Dance Music Culture* 2, no. 1 (2011): 30.
44 Ibid., 42n6.
45 Ibid., 35.
46 Alistair Macaulay, "Fast-Stepped Fury, Rooted in Detroit," *New York Times*, August 11, 2014.
47 Vince Carducci, "Beneath the Pavement, the Beach! Detroit from a Situationist Perspective," *Motown Review of Art*, August 1, 2011; and Donna Terek, "Theatre Bizarre: A Bloody Imaginative Fantasy Party," *Detroit News*, November 1, 2009.

Chapter 6. Surviving in the Postapocalyptic Landscape

1 Susan Sontag, "The Imagination of Disaster," 1965, http://americanfuturesiup.files.wordpress.com/2013/01/sontag-the-imagination-of-disaster.pdf. This essay is included in *Against Interpretation* (Farrar, Straus & Giroux, 1966).
2 Joseph Masco, "Engineering the Future as Nuclear Ruin," in *Imperial Debris: On Ruins and Ruination*, ed. Ann Laura Stoler (Durham, NC: Duke University Press, 2012).
3 Ibid., 253.
4 Ibid., 254.
5 Quoted in ibid., 277.

6 Kyo Maclear, *Beclouded Visions: Hiroshima-Nagasaki and the Art of Witness* (Albany: State University of New York Press, 1999), 36–37. Among the most haunting images of the A-bomb effects are those of nuclear shadows, which are dark stains burned into the ground and onto buildings where the immense heat of the bomb vaporized the people who had been there an instant before doing ordinary things. One such image shows the silhouette of a painter with a ladder, his arm extended. Yet even today such images are scarce. See ibid., 41, 45–48. I also thank Kaleigh James (Winchell) for calling my attention to the imagery of nuclear shadows.

7 On the controversy over the *Enola Gay* exhibition at the Smithsonian, see Steven C. Dubin, "Battle Royal: the Final Mission of the *Enola Gay*," in *Displays of Power: Memory and Amnesia in the American Museum* (New York: New York University Press, 1999), 186–226.

8 Two days after the bombing of Nagasaki, President Harry Truman recorded a statement saying, "When you have to deal with a beast, you have to treat him as a beast," and Canadian prime minister Mackenzie King declared, "It is fortunate that the use of the bomb should have been upon the Japanese rather than upon the white races of Europe." Quoted in Maclear, *Beclouded Visions*, 38.

9 For exhibitions that focus on disaster and destruction, see, for example, *Damage Control: Art and Destruction since 1950* at the Smithsonian's Hirshhorn Museum (2013–2014), which surveys the imagery of destruction beginning with the nuclear blasts in Japan and includes footage of nuclear explosions by Harold "Doc" Edgerton, MIT professor of electrical engineering, made in the 1950s with the Rapatronic camera he helped to invent for this purpose; Jeff Walls's *Destroyed Room* (1978), which presents the wreckage of some domestic disaster and the photographs of Arnold Odermatt, a policeman who spent forty years documenting car crashes along rural roads in Switzerland, as well as other images of spectacular violence and its aftermath; *Under Destruction*, which examines the role of destruction in contemporary art at the Museum Tinguely in Basel and the Swiss Institute in New York (2011); *Gustav Metzger: Historic Photographs* at the New Museum in New York (2011), dedicated to the founder of the auto-destructive art movement; *Utopia/Dystopia: Construction and Destruction in Photography and Collage* at the Museum of Fine Arts in Houston (2012); and the special explosion event produced in conjunction with *Cai Guo-Qiang: Sky Ladder* at the Museum of Contemporary Art in Los Angeles (2012).

10 These include films such as *The Day the Earth Stood Still* (1951), *War of the Worlds* (1953), *It Came from Outer Space* (1953), *20,000 Leagues under the Sea* (1954), *Creature from the Black Lagoon* (1954), *Invasion of the Body Snatchers* (1956), *The Blob* (1958), *The Fly* (1958), and *Attack of the 50 Foot Woman* (1958), among many others. Films by Japanese directors include narratives that deal directly with Hiroshima such as *Black Rain* (1988) by Shohei Imamura, and *Record of A Living Being* (1955) and *Rhapsody in August* (1991), both by Akira Kurosawa.

11 Also see Mick Broderick, ed. *Hibakusha Cinema: Hiroshima, Nagasaki, and the Nuclear Image in Japanese Film* (London: Kegan Paul International, 1996); and Spencer R. Weart, *Nuclear Fear: A History of Images* (Cambridge, MA: Harvard University Press, 1989).

12 See Mervyn F. Bendle, "The Apocalyptic Imagination and Popular Culture," *Journal of Religion and Popular Culture* 11, no. 1 (2005).

13 Wendy Brown, *Walled States, Waning Sovereignty* (New York: Zone Books, 2010),

24, quoted in Slavoj Žižek, *Living in the End Times*, rev. ed. (New York: Verso, 2011), 461.

14 Kyle William Bishop, *American Zombie Gothic: The Rise and Fall (and Rise) of the Walking Dead in Popular Culture* (Jefferson, NC: McFarland, 2010), 30. Bishop provides a superb analysis of the history of zombie cinema. For more on Romero's films, also see Steven Shaviro's chapter, "Contagious Allegories: George Romero," in *Cinematic Body* (Minneapolis: University of Minnesota Press, 1993), 96–118.

15 J. C. Reindl, "CBS '60 Minutes' Bob Simon: Detroit Reminds Me of Mogadishu, Somalia," *Detroit Free Press*, October 12, 2013.

16 Jean Comaroff and John Comaroff, "Alien-Nation: Zombies, Immigrants, and Millennial Capitalism," *South Atlantic Quarterly* 101, no. 4 (2002): 792.

17 Bishop, *American Zombie Gothic*, 100.

18 Ibid., 192–193.

19 André Bazin defines the "Nero complex" as "the pleasure experienced at the sight of urban destruction." Quoted in Johannes von Moltke, "Ruin Cinema," in *Ruins of Modernity*, ed. Julia Hell and Andreas Schönle (Durham, NC: Duke University Press, 2010), 411.

20 Bishop, *American Zombie Gothic*, 30.

21 Romero has followed up with *Diary of the Dead* (2008) and *Survival of the Dead* (2009), which have not been as favorably reviewed by critics as his earlier films.

22 See Gerry Canavan, "'We *Are* the Walking Dead': Race, Time, and Survival in Zombie Narrative," *Extrapolation* 51, no. 3 (2010): 441.

23 Von Moltke, "Ruin Cinema," 411.

24 Bendle, "Apocalyptic Imagination."

25 The Victorian house at 82 Alfred Street in Brush Park that was used in the film was built in the late 1870s, then expanded and remodeled to its Queen Anne style by David C. Whitney, son of lumber baron David Whitney Jr. The architect was Gordon W. Lloyd, who also built the mansion that is now the Whitney restaurant on Woodward Avenue in Detroit. The house is being restored by Jeff Cowin, who bought the home months after *Only Lovers Left Alive* was filmed. See Julie Hinds, "'Only Lovers Left Alive' Vampires Make Themselves at Home in Decaying Detroit Mansion," *Detroit Free Press*, May 2, 2014.

26 Willem Schinkel, "'Illegal Aliens' and the State, or Bare Bodies vs. the Zombie," *International Sociology* 24, no. 6 (2009): 780.

27 Ibid., 784.

28 Ibid., 800. Also see Jen Webb and Sam Byrnand, "Some Kind of Virus: The Zombie as Body and as Trope," *Body & Society* 14, no. 2 (2008): 83–98.

29 The British government, in particular, has stripped citizenship from forty-two Britons who are "suspected terrorists," depriving them of rights "without any public hearing and with only after-the-fact involvement by the courts." It typically does so when people are out of the country, effective immediately, so that that they cannot return to challenge their loss of citizenship. Britain is seeking to expand the practice, and Canada, Austria, and the Netherlands are also considering drafting legislation that gives the government deprivation of citizenship powers. See Katrin Bennhold, "Britain Increasingly Invokes Power to Disown Its Citizens," *New York Times*, April 10, 2014.

30 Jon Stratton, "Zombie Trouble: Zombie Texts, Bare Life, and Displaced People," *European Journal of Cultural Studies* 14 (2011): 277.

31 Ibid.

32 "French Government Crackdown on Roma, Immigrants," *Workers Vanguard*, November 29, 2013.
33 Sean Smith, "'Elysium': Future Shock," *Entertainment Weekly*, July 26, 2013.
34 Eric Cazdyn, *The Already Dead: The New Time of Politics, Culture, and Illness* (Durham, NC: Duke University Press, 2012), 132.
35 Michelle Castillo, "U.S. Has Highest First-Day Infant Mortality out of Industrialized World, Group Reports," *CBS News*, May 7, 2013; and Amy Goodnough, "Infant Mortality Rate Fell Steadily from '05 to '11," *New York Times*, April 17, 2013. As another example, the School of Public Health at the University of California, Berkeley, reports that life expectancy in poor states such as Mississippi and Alabama is six to seven years shorter than states such as Hawaii and Minnesota, and there is a five-year gap in life expectancy between high- and low-wage earners, which is widening. See "A Poor Report Card," *University of California, Berkeley Wellness Letter* 30, no. 3 (2013): 2.
36 Canavan, "'We *Are* the Walking Dead,'" 436–439.
37 Ibid., 446. The quote is from an interview in the *New York Times Magazine*. It should be noted that charges brought against doctors and nurses at the facility have been expunged.
38 Ibid., 433.
39 Quoted in ibid., 448.
40 Ibid., 448.
41 MoJo News Team, "Full Transcript of the Mitt Romney Secret Video," *Mother Jones*, September 19, 2012.
42 See Atlanta Zombie Apocalypse at www.atlantazombie.com/about.
43 See Maryanne Kocis MacLeod, "Zombie Phenomenon Invades Macomb and South Oakland Counties," *Macomb Daily*, October 9, 2012; and Zombie Walk Detroit, at www.zombiewalkdetroit.com.
44 Courtney Rubin, "Survival of the Undeadest," *New York Times*, August 1, 2013. Atlanta also hosts DragonCon, a science fiction and fantasy convention where zombies gather, while Seattle (among other cities) hosts ZomBcon, "The World's Largest Zombie Culture Convention and Survival Expo."
45 Neely Tucker, "Depopulation Boom," *Washington Post*, March 8, 2008.
46 See Daniel W. Drezner, "The Lessons of Zombie-Mania," *Wall Street Journal*, April 5, 2013; and Stratton, "Zombie Trouble," 266.
47 See *The Endangered Coast*, by Detroit-based photographer John Ganis, which documents the effects of Hurricane Sandy along the Atlantic and Gulf Coasts. Also see his *Ruptures and Reclamations*, documenting the BP and Enbridge oil spills, and *Consuming the American Landscape*, on land use and the changing landscape, at http://johnganisphotography.com/galleries/ruptures-and-reclamation/.
48 Alan Feuer, "The Disaster Preppers Next Door," *New York Times*, January 27, 2013.
49 Erik Lacitis, "Preppers Do Their Best to be Ready for the Worst," *Seattle Times*, May 15, 2012; Chuck Raasch, "For 'Preppers,' Every Day Could Be Doomsday," *USA Today*, November 13, 2012; and John North, "'Doomsday Preppers' Casting Director Aims to Be Prepared, Too," *Asheville Daily Planet*, May 28, 2012.
50 Drezner, "The Lessons of Zombie-Mania."
51 Mark Fisher, *Capitalist Realism: Is There No Alternative?* (Ropley, East Hampshire, U.K.: Zero Books, 2009), 2.
52 Sarah Juliet Lauro and Karen Embry, "A Zombie Manifesto: The Nonhuman Condition in the Era of Advanced Capitalism," *Boundary* 35, no. 1 (2008): 98.

Conclusion: Your Town Tomorrow

1 Sarah Cwiek, "What's In a Consent Agreement? Do You Really Want to Know?" *Michigan Radio*, March 21, 2012.
2 "Emergency Manager Information," *State of Michigan Department of Treasure*, 2014, http://www.michigan.gov/treasury/0,1607,7-121-1751_51556-201116--,00.html; and Kate Abbey-Lambertz, "Michigan Emergency Manager Law in Effect in 6 Cities after Detroit Appointment (MAP)," *HuffPost Detroit*, March 15, 2013.
3 Chris Savage, "The Scandal of Michigan's Emergency Managers," *Nation*, February 15, 2012.
4 Timothy Williams, "Many Cities Opt to Clear Faded Areas," *New York Times*, November 12, 2013.
5 Coleman Young and Lonnie Wheeler, *Hard Stuff: The Autobiography of Mayor Coleman Young* (New York: Viking, 1994), 2.
6 Nafeez Ahmed, "Pentagon Preparing for Mass Civil Breakdown," *Guardian*, June 12, 2014.
7 Ibid.
8 Adam Nagourney, "Report Finds a Los Angeles in Decline," *New York Times*, April 10, 2014.
9 Charles M. Blow, "'A Town without Pity,'" *New York Times*, August 10, 2013.
10 Stephen D. King, "When Wealth Disappears," *New York Times*, October 7, 2013.
11 See Don Pittis, "Unlike Marx, Thomas Piketty Wants to Save Capitalism," *CBC News*, May 23, 2014. Also see Gerrit Bogle and Joseph Seymour, "Thomas Piketty's *Capital in the Twenty-First Century*: A Marxist Review," Parts One and Two, *Workers Vanguard*, October 3, 2014 and October 17, 2014.
12 David Harvey, "Afterthoughts on Piketty's *Capital*," *Reading Marx's Capital with David Harvey*, Blog, May 2014, http://davidharvey.org/2014/05/afterthoughts-pikettys-capital/.
13 Harvey, "Afterthoughts." He further notes, "Piketty defines capital as the stock of all assets held by private individuals, corporations and governments that can be traded in the market no matter whether these assets are being used or not. . . . Unfortunately there is no way to value it [initial capital] independently of the value of the goods and services it is used to produce or how much it can be sold for in the market. . . . The rate of return on capital depends crucially on the rate of growth because capital is valued by way of that which it produces and not by what went into its production."
14 David Harvey, *Seventeen Contradictions and the End of Capitalism* (Oxford: Oxford University Press, 2014), 265–266.
15 Ibid., 262.

Selected Bibliography

Agamben, Giorgio. *Homo Sacer: Sovereign Power and Bare Life.* Translated by Daniel Heller-Roazen. Palo Alto, CA: Stanford University Press, 1998.

Alberti, Mike. "Detroit Consigned to an Unnecessarily Bleak Future?" *Remapping Detroit,* December 21, 2011, 1–9.

———. "Detroit's Woes Can Be Eased, but Region's Officials Avert Their Eyes." *Remapping Detroit,* January 25, 2012, 1–9.

———. "Segregation and Racial Politics Long the Death Knell for Regionalism in Detroit Area." *Remapping Debate,* January 11, 2012, 1–5.

———. "Squandered Opportunities Leave Detroit Isolated." *Remapping Detroit,* January 11, 2012, 1–10.

Apel, Dora. *Imagery of Lynching: Black Men, White Women, and the Mob.* New Brunswick, NJ: Rutgers University Press, 2004.

———. *War Culture and the Contest of Images.* New Brunswick, NJ: Rutgers University Press, 2012.

Ashby, Brian, Ben Kolak, Courtney Prokopas, and Kevin Whiteacre. "Ruin Porn, Documentary, and Metal Theft: An Interview with the Co-directors of *Scrappers.*" *Crime, Media, Culture* 8, no. 355 (July 18, 2012). Doi:10.1177/1741659012447127.

Austin, Dan, and Sean Doerr. *Lost Detroit: Stories behind the Motor City's Majestic Ruins.* Charleston, SC: History Press, 2010.

Bak, Richard. *Detroitland: A Collection of Movers, Shakers, Lost Souls, and History Makers from Detroit's Past.* Detroit: Wayne State University Press, 2011.

Bamford, James. "They Know Much More Than You Think." *New York Review of Books,* August 15, 2013, 4–8.

Barr, Nancy, John Gallagher, and Carlo McCormick. *Detroit Revealed: Photographs, 2000–2010.* Detroit: Detroit Institute of Arts, 2011.

Bendle, Mervyn F. "The Apocalyptic Imagination and Popular Culture." *Journal of Religion and Popular Culture* 11, no. 1 (2005).

Bennett, Jill. *Practical Aesthetics: Events, Affects and Art after 9/11.* London: I. B. Tauris, 2012.

Berman, Russell. "Democratic Destruction: Ruins and Emancipation in the American Tradition." In *Ruins of Modernity,* edited by Julia Hell and Andreas Schönle, 104–117. Durham, NC: Duke University Press, 2010.

Bhatt, Ritu. "The Significance of the Aesthetic in Postmodern Architectural Theory." *Journal of Architectural Education* 53, no. 4 (May 2000): 229–238.

Binelli, Mark. *Detroit City Is the Place to Be: The Aftermath of an American Metropolis.* New York: Metropolitan Books, 2012.

Bishop, Kyle William. *American Zombie Gothic: The Rise and Fall (and Rise) of the Walking Dead in Popular Culture.* Jefferson, NC: McFarland, 2010.

Borshuk, Michael. "True Tales and 8 Mile Memoirs: Exploring the Imaginary City of Detroit." *Studies in the Literary Imagination* 41, no. 1 (Spring 2008): 107–134.

Boyle, Kevin. "The Ruins of Detroit: Exploring the Urban Crisis in the Motor City." *Michigan Historical Review* 27, no. 3 (2001): 109–127.

———. *The UAW and the Heyday of American Liberalism, 1945–1968.* Ithaca, NY: Cornell University Press, 1998.

Boym, Svetlana. *The Future of Nostalgia.* New York: Basic Books, 2001.

Burke, Edmund. *A Philosophical Enquiry into the Origin of Our Ideas of the Sublime and Beautiful.* 1757. Edited by Adam Phillips. New York: Oxford University Press, 1990.

Canavan, Gerry. "We *Are* the Walking Dead": Race, Time, and Survival in Zombie Narrative." *Extrapolation* 51, no. 3 (2010): 431–453.

Capeci, Dominic J. Jr., and Martha Wilkerson. *Layered Violence: The Detroit Rioters of 1943.* Jackson: University Press of Mississippi, 1991.

Cazdyn, Eric. *The Already Dead: The New Time of Politics, Culture, and Illness.* Durham, NC: Duke University Press, 2012.

Chafets, Ze'ev. *Devil's Night and Other True Tales of Detroit.* New York: Random House, 1990.

Chanan, Michael. "*Detroit: Ruin of a City*—A Reception Diary." *Journal of Media Practice* 6, no. 3 (2005): 135–144.

Clemens, Paul. *Made in Detroit: A South of 8 Mile Memoir.* New York: Doubleday, 2005.

———. *Punching Out: One Year in a Closing Auto Plant.* New York: Doubleday, 2011.

Comaroff, Jean, and John L. Comaroff. "Alien-Nation: Zombies, Immigrants, and Millennial Capitalism." *South Atlantic Quarterly* 101, no. 4 (2002): 779–805.

Cowie, Jefferson, and Joseph Heathcott, eds. *Beyond the Ruins: The Meanings of Deindustrialization.* Ithaca, NY: Cornell University Press, 2003.

Daskalakis, Georgia, Charles Waldheim, and Jason Young, eds. *Stalking Detroit.* Barcelona: Actar, 2001.

Day, Aidan. *Romanticism.* Hoboken, NJ: Routledge, 2011.

Deane, Darren R. "Louis Kahn's 'Fairy Tales' of American Institutions." In *Nationalism and Architecture*, edited by Raymond Quek and Darren Deane with Sarah Butler, 147–162. Burlington, VT: Ashgate, 2012.

Dillon, Brian, ed. "Introduction: A Short History of Decay." In *Ruins.* Documents of Contemporary Art, edited by Brian Dillon, 10–19. London: Whitechapel Gallery; Cambridge, MA: MIT Press, 2011.

Drooker, Arthur. *American Ruins.* Foreword by Douglas Brinkley. Essay by Christopher Woodward. New York: Merrell, 2009.

Dubin, Steven C. "Battle Royal: the Final Mission of the *Enola Gay.*" In *Displays of Power: Memory and Amnesia in the American Museum*, 186–226. New York: New York University Press, 1999.

Duggan, Lisa. *The Twilight of Equality? Neoliberalism, Cultural Politics, and the Attack on Democracy.* Boston: Beacon Press, 2004.

Edensor, Tim. "The Debris of Industrial Ruins and the Disordering of the Material World." *Journal of Material Culture* 10 (2005): 311–332.

———. *Industrial Ruins: Space, Aesthetics, and Materiality.* New York: Berg, 2005.

Farley, Reynolds, Sheldon Danziger, and Harry J. Holzer. *Detroit Divided.* New York: Russell Sage Foundation, 2000.

Fine, Sidney. *Violence in the Model City: The Cavanaugh Administration, Race Relations, and the Detroit Riot of 1967.* East Lansing: Michigan State University Press, 2007.

Fisher, Mark. *Capitalist Realism: Is There No Alternative?* Ropley, East Hampshire, U.K.: Zero Books, 2009.

Fishman, Robert. "On Big Beaver Road: Detroit and the Diversity of American Metropolitan Landscapes." *Places: Forum of Design for the Public Realm* 19, no. 1 (April 2007): 42–47.

Georgakas, Dan, "Detroit: An Urban Zombie: Motown Images in Three New Documentaries." *Cineaste* 37, no. 4 (2012): 16–21.

Grandin, Greg. "Empire's Ruins: Detroit to the Amazon." In *Imperial Debris: On Ruins and Ruination*, edited by Ann Laura Stoler, 115–128. Durham, NC: Duke University Press, 2013.

———. *Fordlandia: The Rise and Fall of Henry Ford's Forgotten Jungle City.* New York: Metropolitan Books, 2009.

Harvey, David. *The Enigma of Capital and the Crisis of Capitalism.* Oxford: Oxford University Press, 2011.

———. *Rebel Cities: From the Right to the City to the Urban Revolution.* London: Verso, 2012.

———. *Seventeen Contradictions and the End of Capitalism.* Oxford: Oxford University Press, 2014.

Hell, Julia. "Endings and New Beginnings: Ruins and Heritage." *Germanic Review* 86 (2011): 225–231.

———. "Imperial Ruin Gazers, or Why Did Scipio Weep?" In *Ruins of Modernity*, edited by Julia Hell and Andreas Schönle, 169–192. Durham, NC: Duke University Press, 2010.

Herron, Jerry. *After Culture: Detroit and the Humiliation of History.* Detroit: Wayne State University Press, 1993.

———. "The Forgetting Machine: Notes toward a History of Detroit." *Design Observer Group*, January 9, 2012, https://placesjournal.org/article/the-forgetting-machine-notes-toward-a-history-of-detroit/.

———. "Living with Detroit." In *Detroit: 138 Square Miles*, 13–15. Detroit: Museum of Contemporary Art Detroit/D.A.P. 2011.

Herscher, Andrew. *The Unreal Estate Guide to Detroit.* Ann Arbor: University of Michigan Press, 2012.

Hetzler, Florence. "The Aesthetics of Ruins: A New Category of Being." *Journal of Aesthetic Education* 16, no. 2 (summer 1982): 105–108.

High, Steven, and David W. Lewis. *Corporate Wasteland: The Landscape and Memory of Deindustrialization.* Ithaca, NY: Cornell University, 2007.

Huyssen, Andreas. "Authentic Ruins: Products of Modernity." In *Ruins of Modernity*, edited by Julia Hell and Andreas Schönle, 17–28. Durham, NC: Duke University Press, 2010.

Jackson, J. B. *The Necessity for Ruins.* Amherst: University of Massachusetts Press, 1980.

Jacobs, Steven. "*Amor Vacui*: Photography and the Image of the Empty City." *History of Photography* 30, no. 2 (2006): 108–118.

Joselit, David. *After Art.* Princeton, NJ: Princeton University Press, 2013.

Klein, Naomi. *The Shock Doctrine: The Rise of Disaster Capitalism.* New York: Picador, 2007.

Lauro, Sarah Juliet, and Karen Embry. "A Zombie Manifesto: The Nonhuman Condition in the Era of Advanced Capitalism." *Boundary* 35, no. 1 (2008): 85–108.

Leary, John Patrick. "Detroitism." *Guernica*, January 2011.

LeDuff, Charlie. *Detroit: An American Biography.* New York: Penguin Press, 2013.

Loos, Ted. "Picturing Motor City: Julia Reyes Taubman Trains Her Lens on Detroit." *Vogue Magazine*, November 15, 2011.

Macaulay, Rose. "A Note on New Ruins//1953." In *Ruins.* Documents of Contemporary Art, edited by Brian Dillon, 27–28. London: Whitechapel Gallery; Cambridge, MA: MIT Press, 2011.

Maclear, Kyo. *Beclouded Visions: Hiroshima-Nagasaki and the Art of Witness.* Albany: State University of New York Press, 1999.

Marchand, Yves, and Romaine Meffre. *The Ruins of Detroit.* Essays by Robert Polidori and Thomas J. Sugrue. Göttingen: Steidl Publishers, 2010.

Martelle, Scott. *Detroit: A Biography.* Chicago: Chicago Review Press, 2012.

Masco, Joseph. "Engineering the Future as Nuclear Ruin." In *Imperial Debris: On Ruins and Ruination*, edited by Ann Laura Stoler, 252–286. Durham, NC: Duke University Press, 2013.

Maynard, Micheline. *The End of Detroit: How the Big Three Lost Their Grip on the American Car Market.* New York: Doubleday, 2003.

McAlister, Elizabeth. "Slaves, Cannibals, and Infected Hyper-Whites: The Race and Religion of Zombies." *Anthropological Quarterly* 85, no. 2 (Spring 2012): 457–486.

McGowan, Shane. "The Sublime Working of History: Travel, Ruins, and the Romantic Origins of the Post-Apocalyptic Aesthetic." Paper presented at Humanities Center symposium The Apocalyptic Landscape, Wayne State University, Detroit, November 16, 2012.

Millington, Nate. "Post-Industrial Imaginaries: Nature, Representation, and Ruin in Detroit, Michigan." *International Journal of Urban and Regional Research* 37, no. 1 (January 2013): 279–296.

Moon, Whitney. "Reclaiming the Ruins: Detroit's Second Coming?" *Places: Forum of Design for the Public Realm* 21, no. 1 (Spring 2009): 36–41.

Moore, Andrew. *Detroit Disassembled.* Essay by Philip Levine. Bologna: Akron Art Museum and Damiani Editore, 2010.

———. "Detroit Undone." *National Geographic* 281, no. 5 (November 2010): 9–9D.

Morton, Thomas. "Something, Something, Something, Detroit: Lazy Journalists Love Pictures of Abandoned Stuff," *Vice Magazine*, August 1, 2009.

NPR Staff. "Untouched, Thousands of Rape Kits Await Justice." *National Public Radio*, April 21, 2012.

Oramas, Sandro. "The Archaeology of Photography: An Inquiry into the Significance of Ruins in Contemporary Photography." *Camerawork* 24, no. 2 (Fall/Winter 1997): 16–22.

Peck, Jamie. "Zombie Neoliberalism and the Ambidextrous State." *Theoretical Criminology* 14, no. 1 (2010): 104–110.

Perry, Weena. "'Too Young and Vibrant for Ruins': Ground Zero Photography and the Problem of Contemporary Ruin." *Afterimage* 36, no. 3 (November–December 2008): 8–12.

Piketty, Thomas. *Capital in the Twenty-First Century.* Cambridge, MA: Belknap Press, 2014.

Pincus, Julie, and Nichole Christian. *Canvas Detroit.* Detroit: Wayne State University Press, 2014.

Pippin, Tina. "'Behold, I Stand at the Door and Knock' The Living Dead and Apocalyptic Dystopia." *Bible and Critical Theory* 6, no. 3 (2010): 40.1–15. Monash University EPress.

Pope, Richard. "Hooked on Affect: Detroit Techno and Dystopian Digital Culture." *Dancecult: Journal of Electronic Dance Music Culture* 2, no. 1 (2011): 24–44.

Presner, Todd Samuel. "Hegel's Philosophy of World History via Sebald's Imaginary of Ruins: A Contrapuntal Critique of the 'New Space' of Modernity." In *Ruins of*

Modernity, edited by Julia Hell and Andreas Schönle, 193–211. Durham, NC: Duke University Press, 2010.

Regier, Alexander. "Foundational Ruins: The Lisbon Earthquake and the Sublime." In *Ruins of Modernity*, edited by Julia Hell and Andreas Schönle, 357–394. Durham, NC: Duke University Press, 2010.

RomanyWG. *Beauty in Decay*. Berkeley, CA: Gingko Press and Carpet Bombing Culture, 2010.

Rosler, Martha. "Culture Class: Art, Creativity, Urbanism, Part III." *e-flux journal*, 25 (May 2011): 1–24.

Schinkel, Willem. "'Illegal Aliens' and the State, or: Bare Bodies vs. the Zombie." *International Sociology* 24, no. 6 (2009): 779–806.

Shaviro, Stephen. "Capitalist Monsters." *Historical Materialism* 19, no. 4 (2002): 281–290.

———. *Cinematic Body*. Minneapolis: University of Minnesota Press, 1993.

———. "Melancholia; or, The Romantic Anti-Sublime." *Sequence* 1, no. 1 (2012), http://reframe.sussex.ac.uk/sequence/files/2012/12/MELANCHOLIA-or-The-Romantic-Anti-Sublime-SEQUENCE-1.1-2012-Steven-Shaviro.pdf.

Simmel, Georg. "The Ruin//1911." In *Ruins*. Documents of Contemporary Art, edited by Brian Dillon, 23–24. London: Whitechapel Gallery; Cambridge, MA: MIT Press, 2011.

Smithson, Robert. "A Tour of the Monuments of Passaic, New Jersey//1967." In *Ruins*. Documents of Contemporary Art, edited by Brian Dillon, 46–51. London: Whitechapel Gallery; Cambridge, MA: MIT Press, 2011.

Solnit, Rebecca. "Detroit Arcadia: Exploring the Post-American Landscape." *Harpers* (July 2007).

Sommers, Samuel R., Evan P. Apfelbaum, Kristin N. Dukes, Negin Toosi, and Elsie J. Wang. "Race and Media Coverage of Hurricane Katrina: Analysis, Implications, and Future Research Questions," *Analyses of Social Issues and Public Policy* 6, no. 1 (2006): 1–17. doi:10.1111/j.1530-2415.2006.00103.x.

Sontag, Susan. "The Imagination of Disaster" (1965). http://americanfuturesiup.files.wordpress.com/2013/01/sontag-the-imagination-of-disaster.pdf.

Steinmetz, George. "Colonial Melancholy and Fordist Nostalgia: The Ruinscapes of Namibia and Detroit." In *Ruins of Modernity*, edited by Julia Hell and Andreas Schönle, 294–320. Durham, NC: Duke University Press, 2010.

———. "Drive-by Shooting: Making a Documentary about Detroit." *Michigan Quarterly Review* 45, no. 3 (summer 2006): 491–513.

———. "Guest Editorial." *Environment and Planning D: Society and Space* 27 (2009): 761–770.

Stoler, Ann Laura. "Introduction: 'The Rot Remains': From Ruins to Ruination." In *Imperial Debris: On Ruins and Ruination*, edited by Ann Laura Stoler, 1–35. Durham, NC: Duke University Press, 2013.

Stratton, Jon. "Zombie Trouble: Zombie Texts, Bare Life and Displaced People." *European Journal of Cultural Studies* 14 (2011): 265–281.

Sugrue, Thomas J. "Notown." *Democracy: A Journal of Ideas* 28 (Spring 2013).

———. *The Origins of the Urban Crisis: Race and Inequality in Postwar Detroit*. Rev. ed. Princeton, NJ: Princeton University Press, 2005.

———. "The Rise and Fall of Detroit's Middle Class." *New Yorker*, July 22, 2013.

Taubman, Julia Reyes. *Detroit: 138 Square Miles*. Foreword by Elmore Leonard and essay by Jerry Herron. Detroit: Museum of Contemporary Art, Detroit/D.A.P., 2011.

Trigg, Dylan. *The Aesthetics of Decay: Nothingness, Nostalgia and the Absence of Reason*. New York: Peter Lang, 2006.

Trigg, Dylan. "The Place of Trauma: Memory, Haunting, and the Temporality of Ruins." *Memory Studies* 2, no. 1 (2009): 87–101.

Vergara, Camilo José. *American Ruins.* New York: Monacelli Press, 1999.

———. "Downtown Detroit: 'American Metropolis' or Vacant Land—What to Do with the World's Third Largest Concentration of Pre-Depression Skyscrapers?" *Metropolis* (April 1995): 33–38.

———. *The New American Ghetto.* New Brunswick, NJ: Rutgers University Press, 1995.

Vidler, Anthony. "Architecture Dismembered//1992." In *Ruins.* Documents of Contemporary Art, edited by Brian Dillon, 55–66. London: Whitechapel Gallery; Cambridge, MA: MIT Press, 2011.

Vlasic, Bill. *Once upon a Car: The Fall and Resurrection of America's Big Three Automakers—GM, Ford, and Chrysler.* New York: William Morrow, 2011.

Von Moltke, Johannes. "Ruin Cinema." In *Ruins of Modernity*, edited by Julia Hell and Andreas Schönle, 395–417. Durham, NC: Duke University Press, 2010.

Webb, Jen, and Sam Byrnand. "Some Kind of Virus: The Zombie as Body and as Trope." *Body & Society* 14, no. 2 (2008): 83–98.

White, Luke. "Damien Hirst's Shark: Nature, Capitalism and the Sublime." In *The Art of the Sublime*, edited by Nigel Llewellyn and Christine Riding, January 2013, http://www.tate.org.uk/art/research-publications/the-sublime/luke-white-damien-hirsts-shark-nature-capitalism-and-the-sublime-r1136828.

White, Monica M. "D-town Farm: African American Resistance to Food Insecurity and the Transformation of Detroit." *Environmental Practice* 13, no. 4 (2011): 406–417.

Williams, Gilda. "It Was What It Was: Modern Ruins//2010." In *Ruins.* Documents of Contemporary Art, edited by Brian Dillon, 94–99. London: Whitechapel Gallery; Cambridge, MA: MIT Press, 2011.

Williams, Linda. *Hard Core: Power, Pleasure, and the "Frenzy of the Visible."* Rev. ed. Berkeley: University of California Press, 1999.

Woodward, Christopher. *In Ruins: A Journey through History, Art, and Literature.* New York: Vintage, 2003.

Woodward, Richard B. "Disaster Photography: When Is Documentary Exploitation?" *Art News*, February 6, 2013.

Young, Coleman, and Lonnie Wheeler. *Hard Stuff: The Autobiography of Mayor Coleman Young.* New York: Viking, 1994.

Žižek, Slavoj. *Living in the End Times.* Rev. ed. London: Verso, 2011.

———. *Violence: Six Sideways Reflections.* New York: Picador, 2008.

Zucker, Paul. "Ruins: An Aesthetic Hybrid." *Journal of Aesthetics and Art Criticism* 20, no. 2 (1961): 119–130.

Index

Note: Page numbers in *italics* indicate figures.

About the Author

DORA APEL has written three books and one coauthored book, including *Memory Effects: The Holocaust and the Art of Secondary Witnessing*; *Imagery of Lynching: Black Men, White Women, and the Mob*; *War Culture and the Contest of Images*; and *Lynching Photographs*, coauthored with Shawn Michelle Smith. Her work examines traumatic imagery and associated cultural practices of war and violence; race and ethnicity; the merging of documentary, photojournalistic, and artistic practices; the positioning of contemporary documentary within a globalized world; gender and sexuality; and museum practices. She teaches art history and visual culture at Wayne State University in Detroit, where she is Professor and W. Hawkins Ferry Endowed Chair in Modern and Contemporary Art History. She has been living and working in metro Detroit for more than thirty years.